Troubleshooting Relationships on the Autism Spectrum

by the same author

Asperger Syndrome and Long-Term Relationships
Foreword by Liane Holliday Willey
ISBN 978 1 84310 734 7
eISBN 978 1 84642 374 1

Business for Aspies
42 Best Practices for Using Asperger
Syndrome Traits at Work Successfully
ISBN 978 1 84905 845 2
eISBN 978 0 85700 501 4

of related interest

Love, Sex and Long-Term Relationships
What People with Asperger Syndrome Really Really Want
Sarah Hendrickx
Foreword by Stephen M. Shore
ISBN 978 1 84310 605 0
eISBN 978 1 84642 764 0

Alone Together
Making an Asperger Marriage Work
Katrin Bentley
Foreword by Tony Attwood
ISBN 978 1 84310 537 4
eISBN 978 1 84642 623 0

What Men with Asperger Syndrome Want to Know
About Women, Dating and Relationships
Maxine Aston
Foreword by Tony Attwood
ISBN 978 1 84905 269 6
eISBN 978 0 85700 554 0

22 Things a Woman with Asperger's Syndrome
Wants Her Partner to Know
Rudy Simone
Foreword by Tony Attwood
ISBN 978 1 84905 883 4
eISBN 978 0 85700 586 1

The Asperger Couple's Workbook
Practical Advice and Activities for Couples and Counsellors
Maxine Aston
ISBN 978 1 84310 253 3
eISBN 978 1 84642 851 7

Troubleshooting Relationships

ON THE **AUTISM SPECTRUM**

A USER'S GUIDE TO RESOLVING RELATIONSHIP PROBLEMS

ASHLEY STANFORD

Jessica Kingsley *Publishers*
London and Philadelphia

First published in 2013
by Jessica Kingsley Publishers
73 Collier Street
London N1 9BE, UK
and
400 Market Street, Suite 400
Philadelphia, PA 19106, USA

www.jkp.com

Library of Congress Cataloging in Publication Data
Stanford, Ashley, 1969-
Troubleshooting relationships on the autism spectrum
: a user's guide to resolving relationship
problems / Ashley Stanford.
pages cm
Includes bibliographical references and index.
ISBN 978-1-84905-951-0 (alk. paper)
1. Autism spectrum disorders--Patients--Rehabilitation.
2. Autism spectrum disorders--Patients--Family
relationships. 3. Autistic children--Rehabilitation. 4. Social
interaction.. 5. Interpersonal relations. I.
Title.
RC553.A88S828 2013
616.85'882--dc23
2013012245

British Library Cataloguing in Publication Data
A CIP catalogue record for this book is available from the British Library

ISBN 978 1 84905 951 0
eISBN 978 0 85700 808 4

Printed and bound in Great Britain by Bell & Bain Ltd, Glasgow

Dedicated to my best friend, husband,
and partner—one man, many roles.

Also dedicated to Eric and Katie who loaned me their home so
I could have the time and space I needed to write. The world
would be a much better place if there were more people like you.

CONTENTS

PREFACE

In a moment of painful honesty, my husband once said, "I don't know how to do this."

"What?"

"Be in a relationship," were the words he was seeking, but he was too stuck-in-the-moment to find even those words. He simply stood, looking confused and frustrated, like someone who is hungry but does not remember where the kitchen is located.

Despite all the books we had read and advice we had received, the "whole relationship thing" was still very much a mystery.

Is he supposed to agree with me on everything to keep the peace? Or disagree and stand up for himself, to show that he is in the relationship as an active partner? And once he disagrees, how does he get back to a peaceful relationship?

Often he experienced only confusion, but one day he crystallized the overarching problem into one sentence: "There are too many variables."

He could not figure out how to interact in a complex relationship because there were too many convoluted, seemingly erratic, confusing variables to consider. So, we read more relationship books and worked hard to understand and analyze all the important aspects that needed to be considered. The harder we worked, however, the more we saw complexity, not solutions.

The final realization came when we both realized that the books on relationships were mostly counter-productive for us in our autistic spectrum disorder (ASD)-linked partnership. The books were based on foundational assumptions that were incorrect and sometimes even detrimental for our particular, uniquely quirky relationship that was deeply rooted in the traits of autism.

The ultra-logical brain works differently than other brains and this changes how we communicate. A couple's ability to communicate respectfully is one of the most crucial factors in determining their long-term happiness. Perhaps someone with autism may be able to learn solid communication skills, but it is even more complex in an intimate relationship since it is not only the brain, but the body that is part of the equation. A whole different set of foundational principles needs to be in place in order to make sense of one's world from the spectrum-based perspective.

When there is occasional helpful advice in mainstream books on relationships, the advice is often obscured by a format that is not familiar to a logical person. The books talk about feelings as if they are something natural and easy to identify. Once, when reading yet another relationship book, I became so frustrated that I threw the book across the room and said in a mocking tone: "An Aspie would *never* say, 'It makes me angry when you use that tone of voice!'"

For us, mainstream relationship advice books did not work, yet we both needed help.

Since I spent the early part of my career writing user manuals for various computer companies, the structure and style of user manual writing comes naturally. Writing a user manual for relationships would be foolhardy, however; the equivalent of writing a single user manual that would work for every type of computer ever made. There are too many different types of computers, too many different manufacturers, too many different types of components. Similarly, there are too many different types of individuals.

Humans are far more complex than machines. To be useful, everyone would need their own specific user manual since each person is unique enough to be their own "model."

Instead of a user manual, it is far more useful to present a range of strategies that may work with the varying personalities with the assumption, for this particular book at least, that one or both of you has autism. ASD-linked couples of every variety should find useful information within these pages.

The purpose of this book is to present the most relevant strategies that will give you a set of techniques which have the highest probability of working to increase the happiness quotient in your relationship.

It does not matter if you have autism, Asperger syndrome (now considered a type of autism rather than a stand-alone diagnosis), or any other similar condition. The strategies in *Troubleshooting Relationships* are generalized so anyone in a relationship affected by the ASD diagnostic criteria will be able to benefit from them, though the strategies are best suited for high-functioning individuals.

I wrote *Troubleshooting Relationships* for the same purpose that I wrote *Asperger Syndrome and Long-Term Relationships* in 2002: to put all my ideas in one place, creating, "a conglomeration of most of the understandings and solutions that have helped me build a healthier, happier marriage" (Stanford 2002, p.17). I do this so that when there are problems, I can turn to a resource that has been custom-built for couples in relationships where autism plays a vital role.

Disclaimer: *Troubleshooting Relationships* assumes that you know the core diagnostic criteria for autism. I have removed explanations of the basic diagnostic criteria from this book so that it does not:

- dilute the core message

- bore those who have read the basics too many times

- waste precious pages where I could otherwise be giving autism-specific strategies.

It was quite tempting to include the diagnostic criteria, but every time I was tempted to do so, I imagined a couple living somewhere in the world, needing one particular concept to help solve a tough, old issue, but not getting to the correct section of the book because the phrase, "the diagnostic criteria are…" made the couple toss the book aside. Due to the difficult and urgent nature of many relationship issues, the core content needed to be as quickly accessible as possible.

If you have questions regarding, "What is autism/Asperger syndrome/ASD/PPD-NOS/social anxiety disorder?" please refer to *A Practical Guide to Autism* by Fred R. Volkmar and Lisa A. Wiesner (2009).

The goal of this book is to help you solve problems quickly, respectfully, and even lovingly, if possible. If you are having troubles in your relationship, it might be that the solution is simply hidden, undiscovered. Perhaps your solutions are resting, waiting for you, within the pages of this book. It is the available-but-hidden solution that, if left uncovered, is the most devastating in the long run.

My hope is that people who are frustrated and discouraged in their relationships will seek answers in these pages and use the troubleshooting methods to solve their own issues. I know that I have. Even as I was writing, I returned to various chapters when problems arose.

When there are problems, it is all too easy to believe that there is no solution. Yet, as Thomas Edison, one of the world's greatest thinkers said: "When you have exhausted all possibilities, remember this—you haven't."

Over the last twenty-plus years of marriage, during the times when our difficulties seemed unsolvable, there has always been a shadow of belief: "Maybe there's a repair/fix/solution that I just haven't tried yet." I am very grateful for that persistent thought and the way that it opened my mind to possibilities beyond mainstream relationship advice.

As I write this, my husband with autism, originally diagnosed with Asperger syndrome, is out on a morning run with our youngest son, 11 years old, originally diagnosed as high-functioning autistic. I never thought my husband would ever choose to run for any purpose other than escape, or perhaps to catch a plane flight. Running was far too big an assault on his sensory system. After years of problem-solving the issues that prohibited him from regular exercise, however, he is now stretching his legs, feeling his heartbeat, often remarking, "So this is what it feels like to be alive?"

In a few minutes the man I love will walk in the door, sweat on his face and our son by his side. Our son's face will be glowing, pink cheeks, ear-to-ear grin, chattering about who ran fastest, estimating miles per hour, kilometers per hour, wind resistance, stride length, and any other geeky topic. I have seen it before and soon I will see it again—that post-run glow is a sign of his success as a father and as a human being regardless of his particular neurological wiring.

Interestingly, if you could see them, you would see a strong social bond between the two of them and you would also see the trademark signs of autism in some small and some not-so-small tale-tell indicators.

During moments like this, thoughts float across my mind: "What if I'd given up ten years ago? What if I had given up due to 'lack of reciprocity,' or the sensory issues, or all the communication issues? What if I had missed this? What if I had walked away and never had a chance to see the long-term benefits?"

When our son was born with autism, we went through many years of personal discovery and transition. Somehow, mostly through the strategies listed in this book, we persevered. I am so grateful that we made it through those tough years intact. I am sure more strategies will become available to us in the future, but for now, there is more than enough to fill a book. I hope the strategies benefit you, too.

This book is written for spectrum/neurotypical (NT), spectrum/other, or spectrum/spectrum couples. The goal is to have a wealth of strategies available so that when you run into problems and want to keep trying, you have strategies on your bookshelf or on your e-reader that you can try. The effectiveness of the strategies in this book will vary since every couple is different; every person is different; every day is different.

As you read this book, the advice will seem casual, perhaps even "normal" as in mainstream books about relationships, but the content in this book is focused intensely on the logical, rational thinking subset of the population. As couples working within the framework of autism, it is crucial to not be distracted by advice structured for a different mindset. For example, advice on "following our inner feelings" may distract and/or discourage since one or both of you may have a hard time recognizing those feelings. Focusing on your feelings may not solve the problem, but perhaps focusing on a different, more definable aspect will solve the problem.

We need advice that is clear, concise, and specifically aimed at quick, effective solutions so that when we have a problem, we experience it only once (ideal) or as few times as possible (realistic). Scenario: we have a problem; we solve it; then next time we know how to avoid it.

Every relationship is flawed and we all make mistakes, but we can aim for solutions with the highest probability of success. The quality of each day is based on the many little decisions we make throughout the day; the quality of our long-term relationships is based on the multitude of improvements we make in how we support and love each other.

It is to be hoped that you, too, will have moments of joy when you recognize that your hard work was worth it.

PART I

THE TROUBLESHOOTING PROCESS

CHAPTER 1

The Foundational Principles of Troubleshooting

Troubleshooting is a type of problem-solving method often used to repair failed products or processes. Surprisingly, it works effectively in relationships too.

I discovered this one night at the local gym. I entered the stationary bike workout room where each bike has its own monitor so that you can enjoy a TV show while working out. I picked a bike and started pedaling, but the TV would not turn on. I looked down, saw that the power cord had been kicked loose, plugged it in, then sat back down to pedal and enjoy.

The man on the bike next to me was staring at me. When I returned his gaze, he said, "I've been biking for 30 minutes and at least a dozen people have sat down at the bike then just walked away when the TV wouldn't turn on. You're the first one who thought to plug it in."

I forget what I replied, but I do remember thinking smugly: "Well, that's one of the benefits of living with a partner with autism. Logic. Problem-solving. Just fix it." It felt great. I felt capable and confident.

When I went home that night, I encountered a communication issue with my husband. I tried the same troubleshooting process that had worked at the gym: "What's the most obvious solution?" and it worked. Metaphorically I found the power plug and plugged it in. I fixed the problem. Again, I got a surge of feeling capable and confident. Later that evening I began researching whether or not standard troubleshooting strategies could work in ASD-linked relationships.

I found significant information that supported my theory. *Troubleshooting Relationships* is the culmination of that research. This book gives you the troubleshooting process framework so that you can fix your own issues.

Troubleshooting requires identification of the malfunction(s). Identifying the cause of the malfunction is often the process of elimination, trying the most likely solutions first. Once a solution is found, confirmation is needed to verify that the product or process is returned to its normal or preferred state.

In a relationship, troubleshooting is the identification of "trouble" by one or both partners. Once the problem is accurately identified, partners can begin "shooting" at the problem to eliminate it.

If you or your partner is a visual person who thinks in pictures as the well-known Temple Grandin does, then it may help to think of troubleshooting as equipping yourself with a quiver of arrows and using them to shoot at targets (problems). You may miss the target, but you keep pulling those arrows out of your quiver and aiming as best you can. What is most important is that you *never aim at your partner. Aim at the problem.* If you run out of arrows, re-equip yourself with a fresh quiver and keep trying. This is a solid analogy that may help as you go through this process.

Solving problems

In most human relationships, people make the same mistakes again and again without noticing that they are repeating the same mistakes. People who are on the spectrum and capable of troubleshooting in a way that is respectful of their partner's needs may have an advantage since they may be able to identify, troubleshoot, solve, and not repeat the same problems throughout their lives.

The term "troubleshooting" comes from the engineering/ technology sector. Typically, you troubleshoot computer malfunctions. For example, when you press "Print," you expect a hard copy to emerge from the printer. If it does not, you seek to identify the problem and fix it. Potential solutions may be to change a setting, hook up the printer properly, or check that the printer has sufficient ink.

In a relationship, you may find a similar process helpful. For example, if you come home late regularly and find your partner is angry with you for being late, this is a problem. Identify the problem: you came home late and therefore your partner is angry.

Potential solutions may be to call, text, or email your partner when you know that you will be late. If this does not satisfy, try the next likely solution: reset the time which you have agreed to come home. Switch your estimated time of arrival to 7pm instead of 6pm. This way your partner will be happily surprised when you are home "early" and there will be fewer nights when you are technically "late."

Try the obvious solutions first. If those do not work, dive deeper into the complexity of relational thought. Perhaps your partner is not actually angry that you are late; perhaps your partner is worried that you may be attracted to someone else and are staying late at the office in a way that could lead to inappropriate sexual relations with a co-worker. If you have unusual body language and dismissive eye contact, you might easily trigger a partner's worry of infidelity.

The process

Each potential solution is called a "Test." It is part of the debugging process. Here is one example.

Problem: Your partner is angry and you don't know why.

Test 1: Ask, "What is making you angry?"

Test 2: Ask, "What can I do to fix things?"

Test 3: Ask, "What specific action can I do to fix this problem?"

Once a solution is found, write it down in your journal or other location, even make notes on your cell phone. I keep a Marriage Workbook in a spiral notebook, as well as using a notes app on my phone. You can use this information the next time you have a similar conversation. That is the key: each time you solve a problem, you can record it to create your own personalized, highly abbreviated User Manual for _____ (your name) and _____ (your partner's name).

While your goal is to solve the problem once then not experience the problem again, it is likely that you will experience it again, especially if the answer relies on one partner changing, thus the need for a written record of solutions. Archimedes didn't expect humanity to remember the concepts of levers, engines, or hydrostatics by memory any more than we should expect ourselves to remember our own discoveries.

For example, one woman was angry every evening that her husband with autism and sensory processing issues came home late.

They tried several solutions, but nothing worked. She recorded them in her journal so that she knew what didn't work. The abbreviated entries are as follows:

Monday: Tried dressing-to-seduce. Didn't work. Fell asleep crying.

Tuesday: Tried talking it out. Only ended in a fight.

Wednesday: Tried ignoring it. Made me angrier than ever.

Thursday: Tried being super sweet about it. Felt resentful.

Friday: Tried emailing him. Figured out mid-writing that I'm actually worried that he's having an affair.

Saturday: We talked about the issue. Looks like it's solved.

The couple figured out that because he came home on social overload he went straight into "zombie mode" as soon as he walked in the door. In this dazed-out physical condition he looked suspiciously like a man who was disconnected from his wife.

Since he had sensory issues that made sexual relations occur less often, she was worried that perhaps he was seeing another woman. She had been reading magazines and books that stated men thought about sex more than 30 times a day, yet, it seemed like her husband rarely ever wanted sex. In the magazines and books, not initiating sex was a red flag for a cheating husband.

One of the first tests they tried was for her to give a louder message of what she wanted. When he came home, she dressed in sexy night-time wear. She put on her sexy pajamas, showed cleavage, and curved her body in a way that would have the desired effect on another man. This method failed miserably. Despite increasing her cues, her husband ignored her, seemingly oblivious to her attempt to seduce.

She did more testing, including talking to him about the problem. Talking was another failed attempt. So, she tried emailing him. While writing the email she realized that she was not angry at him for being late. She was actually angry at him for the disconnect which gave her the false idea that he was not connected to her as a loyal partner. The only sign missing was that he did not smell of another woman's perfume or have lipstick on his collar. Other than that, he was giving all the signs of a cheating husband. She pressed "Send" on the email and it uncovered the real bug, making the problem solvable.

By troubleshooting the process, going through several layers of testing, they discovered what the problem really was. Once they understood the problem, they both recognized how easily solvable it was. All he needed to do was show her what he already believed: that he was connected to her till-death-do-us-part and that he was fully, completely loyal. He even said, "I can barely handle one woman. Why would I want two?"

A big part of the solution was simple timing. She wanted intimacy, or at least a basic physical recognition when he arrived home, but this was the exact same time he needed distance. By the time he was done needing distance and was ready for intimacy, she was steaming angry, with no more thoughts of intimacy. When she was ready to be close, he was ready for distance and vice versa. Their "I want you" and "I need space" times were mismatched so predictably that they must have looked like a sitcom, night after night making the same mistakes over and over again.

Solutions often come from both sides. For her part, when she began feeling rejected, she reminded herself of his previous acts of love. Also, she recognized that thoughts were not enough. She needed physical affection when he came home and requested that he give her a hug before disappearing into his daily recovery from social overload. For his part, he let his logic overrule his sensory system and gave his wife a hug whether he liked giving it or not.

The end result was two people who loved each other, sensory overload and all, who found a way to sync up their needs closely enough. Their level of intimacy increased and, in proportion, worries decreased.

The goal is to structure life in a way that your days and nights go smoothly, with as few glitches as possible. When there are "crashes" we want to know how to fix them. Quickly. Read on.

CHAPTER 2

Why Troubleshooting Works

TOP TEN REASONS

Troubleshooting helps you to:

1. identify problems clearly
2. make problems fixable
3. deflate escalation
4. empower and equalize both partners
5. give a safe format
6. eliminate the emotional element
7. allow the person with autism to use black and white thinking as needed
8. chart an easily repeatable process
9. outline (or create) rules to the relationship
10. build and secure an environment where solutions are consistently possible.

Specifically:

1. It helps you to identify problems clearly: given the level of confusion that surrounds most social interactions, identifying the problem clearly is the first, most important step.

2. It helps you to make problems fixable: most people with autism are accustomed to experiencing unsolvable problems in social interactions. The standard response to a problem will be to learn to live with it. When you make problems fixable, you may open up a whole new way of interacting.

③ It deflates escalation: "escalation" refers to an argument becoming increasingly heated. By keeping the problems in the framework of logical, scientific troubleshooting, it effectively stops escalation in its tracks.

④ It empowers and equalizes both partners: by giving a person with autism the tools of troubleshooting, you equip him or her with tools equal in power to the inborn social problem-solving skills that many other people have.

⑤ It gives a safe format: one of the most stressful aspects of relationships is how, at any time, something painful could occur without any explanation or reason. The seemingly random nature of social interaction is due to missing the cues. Troubleshooting provides a highly structured format for solving problems, neutralizing the random aspects. It is similar to creating a "safe playground," an area where you can interact with your partner in structured safety.

⑥ It eliminates the emotional element: the act of troubleshooting is taking an emotional experience—dealing with problems in a relationship—and transitioning it to a rational, analytical experience.

⑦ It allows the person with autism to use black and white thinking: typically, in relationships, black and white thinking is too harsh, but if using it within a troubleshooting framework, where you are trying to solve problems for the health and happiness of the relationship, then black and white thinking is not only appropriate, it is needed.

⑧ It charts an easily repeatable process: without a full set of intuitive social skills, when problems are solved, the person with autism may not understand how he or she managed to get from Point A (the beginning of the argument) to Point B (the end of the argument). Outlining a repeatable process gives the person with autism a structure to follow for future use.

⑨ It outlines (or creates) rules to the relationship: people with autism do not know the rules naturally, so having an outline for how to figure out the rules, or how to create rules for situations that need them, is an extremely valuable resource. Rules in personal, intimate relationships are often unique to only the two of you. Figuring out these rules will increase your happiness exponentially.

10 It builds and secures an environment where solutions are consistently possible: the end goal of all troubleshooting is to generate a solution. By following the troubleshooting process, it does not guarantee a solution, but it does make solutions consistently possible.

There are many types of troubleshooting and many different approaches to problem-solving in relationships. Read on to discover the methods that work for you and your partner.

CHAPTER 3

The Troubleshooting Process

IDENTIFY, TEST, EVALUATE

Troubleshooting is a logical, systematic search for solutions to a problem so that the product or process (relationship) can be made operational again. Troubleshooting is needed to develop and maintain complex systems where the symptoms of a problem can have many possible causes.

Metaphorically, troubleshooting is what it sounds like: identifying a problem and shooting it until you hit, eliminate, or neutralize the problem. The goal is to eliminate problems quickly and efficiently so that you and your partner can live a happy, trouble-free life together.

By NT standards the troubleshooting process may be perceived as "being too blunt" or "being heartless," but if used properly, it can be the most compassionate, successful way to bond with your partner and maintain a happy long-term relationship.

Troubleshooting is akin to the scientific process: systematic observation, hypothesis, prediction, experimentation, and evaluation. If the scientific method was the best method for solving relationship issues, however, this book would be named *The Scientific Method for Relationships*. Unfortunately the scientific method can be laborious. Due to the fast speed of emotion, relationship issues often need quick fixes. Ironically, finding a methodology for quick but effective problem-solving for human relationships is quite complex.

In my research, out of all the fifty-plus methods I studied, the methods used by programmers fit best. Like any good programmer, you:

1. identify the problem

2. test a potential solution

3. evaluate whether or not the solution fixed the problem.

Repeat Steps 2 and 3 as necessary.

This ITE process—Identify, Test, Evaluate—is a simple process that can be used to fix problems in nearly any environment. More complex versions of this formula are used in science, technology, engineering, and other similar fields, but ITE is the straightforward, uncomplicated core essence of them all.

Relationships involve complex problems. Who pays for which bills? Do you split costs equally or proportionally based on income? Do you choose to have children and submit to the sensory assault that children cause? Who is in charge of the kids? Who makes sure that they get to the dentist and what do I do when that partner forgets to make the appointment month after month?

In the mainstream population, these issues are difficult enough and they can easily divide relationships between good, intelligent, and compassionate people. If your relationship is affected by ASD, it is far more difficult, making relationship dissection and evaluation a necessity in order to maintain a relationship. Why? Because when you have an autistic brain, there many more unknowns in the social experience. The problems and solutions are magnified by the power of N (a really large number). Once something reaches a certain level of complexity, it becomes an entirely different type of problem. Solving it requires a systematic approach, otherwise you get lost in the details. Simplifying complex problems allows people with autism to create and sustain long-term relationships.

How to apply ITE? The ITE method for problem-solving in relationships probably has not been role modeled for you or your partner. Normally, people in adult relationships use the following process:

1. Repeat relational dynamics from childhood or young adulthood in an effort to heal.

2. Create drama to soothe pain or perhaps make the core, most difficult pains less noticeable.

3. Form friendship circles that often reinforce the dysfunction or soothe discomfort.

4. Adopt other processes the motivations and intentions of which may be unfamiliar to someone with an autistic brain.

One of the reasons why I married a man with autism is that I have little tolerance for drama. I believe that if you are busy fixing real problems in the world, then there is more than enough drama; there is no need to create more. I knew that a man with a highly logical brain would appreciate and encourage quick, efficient solutions to typical marital difficulties.

That said, it took many years and many false starts before we both realized that the methodology we use to fix a laptop, tablet, desktop, server, or other device can also be used to fix a problem in a relationship.

While learning the ITE process yourself will help in many ways, it is optimal if both partners are aware of the ITE process. It gives you the context to say, "Are we identifying, testing, or evaluating right now?" Each step has a different purpose and identifying what you are trying to accomplish can increase clarity which increases your chances for success.

Imagine that you are trying to identify the reason why you are both angry with each other. Skipping the Identify step and going directly to the Evaluate step would sound like: "Our relationship is bad because you're so angry." This makes problem-solving nearly impossible because you do not even know what the problem is. In this situation, the Identify step might sound like: "It looks like both of us are angry. Do you have any idea why?"

Similarly if you skip to the Test step without having finished the first stage, Identify, you and your partner may bounce around blindly, forgetting what started the argument in the first place, allowing the tension and frustration to snowball. People with less logical brains may find this normal. People with logical brains may find this inefficient, silly, and highly frustrating.

Step 1: Identify

Identifying the problem is the most important step. As long as you don't know what the problem is, you have no hope of fixing it. Identifying the problem is the crucial starting point, the pinpoint on the map that helps you navigate from Point A to Point B.

It may help to think of your relationship problems as simple navigation issues. You identify where you are and where you want to be, then calculate how you would like to get there. Many of us know where we want to be. Knowing where we currently are can be more difficult.

Before I had a data plan on my cell phone I would often call my husband and ask him for help with directions whenever I was lost. He would often help me over the phone from his desk as he searched on Google Maps. He would give me directions over the phone and I would follow the directions while driving. But, a typical "I'm lost" phone call started like this:

Me: *"Carl, I need help!"*

Him: *"Sure. What?"*

Me: *"I'm lost. Can you help me find how to get to _____ (destination)."*

Him: *"Sure. Where are you now?"*

Me: *"I don't know!"*

In hindsight the "I'm lost but I don't know where I am" conversations were hilarious. He would Google the end point then search for me in a wide radius. I would describe what I saw, catching glimpses of street names as they zoomed past. For some reason, it rarely occurred to me to pull over, stop, and find an accurate starting point. So much time and energy was wasted when I did not know my starting point.

In contrast, when I knew my location, he could say, "Turn left at Sacramento. Go half a mile then take a left at University Ave. Destination will be on your right in 1 mile." Simple. Logical. Quick.

Our relationship problems can be similar. If all we know is, "I'm mad (lost) and I want to not be mad anymore (end destination)," then figuring out how to get past the problem, Point A, to the solution, Point B, can be bizarrely frustrating.

In contrast, if we can quickly identify our starting point, we can more easily and swiftly zoom to a solution. If we are mad (lost) yet know that the last streets we passed (the last troublesome thoughts) were at the intersection of Dishes St and Division of Labor Ave, then we can more quickly identify the problem as, "I'm angry that I'm always the one doing the dishes." The navigation from a clear starting point is easier.

Identification is relatively simple, but there are three issues that may get in the way:

1. widely differing viewpoints
2. defensiveness
3. denial.

ISSUE 1: WIDELY DIFFERING VIEWPOINTS

As you identify the problem, each of you states what you think the problem is. If you are mindblind, you may think that you both need to agree exactly on what the problem is. Not so. You can both describe the problem in different terms due to your differing points of view.

> Worst case scenario: You end up arguing so much about what the core problem is, that you never get to the next step.

> Best case scenario: If the problem as you see it is very different from the problem as your partner sees it, it means you have two problems to solve.

If you are stuck at the worst case scenario where one or both of you cannot accept that the other person's point of view is just as valid as your own, consider the following analogy:

> Our minds are like a mathematics exercise. If you agree on the situation, you have only one math problem to solve. If you do not agree, then you have two math problems to solve. Either way, it is in your best interest to solve the problem rather than continue arguing about the differing natures of what you, as a couple, perceive as two different problems.

ISSUE 2: DEFENSIVENESS

If one or both of you are defensive, energy will be spent self-protecting rather than solving the problem.

When this happens, it is unlikely that the problem will be solved. When people are defensive they are much like a cat in a cage: they will either scratch or try to escape. It takes time and a safe environment in order for calm to be restored. The best way for a defensive person to shift out of defensive mode and into problem-solving mode is to wait until the defensiveness has passed.

Waiting allows the defensive person's body to recover from the flood of cortisol, adrenaline, and noradrenaline secreted into the bloodstream by the hypothalamus. During the defensive period, nearly all organs of the body respond, trying to maintain internal homeostasis.

Here is a short, incomplete list of the physiological reaction that occurs when a partner is under stress. I included enough to give you a visual idea of what it is happening internally when your partner transforms from his or her regular state to one of defensiveness.

- Respiratory rate increases to get more oxygen into the bloodstream.

- Blood is shunted away from the gastrointestinal tract, spleen and other non-vital organs. It is rerouted to more vital organs such as the heart, lungs, and brain. Additional blood is also sent to the muscles and limbs.

- Blood pressure increases supplying the body with blood more efficiently.

- Stress hormones affect the limbic system in the brain which controls emotions.

- The areas of the brain related to short- and long-term memory are affected, causing possible problems with memory.

- Glycerin stored in the liver breaks down to supply the body with more glucose.

- The body makes additional glucose from sources other than carbohydrates.

- The immune system becomes suppressed resulting in an increased possibility of infection.

- The pupils of the eye dilate and vision becomes sharper.

In order to come out of the defensive state, the person's heart rate must lower, respiratory rate must stabilize, and many other affected systems need time to recover.

"Defensive" is a war-like term inferring two opposing sides. Note the distinction between defensiveness, an aggressive reaction, and denial, the next subject, which is more of a passive habit.

ISSUE 3: DENIAL

There are people who believe that they do not need to actively engage in the process of problem-solving in their relationships. They make comments such as, "Why do you always have to be making problems?" or "Nothing is wrong. Just leave it be."

All human interaction has potential for problems. Every relationship needs problem-solving. Even a relationship with a cat will involve problem-solving. Will the cat be allowed to scratch the furniture? Will the cat be allowed outdoors? Admittedly, your relationship with a pet is quite different from the relationships you have with fellow human beings, but if a relationship with a cat deserves problem-solving strategies, then a relationship with a human who has verbal ability and far more complex thought needs problem-solving even more. Truly, every relationship needs problem-solving.

If either you or your partner is stuck at the denial stage, believing that there are no problems, then you have to get past the denial before you can engage in any useful problem-solving. For example:

Identify: When presented with a problem, one partner denies there is a problem. "Nothing is wrong. Why are you making a fuss?"

Test: Check your own views. Is there actually a problem or are you nit-picking/creating a fuss? If there is any doubt in your mind that the problem needs active problem-solving, then put the problem-solving on hold until you can verify one way or the other that the problem truly needs to be solved.

THE MOST IMPORTANT ASPECT OF IDENTIFYING

The most important aspect of the Identify step is making sure that the problem is one that needs solving.

One example may be: "My partner makes a funny sound when he eats." While it may bother you to hear this noise, it is likely to be a problem that does not need problem-solving. It is most likely something that needs your acceptance.

If the problem is one that needs solving, go back to the Identify step. For example, say one partner is spending more money than he makes. Accepting this problem is not appropriate. Fixing it is necessary.

Test: Try to fix the problem yourself. In the money spending example, if you are the one with the problem, seek help. Get your spending under control.

If the problem is in your partner's control or otherwise is something that needs both partners' attention, then engage in reciprocal problem-solving (made easier by the ITE process). For example, imagine that you are angry with your partner.

If the problem is not temporary and you cannot fix it yourself, then together, discuss what the core problem really is. For example, it might be that you both tend to be angry and frustrated with each other each weekend, all day Saturday and all day Sunday.

Test: Perhaps you are both being overloaded by the change in routine on weekends or the too-close interactions on the weekends. Perhaps you need more time to yourself for silence and work on your own projects. Give it a try—test a solution such as giving yourself dedicated, predictable time alone on the weekends.

For problems that do not have solutions, there are often two final steps:

1 Shift perspective.

2 If a shift of perspective is not possible, choose whether or not to live with the problem.

Step 2: Test

Once you have identified the problem, now you can begin testing potential solutions. Your first attempt may fail and so may your second, but somewhere along the path, like a lost hat or glove, is your solution.

The Test process is simple: you try what you think will work, then evaluate. If it worked, great. If not, try another Test. For example, if you want your partner to stop swearing, you can try the most obvious thing: ask your partner to stop swearing.

If it works, great. If not, try another solution such as having a swearing jar (a simple glass jar) into which your partner must put a dollar every time he or she says a swearword in front of you by mistake. If that does not work you can keep trying other solutions until you find one that works for you both.

Sometimes the solution will be obvious, quick and easy. Sometimes you will try potential solution after potential solution for years and still not find one that works.

"I have not failed. I've just found 10,000 ways that won't work."
(Thomas A. Edison)

The classic example of troubleshooting is a mechanical example:

The car will not start (the symptom).

- *Why?* The battery is dead.

- *Why?* The alternator is not functioning.

- *Why?* The alternator belt has broken.

- *Why?* The alternator belt was well beyond its useful service life and not replaced.

- *Why?* The vehicle was not maintained according to the recommended service schedule.

- *Why?* Replacement parts are not available because of the extreme age of the vehicle.

Solution 1: Purchase a different vehicle that is maintainable (immediate solution).

Solution 2: Maintain the replacement vehicle according to the recommended service schedule (long-term solution).

The goal is to trace the chain of causality until you end up at the original source of the problem. It takes the emotional element out of the equation and makes the problem solvable. If one step does not work, it is not a reflection on your worth as a human being, but instead, is just a problem that needs fixing.

Working through the "Why?" process can take energy and time. You may feel like a failure as you push past the original "Why?" Remember: people do not fail, processes do. Change the process, eliminate the problem. You only fail if you do not try to solve it.

The troubleshooting process helps you to avoid assumptions and logic traps. It helps you to trace the chain of causality in direct increments from the effect through any layers of abstraction to a root cause. The relationship equivalent of the mechanical example above is this:

My partner is angry (the symptom).

- *Why?* My partner is angry at me.

- *Why?* I did not do what my partner asked me to do.

- *Why?* It was an unpleasant task.

- *Why?* I have a sensory issue that is triggered by that task.

- *Why?* Because it is a work day and I am already spent by the time I get home. No more energy for a task that is so difficult.

Solution 1: Do the task at the weekend instead.

Solution 2: Trade tasks so that you each have tasks that are least annoying to you personally.

There is a good chance that you will struggle to recreate the test process in your own unique situations. If you do, refer to this chapter for ideas that will prompt your next test.

If you do not know what to try for the next potential solution:

1. Try the most obvious solution.

2. Try to understand why the problem exists. Sometimes that is enough of a solution.

3. Try stream of conscience; ramble on about the problem until a new potential solution occurs to you.

4. Try distancing yourself from the problem: "If I wanted to solve this problem I would _____."

5. Try the opposite of what you have done before.

6. Read other parts of this book to help you brainstorm.

7. Read other books listed in the Resources section.

8. Listen to podcasts, talks (such as commencement speeches or TED talks), or other content that is not related to your problem, but will generate new thought regarding how you approach your life.

9. Ask a trusted friend for new ideas.

10. Ask your partner for ideas on what to try next—this may seem obvious, but it is easily overlooked if you tend to not seek out the advice of others.

11. Give yourself a break from troubleshooting and try again when you are refreshed.

12. Take a nap and let your subconscious work on the problem.

13 Try doing a favorite hobby or activity such as cooking, carving, sewing, gardening, building, or another hands-on task to allow your mind time to think of a new idea.

14 Try doing for your partner what you would like your partner to do for you.

15 Finish the following sentence, "To make my partner happy I could _____," or, "To get past this problem, I could _____."

16 Think of what you do not want to do the most; it may be what you need to do to solve the problem.

17 Find a great role model and ask, "What would _____ do?"

18 Think of the least likely solution and do it.

One of my favorite suggestions is to try doing what you do not want to do, mostly because it is so often effective. The most obvious application occurred many years ago when our children were young and I was "not in the mood" for sex too often. I found that every time I went ahead and tried it anyway I actually had a wonderful time about 90 percent of the time. In hindsight I was almost always grateful that I had been open-minded. I was nearly always glad I had pushed myself past the initial resistance. Ninety percent is a high rate of being wrong about what I thought I wanted!

After proving myself wrong about "not being in the mood" for many years, I finally learned to ask myself, "I feel like I don't want to do it, but is that just a temporary resistance that will be proven inaccurate in only a minute's time?"

My all-time favorite solution is the last one: try what is least likely to work. Some of our most brilliant solutions have come from trying the least likely solution. One example happened in November 2009. The company my husband worked for decided it wanted to show a profit by the end of the year, so they fired all their engineers and told them they would consider rehiring them in January. It was a terribly unkind thing to do to the engineers—the brains of the company— and it was a terrible time to be looking for a new job in the US.

Since I was working nearly full-time parenting one of our sons with autism and our other three children, I was not much help as a wage-earner. We hit a wall financially and none of the solutions we tried worked. So, I did the least obvious thing: I paid off all credit card debt. Most people would think it wise to leave the debt and keep as much cash as possible at hand to ride out the storm, but instead, I did what was least obvious—pull every dollar I could from every available spot to pay off all debt. It left us poor, but debt-free.

It worked because it gave us financial peace of mind. It lowered our upcoming load (only mortgage and utilities were left to pay). It made us feel good about our ability to "be smart" with our money. It was the least obvious thing to do but it was the right thing to do. We came through the tough time in far better shape than we had been before the lay-off.

As you try potential solutions it may feel like a lot of work. It helps to think of problem-solving as a muscle. The more problems you solve, the better you get. A visual analogy may help:

> Think of a person who has very few problems to solve and notice how that person gets stressed over simple decisions such as getting to a doctor's appointment or what to have for lunch. Contrast that person's life with someone who handles massive responsibility but manages it with the same level of stress that the first person handles their relatively minor concerns.

The examples we use are: Bill Gates (Microsoft)/Michael Dell (Dell computers)/Marissa Mayer (Yahoo) versus Margaret, an elderly woman we know who is very concerned about her knitting, worrying that she may run out of yarn before she finishes a particular scarf when she always ends up with more than enough. Managing multi-billion dollar companies is, logically, more stressful than knitting, but Margaret's body and the bodies of a tech giant are likely experiencing the same amount of stress. This comparison helps me see that a person's stress response can be a choice. It also helps me see that problem-solving abilities can be built, one day at a time, by getting more and more effective at what you do.

The Test process can be the most fun step out of the three steps in ITE. It is fun because it allows you to try things that you would not normally try. It gives you the opportunity to make that mistake for the last time by finding solutions that really work.

Step 3: Evaluate

Troubleshooting is goal-oriented. The problem should be solved by the end of the troubleshooting process, even if it is just a temporary solution, a partial solution, or the decision to leave the problem as is.

The goals of troubleshooting are to:

1. Recognize and unlearn patterns of repeated conflict to allow for more positive, comfortable exchanges.

2. Either develop more social and interpersonal skills or learn workarounds.

3. Create a personal day-to-day sense of satisfaction and overall health.

Most often the evaluation step will be binary: you either solved the problem or you did not. If you did, great, move on. If you did not, proceed to the next potential solution.

The evaluation step is the most clear. It is not as crucial as Steps 1 and 2, but it is most important when you want to make sure that the same problem will not resurface again soon.

Summary/Maintenance

ITE can make difficult, confusing, and unfortunately common social situations easier for someone with a social disorder. For someone on the spectrum, the main value of ITE is that it cuts your workload in one-third. If you are identifying the problem, you do not need to be worrying about testing or evaluating. ITE is a linear process that works within a non-linear relationship dynamic.

PART 2

BEGINNING WITH CORRECT ASSUMPTIONS

CHAPTER 4

Fixing the Problem versus Fixing Each Other

At some time in everyone's life there comes a point (it is to be hoped) when we identify who we are and who we want to be. A person with autism may find it easier or more difficult than it is for others.

It may be harder if you have lived a life with people telling you how to act, what to say, and when to say it. As one man with autism said, "Of course I don't know who I am. My entire life has been scripted." While social skills need to be learned, there is a potential for backlash when even the most minute details such as how close to stand to someone has been specifically learned. You may wonder who you are without all the scripting. Or, if you did not get assistance with social skills, you may wonder what you would have become if you had received help.

Either way, you may have had so much rewiring (or no rewiring) of your self and your actions that the thought of, "Who am I?" leaves you feeling blank. You are who others say you are. Or perhaps you have no "social mirror"—people reflecting back to you their perceptions of you—which makes it more difficult to see the many facets of your identity. If any of this sounds familiar to you, it may be much harder to identify who you are and much harder to assert yourself in your interactions with your partner.

It may be easier if you are a bit mindblind and do not know or care what others think of you. When you separate the reality from the emotion, comments from others affect you far less.

If you have autism, it is likely you have some degree of mindblindness. With mindblindness, the opinions of others are not relevant. So, when in an argument with a partner who wants you to, "be nicer," "be more loving," or, "be polite," the comments are mostly babble. The viewpoints of others fall on deaf ears because how could there be any reality other than the one you currently see?

If this is the case for you, then living with a partner who wants you to change might be annoying, but will not bother you on the same level as it would if you were not so sure of your own reality.

Asking your partner to change who he or she is

When a problem is interlaced with a person's identity, it is not fixable. You cannot ask people to change who they are. For example:

- Asking the partner with autism to check in with you once a day is probably not connected with core identity.

- Asking the partner with autism to, "be more friendly," or, "be nicer," is probably connected with core identity. (It is definitely connected to the diagnosis.)

While we can rewire many aspects of who we are, it is safest to avoid areas related to core identity. Areas to avoid (specific to autism-linked relationships):

- *Physiological aspects*: touch, taste, smell, sight, sound.

- *Social aspects*: quantity or quality of social interaction.

- *Relational aspects*: reciprocal interactions.

Why should we avoid these areas? Isn't it part of self-improvement to tackle these areas and try to make ourselves and each other better? It may sound logical and even good to do so and when we were younger and in our schooling years, this was more appropriate. In adulthood, however, something shifts. You become as self-reliant as you possibly can. Within that context, a request to change who you are (core identity) is more accurately categorized as a veiled attempt at trying to change core identity. Asking adults to change who they are is inappropriate, especially in intimate relationships.

Problems that reside inside the "inner circle of self" are delicate. When they are encroached on, the person is likely to become defensive, channeling all energies towards self-protection.

When a person is in self-protective stance, the respectful reactions are to stop talking, leave the room, and reflect on it later when both of you are receptive again. During this time apart it helps to evaluate:

- Are you asking your partner to change who he or she is? or

- Are you asking your partner to make a reasonable compromise so that you can live together happily?

Fixing your partner

One day when frustrated over a disagreement my husband and I had deemed unsolvable, I went for a walk. While being brutally honest with myself, I confessed that I did want to fix my husband. I wanted him to be different, better.

As I heard the words in my mind: "I want to have my husband fixed," it sounded much like what I also said about the cats we fostered for the local cat rescue group. I often took the kitties to the veterinarian to "get them fixed." Fixing meant neutering them.

I wondered if I was doing the same thing to my husband, emasculating him. Was I? Since I was not sure, I went home and apologized for having suggested changes that might have appeared threatening on the level of identity.

The word "fix" has both a negative and a positive connotation and unfortunately in an argument, one partner could be referring to "fixing" something as a positive act, while the other partner perceives it as negative, especially when it refers to behavior and/or character flaws. Whenever two people are using the same word but have significantly different meanings, miscommunication is inevitable.

It may help to come to a common agreement as to how you both perceive the act of "fixing a problem" and/or "fixing the relationship." There is a good chance that the tendency to hear words literally, without significant emotional involvement, actually gives a person with autism an advantage in this area. If you can look logically at the act of fixing, you might be more able to differentiate between the problem and your sense of self.

The English language has a limited supply of words that mean "fix." When you define the word specifically, you can better explain your perception of the act to each other as partners. Once you identify and verbalize your perception, your partner can have insights into how you see it and possibly agree or disagree with you more accurately.

Adjust	Amend	Correct
Debug	Mend	Overhaul
Rebuild	Repair	Restore
Regulate	Revise	Sort

Some of these words will have negative connotations for you depending on your background. For example, the word "repair" is often used in literature about autism, often in the form of, "a person with autism has a limited ability to repair conversations." The word may evoke thoughts of the person being defective by nature. If so, avoid that word.

Similarly, the word "mend" often refers to broken, ripped, or destroyed things. We mend old clothes; we also mend a broken heart. If mending has a negative connotation, avoid it also.

In contrast, the word "fix" may be your best choice of terminology depending on your background. If the person with autism tends to be curious and likes to take things apart to fix them, then the word, "fix," may be a happy word. In our case, it is. Both my husband and I usually have at least one screwdriver in our backpacks (or my purse) for taking apart laptops and desktops. Both of us are always stopped at the airport when going through security to lose yet another screwdriver that is found buried deep in some forgotten pocket of our carry-on bags. While I only take apart something occasionally, for him, rarely a day goes by when he has not opened the case of at least one computer or other device.

Note that when first using the word "fix" in the context of "fixing" someone, verify that your partner is not equating it to "fix" as a synonym for "neuter" or "spay." People with autism often hear the literal meaning of words or phrases. Metaphors or words with multiple meanings can cause unnecessary confusion. The word "fix" has many meanings and the wrong definition may be innocently assumed.

Hopefully you can use the word "fix" with impunity in your relationship, especially if you can get past the last hurdle: the negative connotation to "fixing" a person.

A highly logical person with autism can see the following contradiction:

Society advocates self-improvement.

versus

"They don't accept me as I am."

The negative aspect comes from a distaste for one person (the dominant teacher, boss, parent) trying to perfect another (the inferior student, employee, child).

The differentiating factor between good fixing and bad fixing is whether or not the person being fixed *is the one making the choice* to be fixed. It is about free will and personal choice.

Outsourcing self-awareness

For highly self-aware people, the decision to self-analyze and make a personal change is relatively natural and common. New Year's resolutions, self-help books, even self-improvement applications on your cell phone, all abound to help people who have identified their own issues and seek ways to fix and improve themselves.

Autism and the accompanying lack of awareness of the emotional self can make this significantly more difficult. People with autism may rely on others to tell them what needs to be corrected. This can be perceived as an "outsourcing of social analysis," rather than a dependent reliance on others.

To see this outsourcing in action, take the example of Matt, a man with high-functioning autism, who often stood too close to his co-workers, making them uncomfortable especially in the current era when staff are on alert for potential sexual harassment. When Matt's boss mentioned this inappropriate behavior during Matt's yearly employee review, Matt had to rely on his boss to discern that this was a problem. Matt could not see it on his own. Matt's self-awareness was low; he "outsourced" this awareness to his boss and then relied on his boss's advice.

In this scenario, it would have been extremely easy for Matt to see this feedback in a negative light, a comment on Matt's "inability to see something he should be able to see." At worst, he could get defensive. The hurt pride and defensiveness would put a barrier up between him and his boss. Even worse, it would cut Matt off from his own ability (albeit outsourced ability) to solve a problem that was hurting him at work and could possibly cost him his job.

At best, Matt would recognize that he had skills which other people did not have and other people had skills which he did not have (such as naturally identifying correct physical proximity to other people).

There are a few "tricks" you can use to help yourself get past the defensiveness and recognize that when someone else comments on something that most other adults already know, it does not necessarily mean that they want to play the boss, teacher, or parent role with you.

As one woman put it succinctly: "A person with autism refusing to take social advice from an NT friend is like a naked person refusing an offer of clothing."

Another woman said, "If I was near-sighted and I refused to wear glasses, that refusal would be colossally undermining my ability to live. When I give my husband (with autism) advice, I'm not being bossy or nagging or negative. I am handing him glasses. I don't know how to help him see that I'm not nagging. I just know that nagging is completely different from what I'm doing. I'm saying, 'Here, wear these glasses for a minute. If you do, you'll see what I mean.'"

Over the years I have found the glasses analogy particularly helpful, especially since it has become a reciprocal act. Sometimes I hand my husband a pair of NT glasses and sometimes he hands me a pair of ASD glasses. I enjoy seeing into his world. The glasses analogy works for us, but may not work for everyone.

One of the reasons why it is hard to accept a partner's advice is because it may indicate that he or she does not accept you as you are (for example, if your partner tells you to, "Please change into nicer clothes before we go out to dinner").

Regardless of whether or not your partner accepts you, the most important step is that you accept yourself. Without taking that step, it does not matter much if your partner accepts you—you will be "unacceptable" and "not good enough" until you can accept yourself.

Ironically, accepting the advice of others regarding social mores is a way of recognizing and accepting who you are. It does not mean that you should blindly follow anyone who gives you social advice; it simply means that accepting (and even requesting) social advice is a sign that you have fully accepted yourself as you are.

A word of caution: despite all the logical reasoning for why people with autism should rely on socially-skilled people for social advice, it is still extremely difficult. Autism is known as the "extreme male" way of being and the common stereotype is that, "Men don't ask for directions." This means that if you have autism, you may have to work much harder than others, extremely hard, to allow people to give you advice. It may not even occur to you that others have advice that may be helpful.

It will be counter-intuitive and unpleasant to ask for advice, but, it is to be hoped, the results will prove over time that allowing others to assist you with social-skills advice makes your life easier and more manageable.

On the flip side, giving social advice can sometimes be just as worrisome as receiving social advice. I was recently reminded of this when my husband had completed a long trans-Pacific flight and had gone straight to work without changing his clothes. He texted me a few hours after he had landed: "At work, didn't stop by house. Relaxing at my desk. Team is doing well." I debated over whether or not to tell him that wearing the equivalent of pajamas to work was inappropriate since he was the company owner and lead role model for all employees. Plus, I knew he hadn't had access to a shower for at least 30 hours of the trans-Pacific travel.

I debated for a long time: "How do I tell him what it means to NTs when you wear stained, ripped sweatpants and t-shirt to the office?" In his segment of the tech sector, programmers judge each other on their code, not on their clothes. Some of the world's best coders dressed similarly, but our mostly NT office was not aware of this and would judge him by NT standards.

I noticed my heart rate increase a little in frustration over basic self-care skills. I repressed the urge to reply with corrective criticism. So much of my NT response was entirely irrelevant in his view. My words would quite literally fall on deaf ears.

I eliminated everything that would not have made sense to him and commented on the one thing that did—he wanted the respect of the people with whom he worked.

I texted one line: "If you want people to respect you, grab some new pants and a new shirt out of your suitcase and go change."

I am not sure if he took this advice since I did not hear back from him until evening. At least it did not result in a fight. Ethically, I felt like I had done the right thing: I had tried to assist the man in my life whose eyes do not see what NT eyes see. I had given him glasses, social glasses, and I knew that if he used those glasses, he would benefit.

Is it fixable?

Which leads to the next concept: when presenting a fix that needs to be made, first determine if it is fixable or not. In the case of my husband's clothing, it was easily fixable in 60 seconds or less.

The clothing issue is a hot topic for many couples. It is the easiest, quickest, least complicated fix, even considering autism-related sensory issues, so it is a great example for this "Fixing the Problem versus Fixing Each Other" chapter.

The reasons why someone might request that a partner fixes (changes) his or her clothing include:

- to look more visually appealing

- to appear "in sync," an NT desire to mirror each other on a physical level

- on a societal level, to appear as if they belong together as a united couple

- to appear "from the same class," especially in an area where class hierarchy is still in place

- to impress others

- to feel good in the clothing

- for sensory purposes so that one partner can touch the other without his or her fingertips being assaulted by an unpleasant texture.

If you wish to request your partner make different clothing choices, the following phrases may help:

"I don't want *you* to change. I just want *your clothes* to change."

"It's just a shirt (or pants, shoes, etc.)."

"It makes a big difference for me so unless it really bothers you to change, this is something you could do to make things significantly more enjoyable for me."

"Seeing you dressed in _____ (whatever style you are aiming for) is a type of foreplay. You look so good when you are dressed like that." (Knowing that something will earn one physical affection, can sometimes act as a powerful motivator.)

In one woman's case, certain colors or patterns were exceptionally unsettling for her. She found that if her husband wore a certain color of shirt, she would be agitated and short-tempered all day, usually erupting in an unpleasant evening.

All he had to do was change his shirt. Simple. He did not mind and it made all the difference between a good day and a bad day for his wife. Once they both understood the problem, it was an easy fix.

Understanding the problem was, however, surprisingly difficult. It required a self-awareness that does not come easily to someone with autism. She figured it out by clinically evaluating the situation. She explained her process like this:

1. "I notice a rise in body temperature, a tightening of my fists and shoulder muscles, even a tightening of the muscles on my face. I want to punch someone or do something bad. I am angry. This is The Problem."

2. "But what am I angry at? It's most likely I am angry at someone near me. Check. Nope, nobody near me has done anything annoying."

3. "Next likely: I am angry at someone who passed me. Check. Nope, nothing frustrating from anybody passing me on the road or while walking."

4. "Next likely: I was thinking about a previous event and it triggered a memory of anger. Check. Nope, I wasn't thinking about much of anything."

5. "Next likely: Something in my environment triggered it, upset my sensory system. Check. I do feel physically uneasy in many ways right now…"

6. "The cause of the problem is now isolated. I scan the environment for what could have caused it. Smell: is someone wearing overpowering cologne? No. Sounds: is a baby crying or other loud noise nearby? No. Touch: is there a tag in my clothing rubbing my skin or is there another physical annoyance? No. Sights: is there anything in my visual field that makes me uncomfortable? Yes!"

7 "Bingo! It's the visual field. It takes a bit of thought to figure it out, but I scanned the area using my eyes as a Geiger counter. When I felt an increase in panic and stress, I found the annoyance. The first time I did this an obvious alarm sounded in my body when I looked at my husband's shirt; it made me queasy."

This realization was pivotal. She noticed her physiological reaction. This previously unseen problem had caused her to:

- Associate panic and overload with her husband.

- Feel pervasive panic. The shirt was in her field of vision all day which put her adrenal gland on overload so that by the end of the day she was flinching at small noises, lashing out like someone who has been attacked because, in fact, her sensory system had been attacked many times throughout the day, every time the shirt was in her field of vision.

- Experience a persistent frustration from not knowing what was causing her problem. She knew she loved her husband so why would she be constantly looking away from him? She knew she loved being near him on other days, so why was she inexplicably repulsed by him on some days?

- Warp her self-image. The lack of awareness about this sensory issue caused her to believe that she was an unpredictable, flighty, emotional woman when in fact she prided herself on being quite predictable, reliable, and logical.

As she explained, "The next step was to remove the object from my field of vision. I can either throw out the shirt, hide it, or just request that he not wear it near me. Once I started doing this, everything improved."

I found it admirable that this woman was able to overcome a difficult situation that required a high level of self-awareness. After hearing of her experience, I found that I was similarly afflicted. I explained the situation to my husband and he immediately tossed out all offensive shirts from his closet. It made a surprisingly big difference to our quality of life.

When making requests, make sure you are asking your partner to change based on what you want and need, not on what you think your partner should want and need. I requested what I needed for my visual comfort, not what I thought he should wear based on the year's current fashion trends. Also, make sure the change is doable and possible before you request it.

The quadrants of fixability

To help you to more easily make fixes, it helps to be able to differentiate between the visible and the invisible and between the fixable and the unfixable.

1 Visible, Fixable

2 Visible, Unfixable

3 Invisible, Fixable

4 Invisible, Unfixable

1 *Visible, Fixable* problems would be clothing choices, hair cleanliness, body positioning, physical behaviors such as standing too close or walking awkwardly. This is the easiest category of problems to fix. It is to be hoped that the bulk of your problems will be in this category.

2 *Visible, Unfixable* problems would be physical appearance choices that cannot be changed, behavior choices such as a tic or a necessary self-calming stim that is better than the alternative (potential meltdown). These problems are by far the most problematic: they cannot be hidden, they don't go away, and they may be publicly embarrassing. They are not solvable so trying to work on them may cause endless frustration. The content of your most common arguments may be found in this sector.

3 *Invisible, Fixable* problems would be ways of interacting, ways of treating each other, sensory issues such as smell. Behaviors and habits would be in this category. These issues are harder to discuss, especially with a visual thinker and/or person who needs concrete examples, but at least they are fixable if you work hard enough to communicate about them and create solutions.

④ *Invisible, Unfixable* problems would be the same as above, but those issues that are either too ingrained or too difficult for one or both partners to handle. For example, sexual performance may be an area where there are too many expectations and too many misperceptions (probably mostly based on Hollywood's view of how sex should be). These issues may be the most painful. It helps to comfort oneself with the thought that these unfixable invisible problems are, "at least not publicly embarrassing." This quadrant needs the most compassionate acceptance.

It may help to see these four quadrants within the framework of common software problems. Perhaps it is the geeky side of me that loves this analogy. We have found it quite useful.

There are two types of software. There is the code that is hardwired into the construction of the machine: it is literally burnt into the motherboard. Then there are applications and software packages (and even the operating system) that you can load on to your computer or wipe from your computer.

The firmware is hardwired and is not changeable. The software is changeable which you can download and delete, add or subtract at will. It may not be easy or cheap or fun, but you can change it. The same can be applied to ourselves and our partners. There are certain things you may want to change and certain things you can't change.

It may be difficult to determine which problems are fixable (software) and which ones are not (firmware). Let's look at a more difficult example—emotional state of being.

For example, the problem might be that your partner seems sad all the time.

Is it fixable? Check if there are any environmental issues that could be causing it. There may be something easy that you can fix that will alleviate some of the sadness. For example, one Saturday I was gone most of the day while my husband and children stayed at home to relax. When I returned, he looked desperately sad. I asked him what was wrong and after a long pause he said, "Nothing." He was so overloaded that he was nearly non-verbal. He was not avoiding the question. He really did not know what was happening in his body. Self-awareness does not come naturally for many who are on the spectrum.

I looked around the home and found that both kids had been playing on their laptops without using their headphones and they had left the game console on. All sound sources had probably been on the entire time regardless of where the children were or what they were doing. I went to each room, pressed mute on each laptop and console and went back to see if there was any effect on Carl. His eyes lit up and he immediately "lifted." He had a general low mood for the rest of the day, but the deep sadness was gone.

What if, however, you have eliminated all potential causes of the sadness and your partner is still sad? Perhaps your partner is naturally a low-mood person. Some of the greatest philosophers, artists and thinkers have been sad as a regular state of being.

All of us have "set points" for certain aspects of ourselves. We have a set point for weight, a weight that our bodies try to return to when we diet or overeat. We have emotional set points and physical comfort set points.

It is not "bad" to have sadness as your emotional set point. If it is not annoying to you, accept it and find a way to appreciate it as your partner's way of being.

Summary/Maintenance

When you see something in your relationship with your partner, identify whether it is fixable or not. If your partner deems it unfixable, then it is unfixable, even if you think it would be easy to change.

Remember, if your partner is requesting a change that does not work for you, one thing you can say that will hopefully garner a respectful withdrawal of the change request:

"Don't fix me; I'm not broken."

CHAPTER 5

Nearly Any Problem Can Be Resolved When It Is Small

Nearly any problem, even global issues such as wars and mass human-caused disasters can be traced back to decisions made early on that caused the situation to escalate out of control. The initial problems are seemingly small in comparison to how large and how out-of-control the problem grew to be eventually.

When a problem is small, it is easier to fix. Implementation of "fixing" is actually quite difficult, however. If it were easy to fix social problems, then the world never would have experienced World War I or II or the Cold War or any of the other mass tensions and devastations. Humans tend to let problems grow and fester, leaving misunderstandings to grow as they naturally do. As a law of social physics:

$P \times T = S$

Where:

S = Suffering

P = Problem

T = Time

First, most crucial rule: keep the T factor small. Seconds become minutes and minutes become hours, then days, weeks, and years. You control the T factor. As soon as you notice a P, problem, solve it as quickly and efficiently as you can.

Keep focus, keep focus, keep focus

As soon as you notice that an interaction is becoming tense, stop and ask yourself and/or your partner:

"What are we trying to solve exactly?"

"Remind me what the main problem is?"

If your partner resists (usually by bringing up other issues) you can say:

"I'm confused. Can you help me identify the main problem we are talking about now?"

"I'm really sorry, but I can only handle one problem at a time."

"If you can't give me just one problem at a time, I'll need to excuse myself from this discussion until you can identify the first problem you'd like to work on. Thanks for your understanding."

As soon as that one single problem is identified, grab it, and hold onto it. If your partner goes off track, ask:

"Is this central to the problem we're solving?"

"Do you mind if we stick to the main problem?"

"Let's solve that one next, but let's solve the first problem first."

"I feel like we have gone off track. Can we talk about the original question?" (Either of you can ask this, whether you started the conversation or not.)

"I can tell you want to talk about a lot of different things. I'm going to write down all these different topics and we can discuss them after we finish the first topic." (Actually write them down. It shows your partner that you believe these concerns to be valid—and they are—even though at this point they are mostly an attempt by your partner's brain to escape handling something difficult.)

"Thank you for talking with me." (Appreciation never hurts!) "I'm glad I have you in my life and that we can discuss things like this."

Next, restate your original concern.

"These are all valid and important concerns. Now, let's discuss the thing that sparked them." (Restate your original concern.)

"It feels like you are trying to avoid the original question." (Call his bluff.)

"I am short on time today and need to get a solid answer to the original question." (Restate the question.)

A few physical things you can do:

- *Take a deep breath.* People will often respond by also taking a deep breath. It is called, "entrainment."

- *Yawn.* Yes, you can fake a yawn. Anything to get more oxygen to your partner's brain.

- *Get a drink of water.* Offer your partner a drink. This is a double-whammy: the physiological sensation of cool water going down your throat calms and soothes. It also communicates that you are a team sharing resources.

If your partner has gone off track, he or she is probably feeling defensive. In a very primal way, people are often scared of those who are larger than them (unless that larger person is their protector). Ensure that your head is lower than your partner's head. If you are standing and are taller, slump a little or sit down. If you are sitting, bend a little to show that you are not a threat. Personally, when solving problems I often sit on the floor and do stretches, explaining that I need to relieve sore muscles. It puts him at ease and I get a few extra minutes of stretching, relaxing my body, a win–win. Remember this is not an NT-appropriate strategy. It is specific for those on the spectrum (and perhaps others). It is a primal approach, reducing social context down to its most primitive elements.

The purpose is not to show submission. I am far too sparky a warrior-type to encourage readers to show submission. I am simply pointing out a primal reaction. When people feel defensive they need reassurance that no one is attacking them. By showing a smaller self for a few moments, it allows your partner to effectively reassure him- or herself that he or she is ok and that no one is attacking him or her.

Squashing the spider

Many years ago, a particularly unpleasant argument snowballed, building momentum over three days. Both my husband and I were miserable. Arguing actually lowers the immune system's ability to fight disease and both of us were literally ill with flu-like symptoms at the end of the three days.

While I was battling insomnia on night three, in and out of sleep, I dreamed that both of us were caught in a spider's web. The problem was the spider in the center of the web, and the silk (the web strings radiating out from the center) were all the difficulties we had been discussing, all the sticky traps that we had argued about.

If the visual image of a spider web helps you, next time you have an argument with your partner, stop for a moment and try to determine the core problem, the spider at the middle. What is the one thing that is causing the fight? Hint: it will probably be an action or inaction such as, "He didn't take out the garbage," or "She said something mean to me."

If the event happened a long time ago and/or has a low risk of happening again, then you are probably mis-identifying the problem. For example, say ten years ago you loaned your laptop to your partner and she spilled water on the keyboard. The problem is not what happened in the past—the problem is what is happening now. "She is asking to borrow my laptop and won't respect my, 'No'." That is the statement of the current action and current desire. The rest is history and detail (important detail, but still detail). By focusing on details that distract from the core problem, we lower our chance of success because the core problem is solvable, the other things are probably not.

In this example, neither partner can go back in time and respond differently to the water on the keyboard. There is no redoing the reactions and consequences. Focusing on it merely makes the core problem more complex. It is interesting to note that unless the argument is quite benign, it is actually dangerous to "look elsewhere." Because once you look elsewhere the spider (the problem) can move and be difficult to relocate.

Arguments become complex very quickly. You need to stop it within the first few minutes, preferably the first minute, and keep your eyes on that nasty little spider so that you can squash it. (To animal rights activists, I apologize for this part of the visual.)

A few things which you can say to help keep your eye on the problem include:

"I feel like we're losing sight of what caused the problem. What do you think is the main problem?" (It helps to ask the NT partner this. It simply off-loads the effort of analyzing complex social dynamics.)

"I need to deal with one issue at a time. What was the first issue?"

"I believe that we can solve this, and make you happy, as long as we stick to the main point. What do you believe is the thing that we're trying to solve?"

Or, for truly elusive problems:

"What is happening right now that made this problem occur?"

This is easier said than done but is well worth the effort. Personally, I pretend that if I lose sight of the spider/the core issue, it will run away and then I will have the constant terror of thinking it will bite me in the night. (I must be tasty because I often get spider bites in any country to which I have traveled.) The fear of losing sight of that spider is enough for me.

If he says something unrelated to the core issue, I interrupt. I wave my hands. I give the "Time Out" sign used in football. I put on the brakes. I make the conversation stop. I say:

"Let's stick to the main problem."

"Let's solve the current problem first."

"Let's not get lost. The main problem we can solve right now is _____."

"I can't deal with that right now. I need to solve the main problem first."

Often, I will ignore the off-topic comment and redirect to that teeny core problem:

"The main problem is..."

It is most helpful to reaffirm:

"Nearly any problem can be solved when it is small. Let's solve _____."

The hope is that you will trigger your partner's best traits. For a partner who is on the spectrum, it might be:

- the ability to compartmentalize, blocking out details and/or complications
- the desire to not deal with complex social relationships
- the desire to keep the problem simple and solvable
- the ability for intense focus
- the tendency to problem-solve clinically, without emotional complications.

If you are NT, you may crave an emotionally complex relationship; you may perceive a lack of sincerity. For a few years of my own marriage, before I had heard about autism, I said, "I want a more sophisticated relationship."

The easiest, quickest way to meet your own need for relationship complexity is to build up your network of friendships. There is nothing wrong with wanting deep relationships in your life. Getting your needs met is possible without minimizing your partnership (unless your partner feels threatened by it). It is a simple problem with a simple solution: get complexity from complex people; do not try to get it from a person who does not want it.

Solving the small problems

To show how small problems can be solved, do a short exercise: think of the top three problems you have in your relationship. Write them down if that helps. They must be specific. For example, the problem "Doesn't communicate" is not fair. It is too big. Instead, get your list of three down to specifics, for example "Doesn't reply to my emails," or "Doesn't pick up the phone when I call." There may be a hundred different problems under the Communication umbrella; just pick out three specific problems for this exercise.

Now, pick one, the one that makes you most frustrated or angry.

When written down in simple words, the problem seems small. "He doesn't answer my emails," is just a simple act that has become a habit. It grows from an unexplained simple fact to:

- He does not want to reply.

- He does not like what I said in my emails; he does not care about my thoughts.

- He does not love me; he does not want me.

- Maybe I should leave him. But what about the children and home?

- What can I do to get back at him? What can I do to show him how much this hurts? How can I hurt him as badly as he hurt me?

All of a sudden it feels like there is a monster in the room trying to attack both of you, causing one single problem to morph into a much, much bigger one.

I have met many couples who have the "Doesn't respond to my emails" problem. In one, the wife with autism wrote epistle-long emails and the husband simply did not have time to reply. But, he knew that it was important to her, so even if he was at work and did not "have time," he stopped doing work, read the emails and gave a complete reply. It calmed her and helped her get through the day. For him, he had calculated how much time it took him to deal with the fallout of not replying and found that overall it was *more* time-consuming to not reply. The arguments that ensued after an unanswered email took hours whereas a reply took 10 to 20 minutes.

He understood from experience that it was better to work late and make up the lost time later than to leave his wife unanswered and susceptible to panic attacks. They had been married 16 years and had agreed that this was one of only a few deal-breakers. She needed to communicate through long emails and since he wanted to stay married, he had agreed to do this for her.

For me, seeing this couple's problem and solution helped me realize how hard it was for my own husband to read my emails. My emails were often only a paragraph or two, typically three to twelve sentences, but they were overwhelming for him. The longer the email, the more variables it contained. Processing the emails word by word was laborious and unpleasant for him. Since I did not have an emotional need to write long emails, I began cutting them down to half or less. I made a game of it: "Can I say the same thing in half the words?" I would like to think that it helped, though absence of pain is rarely noticed.

The smallest problem: Do you want to be together?

If you are trying to keep the problem small but are still confused about your partner's requests and comments, perhaps the fundamental question needs to be addressed: "Do you want to be in a relationship?" This is truly the smallest, most vital question and it will cloud the problem-solving process if it is not clear whether each of you wants to be married (or otherwise together).

Why would someone get married if they do not want to be in a relationship? Possible reasons are:

- because they think they are supposed to

- for certain benefits that are no longer needed

- because the partner asked and they could not think of a reason to say, "No."

Those may sound like odd reasons, but if you do not have autism, there is a chance that it is inconceivable for you to consider what the world looks like when your life has been fully scripted. At some point, a person asks, "Is this what I really wanted?"

Solving problems when they are small and forcing larger problems to reveal their small core is an extremely helpful strategy in that it strips conversations of all the extras, revealing the bare truth. It has been many years, at least a decade, since we had one of these arguments, but we used to have arguments where, after all the extras had been stripped away, the underlying argument was, "I do not want to be married" (him) versus, "I want to be married" (me). Once this truth was revealed several times, we were able to answer the questions of "Why be married?" Giving honest, clear-sighted answers to that question was extremely important in our ability to stay married through the tough times.

Autism was at the epicenter of this decision. For those who prefer computers (or books or other interests) to people, relationships hold less appeal. In this context a relationship can go from fun and rewarding to not-worth-my-time very quickly. In an ASD-linked relationship having a solid reason to explain why you are together can make all the difference.

First, the reasons that did *not* work for answering, "Why be in a relationship?":

- *Because you have to.* Somewhere along the line someone probably told you that you have to be in relationships. "You cannot be alone. There is no other option. Without other people around you, you will be lonely, sad, rejected."

    The "because you have to" reasoning does not work any better than a "because I said so" from worn-out parents trying to get their child to eat vegetables. At some point, you are the ultimate authority of what is best for you. People can force you, but on the deepest level, you choose.

- *Because relationships are good for you.* This is subjective. Broccoli and Brussel sprouts are also good for you but, as an adult, it is your choice whether or not to eat them. Unless you truly believe the relationship is good for you, this reasoning cannot provide sufficient motivation.

- *Because everyone else is in relationships.* One excellent aspect of having a logical brain is seeing past herd mentality. The reasoning "because everyone else is doing it" works surprisingly well for NTs, but falls flat for people with highly logical brains. People with autism recognize that the collective "everybody" often does stupid things.

- *Because your partner requested, "I want you to want to be in a relationship with me."* A natural lack of empathy can make this reasoning fall flat.

- *Because you will feel bad if you do not have a significant other in your life.* That is subjective. Some people are far happier in the peace and quiet of the woods, the outback, the desert, the large, supposedly lonely places where they rarely interact with others. Or, even in the cities, you may be perfectly happy living alone as one of thousands in the everyday anonymous crowd. Assuming you will be happier when you have a relationship is like assuming that you are hungry because others are ready to eat lunch. It is subjective and personal.

There are many more reasons than the ones listed above. When discussing the question of, "Why be together?" with someone on the spectrum, who experiences social relations differently, it might be best to skip the reasoning that holds such weak appeal.

Personally, I tried all the typical reasons with my husband with autism. All of them failed. They were meaningless to him. I tried to force a relationship. He just worked longer hours. I tried to use peer pressure. He found ways of distancing himself from the crowd. There was no reason good enough.

So I gave up. I took a step back. I flew to the other side of the world for a summer and considered whether or not to go back. I knew why I wanted to be with him—I wanted to be in a relationship with him because the happiest moments of my life were in his presence. He was generous, kind, loyal, loving, and extremely well-matched to me in terms of likes/dislikes, preferences, lifestyle, personality, and interests. I liked being near him. He liked being near me. Whenever things were difficult, however, problems that naturally occur in any relationship with children and jobs, he was lightning-swift to detach. There was a shallow loyalty. He would stay married to me under any circumstance, but as a silent marriage.

I decided I could not stay with him unless he could answer the question: "Why be in a relationship?" honestly, for himself.

Once the kids and I were gone, the pressure was off. He had the time and space to consider why he wanted to be in a relationship with me—his own personal reason.

He found that reason. It is not profound. It is simple to the point of being ignorable. It is the reason that makes the most sense to his autistic brain: "Because I want you."

As he explained later, the "I want…" encompassed many other reasons: because I want to have someone by my side as I experience life, I want support for those things I cannot do, I want a lover, a friend, a partner.

The last part, "…you," spoke to what he wanted in a partner. He had chosen what traits he wanted in a partner and they happened to be the exact same traits he already had in his wife.

For several months, he wondered why it was so important to have the realization that he already had what he wanted; but, as in any good results oriented framework, the proof of value was in the results. From that point on, he was far more committed to working through problems.

In the past when he would have gone silent or walked away, now he crossed the room to give me a hug or did a task that he knew I would appreciate. While it does not seem logical that a simple thought can have significant impact on our actions, the realization of "Why be married?" was everything. There was no realization more crucial.

Once he made the decision, he was set for life. He will probably never revisit the question. For me, someone who loves analysis of anything personal or technical, it is tempting to revisit this question daily. Yet, that would violate the first principle of keeping small problems small.

In order to reset my approach, I focused on a concept I first heard from a university professor but have since found it is a common concept. "I don't analyze my marriage every day the same way I wouldn't uproot a tree every day to check its roots."

CHAPTER 6

Using Binary Thinking to Your Benefit

For an NT, social interactions are multi-faceted. For a person on the spectrum, social interactions are much more easily understood in black and white terms. Why? To reduce complicated problems down to uncomplicated terms.

In order to do this, you can both make sure that you only troubleshoot problems that need solving. The following questions will help you do that.

1. Does this situation really annoy me? Is it important to me in particular?

Things that are annoying to people in general do not qualify as a problem unless you, too, are annoyed by it. For example, most people want to hear, "Thank you," when they assist you in some way. If you do not care about receiving a "Thank you," and your partner does not regularly say it, then it does not qualify as a problem and therefore does not need troubleshooting. Before deeming something as a problem, first verify that it is something that matters to you directly. Make sure you do not consider something a problem just because society considers it to be a problem.

2. Does the situation make a noticeable, conspicuous difference to me?

If the situation is minor, such as, "She isn't cleaning up her dishes after meals," but it is only a minor inconvenience, then think long and hard before bringing it up as a problem to be solved. Recognize that your partner with autism will probably not be able to tell the difference between little problems and large problems. Any problem that is mentioned will probably be seen at the same level as any other problem since there are only two settings: on or off.

Also, as your partner matures as a companion, he or she may begin identifying differing levels of urgency for issues. In order to facilitate this understanding, make sure that you do not balloon small problems into larger-than-they-actually-are problems. For people with an intense ability to focus, it is easy to let little things become very big things. Do this too often and you have a lot of big things wrong with the relationship. The goal is to create a trouble-free relationship. Making all the little problems into bigger ones, just shifts the ratio of good to bad.

Also verify that it is a little annoyance according to you. For a personal example, when people jiggle their knee or tap their foot or have some other nervous tick, it is a very quick, severe detriment to my husband's ability to stay calm. His reaction is unusual in intensity. If he were to sit next to a knee jiggler for a few minutes it could send him into mental meltdown requiring that he spend significant time at his computer in order for him to calm down.

Before I understood this aspect of his sensory system, I read in a magazine that it is healthy to bounce one's knee when you have excess energy: it burns calories and increases blood flow. So, when I was both sitting and standing I found ways to bounce my knee, tap my foot, or otherwise stay active. Our relationship took a nose dive. He was always angry. He never wanted to be with me. He was spending nearly all of his time at his computer. Once we figured out what was happening, the problem was immediately solved.

3. Is this an ambiguous problem?

Some issues may not fit neatly into the regular problem-solving process. For example, perhaps there are times when you need your friend or partner close for physical and emotional comfort; then there are times when you want to be alone for a month or more at a time. If you make a "rule" out of something that changes, the rule will not stick well.

In order to understand each other clearly and make life easier for both of you, tackle the big unambiguous problems first. The ambiguous ones can lead to confusion. For example, say the problem is, "She hums all the time," but sometimes it bothers you and sometimes you like it. If you say "I can't stand the sound of people humming. Could you please not do that?" you may, after a while, miss the sound of her humming on a sunny Saturday morning. Explaining that you only like it sometimes and not others puts her in a position of always having to wonder what you are feeling, wonder what you are thinking, analyze the environment to see if it is ok to hum around you. Ambiguity can cause stress.

Ambiguous problems, unless they are tremendously, overwhelmingly difficult, should be second or third tier to the clear-cut problems that are constants throughout a person's life.

4. Is this a reasonable request?

There are some requests that are simply asking too much. Your request needs to be reasonable. I once heard a man request of his fiancée, "Your body needs to be fit, toned, tan, soft. Show me what you look like in a bathing suit and I'll decide if it is good enough." While this made sense from a sensory standpoint (it was difficult for him to touch things that were not soft) and from a visual standpoint (it was difficult for him to look at things he did not deem beautiful), his request was not only unreasonable, it was extremely rude.

If you have autism and cannot see how the above request was unreasonable (and offensive) then ask: "Is this something my partner or friend could actually accomplish? Is this something my partner may want to accomplish?"

If in doubt, ask someone who can give you an unbiased opinion on whether or not your request is reasonable. In the example above, even though this man's request was unreasonable, the woman ended up marrying him. Not surprisingly they were divorced soon after. While their experience provides an extreme example, unreasonable requests can cause insurmountable problems.

5. Is this the most annoying of all the problems which we are currently encountering?

There is a common phrase: "Pick your battles." It means that you cannot solve every problem all at once, so choose only a few things to work on at a time. If nearly everything your partner does is annoying (and most of us experience this at some time or another), then pick only the top three. For example, you could pick, "Makes loud noises early in the morning. Can't keep his hands off my stuff. Keeps introducing me to people even though he knows I hate it."

Take it slowly. Work on one at time as a minimum, three at a time as a maximum. All relationships have problems, but as long as you are moving forward, making healthy improvements, then you are headed in the right direction.

6. Is this the core of the problem?

Decide whether you are working on the core of the problem or tackling it bit-by-bit. Be clear about your approach so that it can effectively reduce your workload by half.

Some problems are quite large. Sometimes you can solve the problem by biting off small chunks at a time. For example, if you have children with your partner and he does not know how to play with them or otherwise interact with them, you can focus on one task at a time. Encourage him to read to your child, play computer games with your child, or otherwise interact, one task at a time until it builds up to active parenting. It would be too overwhelming to try to solve the core problem (be a good parent) all at once.

For other large problems, it is best to attack the root, in the same way that you pull up a weed. If you try to pull up a weed by pulling off a small leaf or two or a stem, you will make no progress over time. You have to grab the whole thing and get the root out of the soil. A prime example of this is found in Chapter 9, "Troubleshooting Communication: Meta-Discussions." If you are having trouble communicating and seem to always be fighting, first, find the root and deal with that first.

In our relationship it was not just a weed, it was a tree. I often said, "I'm tired of messing around on the branches. I want the root of the problem, the trunk." To which he would reply, "But I like branches." We finally figured out that together we provided a good balance of troubleshooting strategies. If he preferred to work on the branches (the details) and I preferred to work on the trunk (the core issues), then at any time at least one of us would be happy.

Summary/Maintenance

The goal of all of the above strategies is to identify:

1. what needs solving and what doesn't

2. what is solvable and what is not

3. what is most important so that you can ignore the rest and deal with only a single problem (or a few problems)

4. whether it needs a detailed approach or a core issue approach (thus cutting your work in half).

If your partner or you live in a binary world, use that viewpoint to simplify and more quickly solve any problems so that you can move on to the more enjoyable parts of life.

CHAPTER 7

Assumptions

HOW TO BE A PARTNER (NOT A PARENT)

We all interpret the world based on a set of assumptions, the programmed code in our minds. As we live from day to day, sometimes we find that our understandings (our code) may be wrong (have bugs).

When you have a problem, it is in your best interest to check if you could possibly be wrong. If you have mindblindness, this chapter will seem bizarre to you. In mindblindness there is a good chance that you believe that all problems exist outside of yourself, no problems are your "fault." If you are mindblind this is a particularly important chapter.

People tend to make assumptions about relationships based on what we learned as children. This is normal and natural. The only problem is that it is childish. An adult using childish ways of interacting is wrong, the same way in that it would be wrong for a 30-year-old to suck his thumb in public. It is shameful.

The first, most important step in adulthood is to ask yourself, "Am I using the ideas and ways of interacting from my childhood? Or are they my own ways, my own choices, my own way of interacting?"

Do not lazily accept the beliefs of your parents as your own unless those are the beliefs you want to retain. Do not lazily accept the beliefs of your partner—to do so is the definition of co-dependence, a dangerous and self-destructive state of mind. Choose your own beliefs, see things from your own point of view.

It is common for a young married man to make assumptions about his wife based on how his mother behaved, and vice versa. We may fall into the easy trap of seeing our wife as we saw our mother and our husband as we saw our father. This is common in all relationships and, it is to be hoped, in a highly logical and unusually literal brain that it will be less likely since you will be able to see logically that the person with whom you are now is not your mother or father. This tendency is, however, strong.

How do you break a previous misconception? If you grew up with Applied Behavioral Analysis (ABA) or any type of behavior modification, you may be better suited to adjust your behavior. You know that certain behaviors can be changed.

In our case, my husband, a man with autism, did not experience ABA or anything similar. When he is under stress, he often switches to seeing me as if I was his mother. He makes assumptions about my behavior and reactions that are entirely inaccurate. This is annoying, insulting even. It can lead to explosive arguments if the basic foundational misunderstanding is not addressed: "I am not your mother. You are making inaccurate assumptions about what I am saying. I am not your mother."

I can say those words, but they do not break through the fallacy. When people are under stress their minds tend to be closed. They get stuck in a rut, a mental war bunker, and stay there until the "danger" is over. Sometimes it is safer to simply let your partner stay protected until the imaginary war scene has passed. If possible, however, it is most helpful to try to break through the fallacy, to rewire thought processes and behavior patterns.

I found a way to break this particular fallacy. *I do something that his mother would never do.* I break the mirror that he has held up in front of me, and do the one thing his mother would never do—swear.

A long time ago, I noticed that if I swore, he would laugh, the same laugh that people have when you have struck truth and they see the absurdity of a situation.

I needed to present a truth that would show him (not just tell him) that I was not his mother. I was an entirely different woman with different motivations, different aspirations, different desires, and different outlook on life. This is the archetypal experience of growing up—figuring out that you are no longer with your parents, but are instead forging your own relationship with an entirely new person.

The following example will enable you to visualize this dynamic in action:

Him: *"Nothing is good enough for you. You want me to work harder, be better, be perfect."*

Me: *"What? Really? Where did you get that idea?" (pause to realize that the incongruity is coming from a misconception) "Please drop that **** idea and let's get back to being loving friends."*

This pulls him out of the misconception a little. He laughs, the tale-tell sign that the mirror is breaking. Note that the deeper he is in the illusion, the longer it takes and the harder I work to shatter the glass of misperception. At times, the glass seems bullet-proof. Then, sometimes I swear like a sailor and that works. Sometimes distance and time heals it better.

A word of warning: consider that what your partner sees is very much reality in his or her eyes. One of my initial attempts at "breaking the mirror" with my husband was by initiating intimacy with him, thinking that since his mother was never "in the bedroom" with him, it was a great way to break the mirror. Unfortunately, I failed to recognize what it would feel like from his point of view. While he is in the mindset of seeing me as his mother and I show cleavage or otherwise give a sexual indicator, he has a visceral, "Oh gross!" reaction. This interaction hurt us both. So, consider what method you will use to break the mirror carefully and keep in mind that he literally sees his mother, not you. Do not take it personally; just find a way to fix it.

Now, on to the rest of the conversation:

Me: *"Thanks. Now, for the record: you are good enough just the way you are, perfect actually. I do not want you to work harder. In fact I want the opposite—you have been working too hard lately. I just want you to drop these false assumptions so that we can relax around each other again."*

Him: *(deep sigh) "Ok."*

At this point, he is still not seeing me for who I am, but at least he is not seeing his mother. After his body recovers from the adrenal overload and cortisol rush he will slowly ease into seeing me again.

The relief that can come when people see the problem clearly and have a way of handling problems quickly leads to true, enduring happiness.

Summary/Maintenance

If you are experiencing the same inexplicable miscommunication often, perhaps review your own assumptions—do you see your partner in the same way that you see your parent? If so, give your partner a chance. Get to know him or her.

CHAPTER 8

Troubleshooting Mindblindness

THE UNIVERSE IS US

Mindblindness is a mental condition where one cannot see that other people have their own unique point of view. A person who is mildly mindblind may appear self-centered and egoistical whereas a severely mindblind person may appear psychotic or disconnected from reality.

Imagine that a mindblind person is standing on the sidewalk when nearby a pedestrian crossing the street is struck by a car and killed. The mindblind person will react "callously," ignoring the situation or perhaps even laughing at it. It might seem funny because the mindblind person's point of view is of people acting oddly, inappropriately calling 911, perhaps crying or running into the road to help the injured person. The mindblind person may be baffled: "Why are people yelling? What's the big deal? Why are they looking at the guy in the road?" This is because the mindblind person only experiences her own reality. If she does not feel pain herself, neither does anyone else. There is no purpose to crying (no empathy), calling 911 (social reaction), or running to help the injured person (no concept of motive or intent for anything other than self-interest). A fully mindblind person sees her own mind as the only mind and is incapable of seeing that others have minds of their own.

In some ways mindblind people show, however awkwardly, a fully logical perception of the world. As the great scientist Edwin Hubble discovered in the 1920s, the center of the universe is wherever you are. Occasionally it is useful to be a little mindblind. The center of the universe is relative; the center of the universe is wherever you are. Therefore, according to physical cosmology and Hubble's Law in particular, the mindblind person is fundamentally correct. Their view of the world is *the* view of the world. The difficulties of mindblindness come into play when a mindblind person cannot comprehend the illogical multiplicity of Hubble's Law.

Mindblindness is a comorbid condition of autism. The inability to attribute thoughts and emotions to others creates a barrier when the person with mindblindness tries to create and maintain relationships with others.

Note that mindblindness has as many shades of gray as does autism. There can be varying degrees of mindblindness, ranging from a temporary bout of self-centeredness to a fully-blown blindness that is a limiting disability, prohibiting the mindblind person from many aspects of adulthood, such as having a driver's license due to the inability to understand the intent of other drivers. Mindblindness can be a severely limiting disability.

How do you troubleshoot such a disability? The same way you troubleshoot mobility for a paraplegic. *You build a wheelchair.* The difficulties related to mindblindness can be overcome using certain tools, recognizing and accepting limitations, then making the best of the resources available.

IDENTIFY: MY PARTNER DOES NOT ALLOW ME TO HAVE MY OWN OPINION. MY PARTNER CANNOT SEE THAT I HAVE A POINT OF VIEW DIFFERENT FROM HERS

Test 1: Discuss and define

Introduce the concept of mindblindness to your partner in whatever format she can understand most easily.

- Email your partner a link to an article online describing mindblindness.

- Talk to your partner about mindblindness.

- Show your partner the description in this book, above.

Evaluate: If explaining the concept helps your partner recognize and cope with the negative aspects of mindblindness, great. Note that a temporary lapse by the person with mindblindness is ok. We are only looking for the ability to overcome mindblindness when needed. If an explanation does not help your partner understand that there are points of view other than her own, continue to Test 2.

Test 2: Create a visual image

Draw a quick cartoon – several stick figures, each with their own minds and their own eyes. Show that one stick figure cannot be the eyes and ears for all of them. Discuss the following through pictures:

- relativity
- point of view
- unique individuals.

Note that this will not cure mindblindness. Instead, it will create a logical, visual frame of reference for a person who needs to understand the world logically. The person with mindblindness will still need to overcome the incorrect assumptions caused by the limited perception every time there is an issue. It will not come naturally, but may possibly be taught mechanically.

Evaluate: If the visual image of cartoon stick figures helps your partner accept the fact that her view of the world is not the only view of the world, great. If your partner still believes that there is only one right way to do things—her way—then try Test 3.

Test 3: Explain scientifically

- *Science*: Explore the theory of relativity which states that there is no absolute point of view. Measurements are always based on the viewer's position. Check out books from the library regarding the theory of relativity or research it online.

- *Technology*: Use an analogy that makes sense based on your partner's understanding of the world. One analogy that is probably universal in the tech sector is related to internet connectivity: "Just because you have a good connection to the server doesn't mean that everyone has a good connection to the server."

- *Engineering*: Visit a large parking garage and bring your camera with you. Drive to different floors of the parking garage, taking photos out of the same side of the garage, for example, the west side of the garage, at different angles. Return home and print out the pictures. Discuss how the view is slightly different from the different vantage points. Perhaps label these locations, "Joe's point of view," "Sam's point of view," and the names of other people your partner knows. The view from the top floor of the parking garage is probably different (brighter, wider viewing range) than the view from ground level (darker, mostly sidewalk and a limited view of the building next door).

This will probably be frustrating. See it as a "no loss" experiment. If she does not see her own blindness, then you have lost nothing. If she does open up to the possibility of other minds outside her own, however, you have both taken a large step towards a healthy relationship.

You may be able to use this visual image later in discussions where mindblindness is causing a miscommunication: "I'm seeing this issue from the second floor and you're already way up on the roof. We both have valid views, just see differently. Can you grant that I am on a different floor?" It will not make sense and it will not seem real, but it can be a learned concept for a person with mindblindness.

Evaluate: If your partner is able to see the minds-of-others concept, affectionately referred to as MOO, great. Latch onto the explanation that worked for you both so that you can reference it when future problems occur. If the analogy explanations and visual representations did not work, however, try Test 4.

Test 4: Take it on faith that other people have minds of their own

Ask her if she believes that you might have information about how the world works that she does not have. There is a good chance that she already relies on you for information about social relations.

It is likely that having faith in you will be next-to-impossible for her. Be careful not to confuse mindblindness with a lack of trust. They are different cognitively; they have different motivations and different solutions. Try one of the following:

■ Explain how kids need to have faith in their parents or older siblings. My favorite example is when a parent says to a child, "Don't run into the street." The kids, at least at first, don't understand why, but with time they begin to understand the rules of the road and also understand what happens when a car made of metal hits something soft like a body. Until they have full understanding, the child is exhibiting faith in the parent in order to overcome her limited understand of the world outside her own head.

- Find one interaction you had in the past where you were able to give your partner information that she did not already have. Perhaps it was something simple; perhaps it was one of the biggest turning points in your relationship as a couple. Use that experience as a tool. Name it so that you can reference it easily, so that in the future you can say, "This situation is like The Yeller and I need you to have faith that my opinion may be helpful to your situation right now."

Evaluate: Having faith may be an impossible concept. I have met some highly logical people who find the faith concept revolting. If so, try Test 5.

Test 5: Ask your partner to fake it

Ask her to just pretend, for a moment, that what you are saying is true. Ask her to do it as a favor to you.

The fake-it-till-you-make-it approach is sometimes functional; sometimes not. In some situations it may be appropriate. For example, if you are at a social event and she has misunderstood some social cues, ask her to fake the socially acceptable behavior until the party is over.

Warning: faking it long-term can cause devastating repercussions. Whether or not you have the neurological makeup of someone with autism, some people spend so much of their lives faking it that they fail to develop their own ability to act of their own free will. This is a difficult ethical dilemma. Just be aware of both sides and make the choice that works for you.

Evaluate: If faking it is a sufficient crutch for overcoming mindblindness, fantastic. If not, see Test 6.

Test 6: Train the mind to open to others

Whether she is faking it, having faith, or seeing the logical possibility of minds-of-others, see it as a training exercise. This is valuable if the previous methods worked a little, but not enough to be fully successful.

Take whatever method worked best and use it again and again and again until she has smashed down the door of mindblindness. This worked for my husband. He was truly mindblind with the Dilbertian belief that "people are stupid." He tried tirelessly to see the seemingly invisible world known as the minds-of-others (MOO).

In the mindblind world, he saw that people were as mindless as cows; in the post-mindblind work, he was able to see and respect others' opinions, even if he occasionally mistook one of us for a cow.

Now it is a semi-natural reaction for Carl to consider the minds of others. Just like an athlete learning how to complete a maneuver with accuracy and speed, Carl practiced until he developed the ability to see others' opinions as valid and potentially useful. That is a tremendously powerful ability for someone who has previously experienced the limitations of mindblindness.

Evaluate: If marathon level training works, fantastic, you deserve the gold medal! If not, see Test 7.

Test 7: Accept fully
Accept that your partner with mindblindness will never actually believe that others have minds of their own.

Evaluate: At this point, you decide whether you either live with the mindblindness or you do not.

IDENTIFY: MY PARTNER SEES EVERYONE AS IDIOTS. IT IS LIKE HE IS THE ONLY ONE ON EARTH WHO KNOWS WHAT IS RIGHT

Test 1: See blindness
Understand that this is not arrogance, not something very negative. It is simply a blindness similar to visual blindness. This understanding allows you to have compassion rather than experience frustration. If you see it as a disability rather than arrogance, it makes life much easier for you.

Evaluate: If you do not see it as a disability or otherwise feel that doing so would be allowing him to "get off the hook," try Test 2.

Test 2: Agree!
In large part, we are all idiots. We do relatively stupid things every day. Many of us are partly mindblind every day as we bumble around in our daily work. The cartoon Dilbert often revolves around mindblindness issues. Dilbert has been successful in large part because of its theme: we are all idiots.

Evaluate: If this relaxed approach works and both you and your partner are comfortable with your points of view, then this solution works for you. If not, see Test 3.

Test 3: See the silver lining

People with visual blindness often have other sharpened skills. Mindblindness often comes with an intense ability to focus on a deeply immersive level. While at times it may appear that your partner is ignoring you, there may be hidden benefits to his ability to ignore the rest of the world. Note that this is not ignoring which implies seeing-and-dismissing; he is not seeing in the first place.

Evaluate: If you cannot see a silver lining (or perhaps there is none), try Test 4.

Test 4: Make accommodations

Be aware that this belief is not going to go away and build your life around that fact. If his "you're an idiot" approach is going to cause trouble when you spend Christmas with relatives then go alone or spend Christmas together elsewhere. Make accommodations.

Evaluate: If it appears impossible to make sufficient accommodations and all previous methods were unsuccessful, take an honest look at how the mindblindness is affecting you. If you have a strong support network and the mindblindness is only annoying rather than destructive, then perhaps you can simply laugh it off or ignore it. If there are significant negative consequences related to the mindblindness, choose whether or not you wish to live with the condition. The long-term consequences may be more than you are willing to accept.

IDENTIFY: I AM SO FRUSTRATED BY MY PARTNER'S MINDBLINDNESS/INABILITY TO SEE WHAT I NEED/ LACK OF DESIRE TO GIVE ME WHAT I NEED

Test 1: Claim your reaction

Recognize that the mindblindness can only upset you if you let it. If you accept your partner "as is," the mindblindness is far less frustrating. It is similar to having a partner in a wheelchair. You would not experience constant frustration over your partner not being able to walk and run; you would accept that the wheelchair is part of life. Recognize that your reaction to mindblindness-based issues is your choice.

Evaluate: If you can take responsibility for your reaction to your partner's way of seeing the world and this allows you the peace of mind needed to exist happily as a couple, great. If not, continue to Test 2.

Test 2: Identify mindblindness as a trigger

Notice the connection between a mindblind comment or action and the frustration as it surges inside you. Compare it to how you react to other triggers in your life: someone cutting in front of you at the grocery store, a bad driver on the road, or a person who is being difficult.

If your response to mindblindness is similar to the way you respond to regular daily frustrations, then you can relax knowing that your partner's mindblindness is just one of many things that bother you. No one is perfect and it is ok to be frustrated sometimes.

Evaluate: If recognizing your reaction as a typical response helps calm your frustration, great. If not, continue to Test 3.

Test 3: Use diagrammatic reasoning

In Chapter 24 I have included a long list of strategies to try if troubleshooting a problem does not work. One of these strategies is diagrammatic reasoning wherein you sketch out the problem, parsing out a solution in the diagram.

I tried this one day when I was frustrated. I simply began writing and drawing. I ended up with a cartoon representation of how our conversations often appeared from a bystander's point of view.

Evaluate: Drawing the problem in a visual format may help you work past the mindblindness. If not, keep trying.

Test 4: Work your way into your partner's inner circle

If your partner believes you to be a part of his or her "self" then he or she will consult you on matters the same way he or she checks in with him- or herself: "What do you want to do today?" will no longer be a question only inside your partner's own mind. Your partner will begin to ask the question out loud. Essentially he or she is training him- or herself to think out loud. You will be interspersed with your partner's internal dialogue.

This idea sounds far-fetched until you consider the well-known "one mind, one flesh" concept where, when people marry, they unite as much as possible. In our individualistic focused world, this concept seems at odds with the mental construct of a healthy adult relationship. It works in many relationships, however, and may be a much-needed work-around for people in a relationship where mindblindness is part of the equation.

Personally, I am fiercely independent, but in order to work together with my husband I needed to be part of his inner circle, part of his mental processes. There is no way I could have written this book and my previous book, *Asperger Syndrome and Long-Term Relationships* (2002), if I was not intimately close to him mentally as well as physically. There is no inclination to share information with me, so without this redrawing of the circle-of-self we would only be roommates instead of soul-mates.

How to get into the inner circle

On a piece of paper, draw stick figures representing you and your partner. Draw a circle lightly around each stick figure. Explain that the drawing represents how you were when you first met.

At this point it may be tempting to erase the inner parts of the circles and join them as one circle. Don't. This makes sense in the NT world, but asking a person with mindblindness to accept that as a reality is like asking people in wheelchairs to pretend that they have wings instead of wheels. It is a senseless notion.

Instead, draw a stick figure representing your partner and around him or her draw the things he or she has let into his or her inner circle: laptop, favorite hairbrush, perhaps a cat. Draw a circle around the figure representing your partner and explain, "This is your inner circle, the things you consider to be part of you." Draw a small stick figure of you in the circle and ask, "I would like to be part of your inner circle. Is that ok with you?"

There may be some hesitance and perhaps confusion, but give your partner the opportunity to agree or disagree. If he or she says, "Yes," erase the stick figure of yourself and redraw yourself inside your partner's circle, along with the laptop and the cat.

Note that if you are not mindblind, this visual image may be just as hurtful for you as it is helpful for your partner. Remind yourself that you have an entirely different view of the relationship, perhaps as two individuals joined in one circle. Make sure you do not fall into mindblindness yourself. You do not have to have the same view as your partner. Maintain your own view and enjoy the relationship.

Evaluate: You may sense a whole new level of intimacy if this works. If your partner says, "No," to allowing you in his or her inner circle or if it backfires in some other way, see Test 5.

Test 5: Build crutches for the mindblindness

See Tests 1–6 in the first troubleshooting section of this chapter for a half dozen types of crutches that may work for you and your partner. For quick reference, they are:

1. discuss and define

2. create a visual image

3. explain scientifically

4. take it on faith that other people have minds of their own

5. ask your partner to fake it

6. train the mind to open to others.

Evaluate: If none of the previous methods worked and if you have built all the different types of crutches you can think of and none of it has eased your frustration, then try Test 6.

Test 6: Check to see if you are co-dependent

You may be frustrated at your partner's mindblindness only because it causes you to counter-balance with co-dependency.

There are many self-tests online to see if co-dependency is part of your relationship, but they are all based on the premise that neither partner has autism.

To see a test for co-dependency adjusted for ASD-linked relationships, see Appendix C. The text is in the form of statements asking the respondent to agree or disagree about issues such as:

- Arguments with my partner make me want to change my partner.

- I sometimes think that if my partner could see things my way life would be much better.

There are 22 questions total. Please see Appendix C for the full self-test.

Evaluate: If you are not co-dependent and none of the previous methods worked, try Test 7.

Test 7: Get your point of view validated from somewhere/someone else

You may be experiencing frustration because you really, truly need to be heard. Trying to be heard by someone with mindblindness will only cause frustration. Remind yourself, "I'm talking to the wrong person, that's all." Make new friends; join online groups that are discussing similar issues; talk to people you know. Satisfy the need to be heard.

Evaluate: Check to see if this extra support has lessened your frustration with your partner. If being heard by others eases your frustration, even a little, then you have found a solution. You can build on this success by restructuring your life to include more friendships or other interactions with people who help satisfy this basic need for social validation. If this does not work, see Test 8.

Test 8: Be strong enough in your own sense of self to not need external validation

There is a chance that no one, even the most spectacular person could satisfy what you need and the fix needs to be internal. Also, there is a chance you are so invested in that feeling of frustration that there is no solution.

Evaluate: To see if this is the case, read Love and Stosny's (2008) *How to Improve Your Marriage without Talking About It* (see References section for details). The second half of the book will walk you through the steps to become more independent, secure, and loving (and less frustrated!). If this does not work, try Test 9.

Test 9: Unrelated?

There is a chance that you are experiencing frustration with your partner's mindblindness that is not related to your partner in any way. Perhaps you are afraid to speak up for yourself and feel that it's easier to complain about your partner's mindblindness. Perhaps you actually want to quit your job, but do not want to consciously see that because it is a terrifying thought to be on the job market again. Instead, it is easier to be frustrated at your partner than to be frustrated with yourself.

Next time you experience this frustration, walk out of the room or otherwise distance yourself from the situation if possible. Take a long, quiet walk (or whatever you do to encourage deep thought) and ask yourself over and over again, "What am I mad at? What is frustrating me?" If you give yourself time and space it is likely that the real problem will surface.

Evaluate: If you find what was actually frustrating you and notice that your frustration with your partner has decreased, great. If not, try Test 10.

Test 10: Accept

Accept mindblindness as one of your partner's many quirks. If you have made it this far through the troubleshooting process, then the frustration is not from anything either of you can fix. Instead, accept it, embrace it and let go of the frustration, reminding yourself that it's in your best interest to just let it go.

Evaluate: If you can let go of the inherent frustration, you have been successful. If not, try reevaluating the original problem. Perhaps the starting point was incorrect.

Test 11: Enjoy the benefits

After all your efforts trying to overcome mindblindness, if you still experience frustration, one final potential solution might be to focus on the benefits. A personal example: one evening my son, a young man with autism, and I were driving to an event and I told him about the person who would possibly be his manager for this event. I had spoken with her earlier on that day and could tell that the situation might be difficult since we were going to be late due to a previous engagement before the event.

> **Me:** "The lady who may be supervising you is a guilt-tripper. She will probably make you feel bad about showing up late. Just let her know that [extensive advice]."

> *(After a few minutes he cut me off)*

> **Teen son:** "Mom, don't worry! If she's angry, mean, or trying to guilt trip, I won't see it! Remember, I don't read facial expressions and if she tries to communicate something through her tone of voice, I won't hear it! If she scowls at me, I won't see it! I have to try hard to figure those things out. I just won't bother, no worries."

I had forgotten that, thanks to his autistic brain, he was free from many of the less-pleasant human interactions.

Evaluate: If focusing on the benefits of mindblindness alleviates some of the frustration, then you have managed to make the best of it, focusing on the "ability" part of "disability."

Summary/Maintenance

There are benefits to mindblindness. Enjoy them. And for the barriers? Learn to jump over them, walk around them, kick them down, or in some cases, enjoy the barrier—turn it into a comfortable bench.

PART 3

TROUBLESHOOTING EVERYDAY PROBLEMS

CHAPTER 9

Troubleshooting Communication

META-DISCUSSIONS

A man with autism once explained to me: "I wish people would stop telling me I need to communicate. Talking with someone, trying to communicate, feels like kayaking down a river. In whitewater. Without a paddle. On a stormy day. Knowing there is a waterfall up ahead. And stinging piranhas in the river. Why would I want to do something like that? (Pause) It's a heck of a lot easier to just not communicate, then apologize later."

In his socially muted perception, at any moment, without warning, he could say something that would cause a flurry of reaction (whitewater), an unintelligible response with painful consequence (piranhas) and he could fall off the edge (waterfall), completely unaware of why the discussion was falling and failing so quickly. Without the ability to repair the discussion, he had no way of redirecting a misunderstanding (no paddle).

He was helpless, at the mercy of a fast-moving interaction that he did not understand. He said, "It's scary," and I could tell from his body language (hunched shoulders, knit brow, arms folded tight) that he was truly scared; his body was in protective mode, as it should be in such a hazardous situation.

You can give your partner a paddle—the ability to navigate a discussion—by engaging in meta-discussions regularly.

What is a meta-discussion?

A meta-discussion is a discussion about having a discussion. It establishes issues such as:

- the style of the discussion

- the tone

- the setting in which the discussion occurs

- topics that are off-limits

- triggers for one partner

- any limitations or preferred ways of interacting

- any other ground rules that are important to one or both of you.

A meta-discussion describes the safe environment where an effective, healthy, mutually respectful discussion can occur.

In relationships, meta-discussions can provide the structure needed for people with social awkwardness or communication difficulties to maintain long-term relationships. The meta-discussion allows us to form a solid foundation of mutual agreement that will last for many years to come.

For example, if you are arguing over who does the dishes, your meta-discussion may be about:

- whether or not you should talk about these matters after 9pm at night when you are both exhausted

- the tone of voice one of you was using

- whether or not swear words are acceptable in the home

- whether or not name calling is allowed in your relationship

- whether or not sarcasm is acceptable

- the level of acceptable joking around that can be used in discussion.

What a meta-discussion is not

A meta-discussion does not mean a simple change of subject. A change of subject is actually an avoidance technique instead, which is covered in Chapter 15, "Troubleshooting Blame and Avoidance."

A meta-discussion is not a deeper discussion about the details of your current disagreement. A meta-discussion would *not* include details such as:

- who did the dishes last
- how to determine whose turn it is to do the dishes
- why it is important to you that your partner helps with the dishes
- how often the dishes should be washed.

The word "meta" is a Greek preposition meaning "adjacent" or "beyond." If you or your partner have serious communication difficulties, the meaning of a meta-discussion may be hard to grasp, in the same way that words from a foreign language are hard to grasp.

Nevertheless, it is important to differentiate a meta-discussion from a regular discussion because of the clarity and simplicity it grants.

The value of a meta-discussion

A meta-discussion takes time upfront, but is very much an investment. A small deposit pays dividends later on in the relationship. Once you establish rules of the relationship, whenever you find a discussion going awry, you can quickly adjust through a quick meta-discussion to re-establish the ground rules.

To see the value, let's compare a single situation both with and without a meta-discussion.

First, the example *without* a meta-discussion:

Partner: *"Every time we visit your parents you act like you don't even know me. We're married. Could you at least hold my hand?"*

Partner with autism: *"Why?"*

- Due to mindblindness, she does not perceive the purpose of a public display of affection.

Partner: *"We've talked about this a million times! Why don't you ever listen? It hurts so badly when you do this to me in front of your family. You must really hate me."*

- Due to a need for attachment to spouse, the lack of public display of connection triggers a feeling of being unloved along with a fear of abandonment.

Partner with autism: *Silently terrified, wondering what just happened.*

The same example *with* a meta-discussion:

Partner: *"Every time we visit your parents you act like you don't even know me. We're married. Could you at least hold my hand?"*

Partner with autism: *"Why?"*

■ Do not expect the person with autism to initiate the meta-discussion, at least not at first.

Partner: *"We talked about this earlier and already established the ground rules that you will hold my hand while we are at your parents."*

■ Notice that there is no mention of her emotional reaction. She does experience an emotional reaction but it will be dealt with after the ground rule has been re-established.

Partner with autism: *"Oh. Yeah. I forgot."*

Partner: *"And we agreed that whenever you forget about a previous agreement you will recognize it verbally and apologize for hurting me."*

Partner with autism: *"Darn it. I'm so sorry."*

■ Thinks of what she can do to show her appreciation for her partner's patience in such situations.

If one or both of you are having a hard time understanding why meta-discussions are important, consider that:

■ the meta-discussion is the railroad tracks; the discussion is the train

■ the meta-discussion is the road; the discussion is the car

■ the meta-discussion is the hiking gear; the discussion is the steep mountain to climb.

In the last two analogies, you can actually continue the drive or hike (the discussion) but it will be far more difficult to drive across rough terrain or hike with inadequate gear. In the first analogy, appropriate for times when you absolutely need a meta-discussion, the tracks are an absolute necessity.

Meta-discussions every couple should have

During a meta-discussion you write your own rules which then provide a solid foundation for communication ability that will last for many years to come. A meta-discussion is an investment in the relationship, a deposit that earns a high interest rate. A meta-discussion may take a few extra minutes (or hours) today, but may save you days or weeks in the future, or perhaps save the relationship itself.

There are a dozen meta-discussions which people in long-term relationships can have and should have. These discussions can make your lives together significantly easier and more enjoyable.

1 If you feel yourself getting too angry/frustrated/upset to think clearly, what should be the protocol?

Example: "When I feel too angry to think clearly, I will retreat to a different room, and set my timer for 15 minutes. If I feel better after 15 minutes, we can retry the discussion, but under no condition will I restart the discussion before then."

2 If you see your partner getting too angry and he or she does not recognize it in him- or herself, what should be the protocol? Note that once a person is angry, it is far more difficult to be self-aware.

Example: "When you are angry I will ask you to notice it and see if you need a break. If you don't take a break and are still visibly out of control, I will call a Time Out for 15 minutes."

3 If your partner uses language during the discussion that distracts or hurts you, define what is and what is not acceptable.

Example: "I get anxious when you are sarcastic when we are talking. Usually I don't understand what you are saying and it makes me feel lost."

4 If your partner does not give eye contact or forces eye contact during difficult discussions, determine what is acceptable.

Example: "I can't look directly at you when we are talking about difficult things," or "I need you to give eye contact when we are talking about something that is very important to me." Together you determine what works for you both.

5 If your partner uses unacceptable volume, tone, or vocabulary, decide what is allowed and what is not.

Example: "No yelling. No screaming. No swearing. No whispering. No saying _____ (words that are off limits)."

6 While this may seem obvious, you may need to determine parameters of physical touch during arguments.

Example: "No hitting. No slapping. No scratching. No pushing." If your partner comes from a culture where these things are considered acceptable, you may need to be clear about what is acceptable to you. Also, your partner may be getting ideas for what is acceptable based on TV or a particular movie that has a relationship dynamic that is not acceptable in your view.

A meta-discussion also helps people think more logically and clearly. Once you step back from the hot topic, your body and mind begin to cool down, returning to their more natural logical state. The act of engaging in a meta-discussion can lead to a calmer exploration of the question you asked in the first place.

Below are a few examples of meta-discussions.

Partner A says something hurtful and spiteful, calling the other a mean name.

Partner B says, "I know you are a good person and would never hurt me on purpose. We agreed that we would not engage in name calling, yes?"

This is stepping back from the discussion to review a previously agreed upon Rule of Engagement.

Partner A says something that avoids a difficult topic of discussion/a difficult question.

Partner B says, "Please answer the question directly. When you do not answer the question, we waste time in avoidance. Honestly I would rather be _____ (favorite hobby) than arguing."

Often, when presented with a difficult question or topic, people will try to avoid answering. Many common avoidance techniques are outlined in the second half of this chapter so that you can identify them.

Avoidance techniques are detrimental because they:

- fail to address the original question, and

- cause many more questions, often twisting the discussion up in knots.

By calling it what it is—avoidance—and not getting distracted by an avoidance strategy, we can stay on topic.

Note that a meta-discussion does not mean a simple change of subject. If one of you starts exploring another subject, no meta-discussion has taken place. A change of subject is actually an avoidance technique.

Partner A responds in a way that shows disrespect.

Partner B says, "When you show disrespect I cannot speak with you rationally. It makes me angry when you _____ (turn your back on me, walk away while I am talking, click your fingernails, any annoying behavior). If we are going to discuss this respectfully, I need to you stop that for just a few minutes. Thank you."

There are certain things that are just too hard to ignore. Recognize that you have limited willpower and request that your partner makes the discussion easier for you.

Once the concept of a meta-discussion is in place, both of you can use it as a tool to create more stability and comfort in the relationship. Personally, when my husband is kayaking down the rapids without a paddle (perceiving danger in a discussion), I literally take a step back. If I am sitting, I move backwards and say, "Meta-discussion. Let's get back to safety. I am not attacking you, just asking a question. Can you see that?"

The physical step back indicates that I care more about his sense of safety than I do about getting a quick answer to a question.

Summary/Maintenance

The content of a meta-discussion includes the style of the discussion, the tone, the participants, the setting in which the discussion occurs, and other mechanics.

A meta-discussion allows you to set clear ground rules in the relationship. It would be inappropriate for us to list anything other than sample ground rules—each relationship is unique and the meta-discussions you have will be based on your unique preferences. Many meta-discussions will probably be the same thing over and over again, reminders that you live with a unique human being. For example, I often forget that when my husband disagrees, he is silent. Silence equals lack of agreement. For me, if I disagree, I speak up, regardless of discomfort or the advisability of disagreeing. A typical meta-discussion would include me saying, "Hey, I just took a step back from the discussion and realized that I am basing everything on an incorrect premise (thinking he had agreed with me when the silence was actually disagreement)."

A meta-discussion may take a few extra minutes (or hours) today, but may save you days, weeks in the future, or perhaps the relationship itself.

CHAPTER 10

Troubleshooting Executive Function

PLANNING AND SCHEDULING

Executive function covers many areas of ability: working memory, attention, verbal reasoning, inhibition, mental flexibility, task switching, and—what is most important for those on the autism spectrum who are living with someone in an adult relationship—planning, scheduling, and organizing.

Unusually weak or unusually strong abilities can create interesting imbalances in relationships. While autism tends to come with weak executive function, it is not actually part of the diagnostic criteria.

I married a man with autism, which means he has skills other than executive function: planning, scheduling, and organizing are laborious and unpleasant for him. In contrast, I have hyper-executive function. I plan things for the fun of it. It is hard for me *not* to plan, organize, and schedule. It makes me happy to exercise executive function.

Extreme differences

On days when I am frustrated by our extreme differences, I wear a silky black necklace with a yin and yang engraved in silver. When I wear it, it reminds me to love the differences in people, even the extreme differences.

One aspect of weak executive function is an increased ability to be in the moment, an unusually strong ability to focus. My husband has used this ability to great benefit by using it to enhance his parenting abilities. When he is with one child, he is only with that child. He is not thinking of what to make for dinner or how he needs to get back to work. Yogis and meditation practitioners would envy his ability to be fully in the moment.

One aspect of the hyper-executive function is a persistent ability to plan and organize. It is most evident when I am talking with someone. I see a flowchart of dozens of possibilities. If we are arguing and he says X, there is an 85 percent chance that I will respond unpleasantly, a 10 percent chance that I will be able to keep my cool, and a 5 percent chance that I will storm out of the room. Each of those choices branches out to other potential outcomes. Conversation fascinates me. The tree shifts and reshapes with every comment the other person makes. I usually see two to three moves ahead, four or even twenty moves ahead in predictable situations. My mind considers it a game, a way to relax and play.

Because of our extreme differences, my partner has been able to communicate to me how wonderful it feels to be fully present in the moment and I have been able to communicate to him that planning, organizing, and scheduling can be enjoyable. It makes it easier for both of us to build ability when we can consider that, "It may not be easy or fun for me to do this, but at least for someone it is fun."

IDENTIFY: MY PARTNER WITH AUTISM LACKS THE ABILITY TO PLAN FOR THE FUTURE, WHICH CAN BE FRUSTRATING FOR BOTH OF US

Test 1: Let a fish be a fish

Strong executive function is nice, but not necessary, to live a good life. If your partner experiences difficulties in planning, take a "nobody's perfect" approach. Stop expecting your partner with autism to plan. Assume that your partner will not plan, and go from there. Relationships thrive when each partner focuses on the other's strengths (and lets weaknesses blend into the background).

Perhaps keep in mind that everyone has their own brand of genius, but if you judge a cat by its ability to sing, it will live its whole life believing it is inferior. There are many variations of this saying. Insert the animal you like and a task which that animal is not built to do. The original quote, usually attributed to Einstein is, "Everyone is a genius, but if you judge a fish by its ability to climb a tree, it will live its whole life believing it is stupid."

Evaluate: If you are feeling frustration over your partner's lack of ability to plan, it means that:

- you are human, and

- you have not fully accepted that your partner is not naturally capable of planning.

Once you stop expecting it, you can stop being frustrated. Once you stop being frustrated, you can relax enough to do productive troubleshooting.

If this strategy has worked, you will feel a sense of relief. While it means that you will be doing the planning for both you and your partner with autism, it also means that you no longer have to deal with the element of frustration.

Stop expecting it and the suffering will lessen in proportion. Remember: suffering is the distance between expectation and reality. You may still experience pain, but suffering (frustration) is optional.

Test 2: Recognize the sub-tasks

Some productivity psychologists say a person can get seven (or three, five or other number below ten) things done every day. For a person with autism, these seven things might each involve sub-steps that would not apply to someone who does not have autism. The sub-tasks multiply the number of tasks to 20, 30, or more.

For example, imagine that your partner needs to communicate to his boss that he is going to miss an important deadline.

For an NT, this is a single task: the NT tells his boss that he won't be able to meet the deadline—one single task.

For a person with autism, this task might involve:

1. Recognizing that the boss is not aware that the deadline will be missed. It might not occur to the person with autism that the boss does not already know this. Forcing an unnatural level of awareness about his boss's state of mind involves effort.

2. Deciding whether or not the boss needs to know. There are many social rules about not communicating versus over-communicating. There is a chance that this deadline is so small that the boss does not care and would be annoyed by being bothered with the information. An NT would intuitively sense what the boss needs to know. A person with autism might have to consider this consciously and methodically.

3. Figuring out the best method of communication. Has the boss given an indication as to which type of communication she prefers? Will she respond more favorably to an email or by telling her in person? This is also an intuitive social skill. People usually drop hints as to what type of communication they prefer.

4. Choosing words correctly so as to make the person with autism look like a responsible person. Whether the person with autism was responsible is often irrelevant. It is how the boss perceives it that determines a person's pay scale and position in the company.

A person with autism might not know to use words such as "best," "quality," and "I…care." For example, a person with autism might say, "I'm not going to be done on time." The word "not" is negative, especially when you use it in an "I…" sentence. The person with autism takes full blame with no explanation of why he is reporting this poor performance. Compare this to an NT who may say, "I'm really excited about this project and I want to submit the best final version. Since the graphics department took an extra week, it looks like final submission will also be a week late. I really care about the quality of the final product and just wanted to let you know since you also really care about this project."

Evaluate: If recognition of the sub-tasks allows you to be more compassionate, then this test has worked. If you continue to be frustrated by your partner's lack of planning, see the next test.

Test 3: Get planning crutches

If planning does not come naturally, you can both get tools that will help make your life as a couple easier.

A few tools to try:

- a To Do organizer such as Evernote, Astrid, or similar

- a coach, perhaps a partner who has strong planning abilities

- many routines so as to minimize the mental workload

- reliably scheduled quiet time where you can focus only on planning out the next few hours or the next day.

Executive function gives you freedom and control over your life. People who are able to plan out their day, their week, their life, is able to actually create their life rather than just get whatever is given them. If executive function does not come naturally, you can still build a life where the effects of executive function are felt whether or not that ability came naturally from your own thought processes or not.

Evaluate: Are the tools making your life easier? Are you experiencing more or less stress now that you are using organizing skills? If the tools lower your stress levels and give you more control over your day-to-day life, this test has worked. If not, keep going in the troubleshooting process.

Test 4: Make executive function less important

Build a highly routinized day. Both put your keys in the same spot each day. Eat the same cereal every morning. Always turn off the light and sleep at the same time each night. Develop routines at work. If you see this as odd, consider that Steve Jobs, one of the most successful men of this century routinized his life to the point that he wore the same type of clothing every day: a black turtleneck and jeans. It simplified his life so that he could devote his talents to other things.

Routines save you time, energy, and mental willpower

Evaluate: If either of you notice that you experience a sense of your days being easier, then this has worked. The routines have left more brainspace available for other things; but if you notice that you are still stressed by the lack of planning, organizing, and scheduling, try the next test.

Test 5: Quantify level of executive function needed

Since there are so many elements to decision-making, it may be helpful for you to review the number of life planning tasks for which you and your partner are responsible. Seeing them on paper, especially when you can tally them, can help make difficult tasks more concrete and doable.

Personal example: I realized one day that my husband and I were both taking care of many responsibilities. Both of us worried about getting the rubbish bins out on time each week. Both of us worried about the kids getting their homework done each night. Both of us worried about what to make for dinner. Once I realized that we had twice the number of difficulties, I asked Carl if we could divide the responsibilities fairly according to our relative strengths.

Once we had put this in action, we both felt like half of our load had been lifted. Occasionally one of us would not trust the other to complete a task on time and that task would end up on both of our lists so we occasionally met to re-divide the tasks fairly. It worked.

Evaluate: If dividing your mutual workload in half with your partner helps you both feel like you have less work to do then you have struck gold (relationship gold). If you both still worry about too many tasks, then keep trying other solutions.

Test 6: Outsource your executive function

Have someone else do the planning, organizing, and scheduling for you. Hiring a VA, virtual assistant, is how many professionals get help with their too-heavy workload, but it is unlikely to work for someone on the spectrum. Working with a VA requires strong social skills, negotiation, and crystal-clear communication. Instead, outsource to those with whom you already live and work.

Evaluate: If you or your partner find it easier to think clearly when you have someone assisting, then this is working. If it does not yield clarity of thought or if it annoys your partner, then refer back to Test 1. The ultimate way to solve any problem is to accept it.

There are two other major issues for adult relationships in regards to executive function: end-of-life planning and financial planning. Instead of using the regular troubleshooting methods, I am listing them in rapid-fire style, so that you can see other types of troubleshooting role modeled throughout this book.

IDENTIFY: WE HAVE NO WILL, NO END-OF-LIFE PLANS

1. Take it step by step in a logical, linear way. First, write a will. Looking for free will-writing software online can be less than pleasant since many sites have paid links and distractions. Talking to a lawyer in person to get a will written can be expensive. Writing your own won't have sufficient legal underpinning unless you are an estate lawyer by training. The easiest method is to get a book about writing a will, good examples of which are published by Nolo. They have many different types of books and can make the process painless. I used *Quick and Legal Will Book* by Denis Clifford (2008) and was able to complete and print my will within 20 minutes of starting.

2. Next, discuss social support. There is a good chance that your partner with autism does not visualize the social support of family and friends in the later years. Try to create that image of continuing support so that if you die before your partner does, he or she is able to anticipate and welcome the support of others.

3. Finally, discuss the following questions about your retirement years:

   a. Where will we live?

   b. What funds will we use for daily expenses?

   c. How can we prepare for that now?

   If your partner has weak executive function, these questions will be particularly difficult. Ask them rarely and write down the answers, putting the To Dos into play so that they are automated. For example, if you decide you need to save $100 from every paycheck and put it into retirement, then set up an auto-pay/auto-deposit so that you don't have to think about it until you review your plans next year, every five years, or whatever interval makes sense for you.

IDENTIFY: ONE (OR BOTH OF US) IS HAVING A HARD TIME FINANCIALLY

1. Budget! It doesn't make sense that tracking funds would do anything other than leave a paper trail, but try creating and maintaining a weekly budget then judge the results. Calculate what you make each month and subtract monthly expenses.

2. Recognize that everyone has a level of financial intelligence. This approach makes it easier to:

   a. improve by learning more about how to manage finances

   b. identify that current financial state is only a less-mature starting point and that you will continue to grow in financial acuity

   c. recognize that increased knowledge can be found outside one's own head (a difficult concept to grasp for people with theory of mind issues).

3. Get financial crutches. Seek the appropriate level of support. If your partner is irresponsible with money on the level of a gambler

or compulsive shopper, then remove all access to money, slowly increasing access as your partner matures. If your partner is only mildly irresponsible, having an occasional misstep with finances, use tools that help keep you both on track. Tools such as Mint, budgeting software that works on your phone and laptop, can help correct minor mistakes and help keep you on track.

Summary/Maintenance

Executive function is a crucial element for your adult life. It allows you to learn from the past and prepare for the future, enabling you to build the life you want. Fortunately, you do not have to have executive function naturally in order to build a successful life. You can use many different workarounds, many different types of support resources. The desired end result is for you to have the power to build the life you want with a partner who loves and supports you, regardless of whether or not the frontal lobe area of your brain is allowing you to plan, schedule, and organize naturally.

CHAPTER 11

Troubleshooting in the Bedroom

SENSUAL SHARING

To be honest, this is my favorite part of the book. By working through many geeky sensory issues and personal body issues, I am finally at a place where this part of my life and my relationship brings the deepest joy and most profound sense of bliss.

It all started when I began going to the local YMCA. There was a yoga class on Monday nights at 6:15 that worked well with my schedule so I attended often. It was Kundalini yoga, a regular yoga class as far as I knew. During the first year I did Kundalini yoga I noticed that my body felt more alive and aware. It was not until two years later that I realized why. In a conversation with a doctor he asked, "You look great. What's your secret?"

I replied, "Well, I've really been enjoying my Kundalini yoga class."

He did a double-take as if he wondered if I was serious. I was. He pulled out his cell phone, did a quick online search and read me the wikipedia definition of Kundalini, "An erotic yoga…"

I blushed a red deeper than a ripe strawberry. No wonder! The yoga class has nothing explicitly sexual in the exercises. It simply made my body come alive. I realized with regret and embarrassment that I had raved to dozens of people about how much I loved Kundalini yoga. How many of them had heard me say, "I love Kundalini yoga!" and heard, "I love erotic yoga!" My comment had been unintentionally inappropriate to mention to casual acquaintances. Whoops.

This experience gave me a sense of what it may feel like for people with autism when they are told that their behavior is inappropriate. It is embarrassing. I found the sensation unpleasant.

Armed with this new knowledge of the intended benefits of this particular type of yoga, I kept doing Kundalini yoga, but I was more restrained in how I spoke about it with people I did not know well.

For many people on the spectrum, body awareness may be low, but perhaps it can be learned, trained, or explored at the very least. The upside is that if you do learn body awareness, you will have learned it to a depth and with a passion greater than anyone who has not had to work so hard for it.

There are three things you need to know about sex:

- Sex is supposed to feel good.

- Great sex starts with self-awareness/body-awareness.

- It is ok if you are bad at sex. Many people are.

Using the intense focus to your benefit

In an intimate relationship with someone who has both a social deficit and a communication deficit, you may find that non-verbal one-on-one physical interaction is most successful since it avoids barriers which abound in normal non-sexual interaction.

In contrast to everyday interactions, in sexual interaction eye contact is a bonus, but less necessary than in regular conversation. Body language messages become more obvious and are far less nuanced. Gestures are only important in the flirtation or foreplay part of the time-line and verbal communication changes from sophisticated repartee to a more primal expression of physical sensation.

On the other hand, you may find sexual interaction to be particularly difficult if you or your partner have sensory issues or if theory of mind problems prohibit you or your partner from sensing cues given during a sexual encounter.

The Kama Sutra for those with autism

The Kama Sutra is known as the most time-honored sex guide. It contains both pictures and text: the pictures show various positions for intercourse and the text describes how women are to treat men and how men are to treat women. It is culture specific and time specific.

Note that I did not include the Kama Sutra in the References section of this book. It is a 2,000 year old text and, if taken literally, the text gives some terribly destructive ideas of submission, social hierarchy, and interaction protocol that would have been appropriate social behavior in ancient times but not now.

Thankfully there are many other appropriate manuals, including *The Modern Kama Sutra: The Ultimate Guide to the Secrets of Erotic Pleasure* by Kamini and Kirk Thomas (2005) and *Loving Sex: The Book of Joy and Passion* by Laura Berman (2011).

If seeking further reading, look for the following criteria:

- The book should start with a medical description of arousal, especially the classic graph showing the sexual response cycle and how it differs for men and women. This is a good sign that the book may be appropriate for a literal thinker.

- If there are pictures, the majority of people are smiling. This is a quick and easy indication that the book is of the healthy variety (as opposed to pornographic or social-seeking sex).

- If the book states "rules," it states regularly that each person needs to make their own rules within their own relationship. A couple's goal is to have their own Kama Sutra, probably not written, but mutually understood.

For someone on the spectrum, the main value of books is that they give much needed information that other people get from friends or by "asking around." One of the diagnostic criteria dictates that the person with autism does not naturally reach out to others for information, but may, perhaps, reach out to books.

What *not* to do

- Do not view pornography. It may be particularly appealing if you are a visual person, but viewing porn creates the following logic pattern: "I am attracted to various types of bodies." This is a confusing and even dangerous message if you both have agreed to be monogamous. (For simplicity's sake, monogamy makes sense.)

    Note that some people advocate that you should view porn as a couple to heighten the sexual experience. Before you do, consider what messages your partner with autism will get from viewing porn. Remember that the porn will be viewed as literal scripting. If you want to be married to a porn star, then it is appropriate, but for many that is unappealing.

- Do not seek information about sex online. The common saying is that the growth of the internet was fueled by porn, but that doesn't make the internet a good source. People put sexual content online usually to make money; there is no other good reason to do so. Consider looking for sexual information online as akin to hiring a prostitute or gigolo (female or male who is paid for sex) for advice. That mental connection will probably make searching online unappealing enough for you to avoid it.

- Do not talk about sex with others unless you are fully sure it is an appropriate time, place, and person. It is far too easy for someone with autism to say inappropriate things and/or fall prey to a regrettable situation. It is always best to err on the side of caution. If you have no one to talk to about your questions, remember most questions can be answered by your doctor.

Three most important aspects of sex

If you and/or your partner has autism, there are three particularly crucial elements to a good sex life:

- loving your own body

- loving your partner's body

- having an awareness of what feels good to you in particular.

LOVING YOUR OWN BODY

Many years ago I knew a woman who was particularly beautiful. She wasn't beautiful by birth; she was beautiful by habit. The way she moved, walked, talked, and interacted was naturally sensual. Needless to say she was admired by many. For someone with autism, having a naturally beautiful body or appearance can be a tremendous asset because it allows you to leapfrog over so many social faux pas. Sensual beauty gives you a free pass on so many things.

I observed this woman the same way an occupational therapist (OT) or a physical therapist (PT) would evaluate someone. The main trait this woman had was that she obviously loved her own body and the way it moved.

As I observed over the span of several years, I adopted some of her behavior patterns. I enjoyed the clothing I wore, choosing clothing that felt particularly good against my skin, throwing out all the clothes that were not optimal. I began enjoying the swish of my skirt when I walked. I began relishing the feel of a shirt with a fitted waistline. Slowly, I noticed that I walked with more hip movement than previously. My hair grew longer as I enjoyed the feel of it around my face and on my neck.

One day I unpacked a box of clothing that had been stored for several years. I noticed that previously I had worn clothing that was utilitarian and unisex, but now my clothes were more fitted and my shoes were far more feminine.

There was a direct correlation between my clothing and my sexual satisfaction. The more I enjoyed my own body, the more I enjoyed sexual interactions with my partner.

Improving your body

For a person with autism, body movements such as walking or hand gestures may seem forced or odd. You may have a tippy-toe walk or an awkward gait. These things can be overcome the same way Olympic athletes train their bodies to learn certain patterns of movement.

For example, when our oldest son was a teen I noticed that his gait was so awkward that it would be off-putting for any potential girlfriend. At the time we lived in downtown Austin, Texas near a three mile walking path that went along the river and across two bridges. Nearly every day we walked along that river with me pushing his younger siblings in the stroller and his other sibling walking alongside, bored but entertained by watching the river.

While we walked, I coached, "Heel, toe, heel, toe." When his foot simply would not do what was necessary I would ask the bored son to push the stroller while I bent down and moved my oldest son's feet for him, pivoting the ankle at the appropriate angle and making contact with the ground with the appropriate part of the foot. He hated this. There were many tears both from him and from me.

At home we did research, watching short video clips of how the foot moves while walking. We walked along this river nearly every day for two years until we moved to California.

In California, yoga was popular with the teenage boys in the neighborhood and he went to yoga practice every other day. We also did walking meditation, possibly the most boring type of exercise possible, but it was necessary to train his body. He took Tae Kwan Do and went all the way to black belt. He still hated it.

Occasionally he says thank you for helping him learn how to move his body. The best part now is when I see him walking with his girlfriend, the woman he will probably marry in a few years' time, and I see him radiating confidence, it is obvious that those years were worth it. Now he loves how he walks. He walks with confidence. He feels good about himself.

I tell this story in part to highlight the difference between what a parent can do with a growing child and how that changes once a person becomes an adult. For many reasons, it is inappropriate for adult partners to coach each other in OT and PT issues. We can assist each other when desired, but generally it is inappropriate to make comments such as:

"You walk incorrectly. You need to fix it."

"You are not making appropriate eye contact. You need to work on that."

"You are awkward in how you move. You need to move more smoothly."

The above comments would be crossing-the-line criticism that would hurt your relationship. It would be painful for one adult partner to share such comments with the other.

Instead, the following comment would be appropriate:

"I love you just the way you are. If there's ever anything I can do to help you feel better, please let me know."

LOVING YOUR PARTNER'S BODY

Half of the puzzle to good sex is loving your own body. The other half is loving your partner's body.

Thankfully I have an exceptionally good role model in this area. My partner with autism has always accepted my body as the model of perfection. (It is not.) He does not see flaws. He just sees what he likes. This is unusual and rare. I am grateful for his perception. Unfortunately he does this naturally and I have no idea how he does it. It just is what it is.

It is likely that one or both of you will have a hard time accepting the flaws in your own body or your partner's body. To help with this section of the book, I sought advice from the general literature on how to encourage acceptance of physical flaws.

IDENTIFY: I AM HAVING A HARD TIME ACCEPTING THE FLAWS IN MY PARTNER'S BODY AND/OR I HAVE A HARD TIME ACCEPTING THE FLAWS IN MY OWN BODY

Test 1: Explore

When you have time to be together, go on an observation expedition of your partner's body. Notice it. Spend time touching and observing. Notice every unique aspect of your partner's body. For example, notice the particular curve of her collar bone, the way her hair drapes, notice the color of her skin, the texture of her lips, notice all of it. No one will know your partner's body better than you if you spend time noticing. "To know me is to love me." It can be a great first step in acceptance.

Evaluate: This is the most valuable and most powerful first step, but the likelihood of it backfiring is relatively high. There is a good chance that you will mention a detail about your partner's body that you noticed but that your partner wishes you did not mention. If this occurs, see Test 2.

Test 2: Become comfortable with your body

See the movie *Naked States*, a documentary that de-inhibits the naked human body. It is not porn. Instead, it shows acceptance of the human body in all its forms.

Evaluate: If you feel more comfortable with your own naked body and your partner's naked body, then this movie has accomplished its goal. If not, try the next test.

Test 3: Accommodate, accommodate, accommodate

Your partner may be uneasy due to sensory issues. Perhaps your partner's skin is particularly sensitive to temperature changes. Perhaps arousal heightens his or her other senses to an uncomfortable level. Ask questions and when your partner tells you of unique sensory issues, accommodate the unique needs of your partner's body.

Evaluate: If you are able to accommodate your partner's unique needs and this leads to full acceptance then this has worked. If not, see the next test.

Test 4: The scientific approach

Make it a personal experiment. When you kiss your partner at one particular spot does he or she react positively? Since you will not be able to read other body language to get cues for what is appropriate you will have to learn from experience and play the odds. For example, maybe 75 percent of the time your partner likes it when you kiss him or her on the neck. If you kiss your partner on his or her neck and he or she does not like it, make note and keep trying new ways of pleasing your partner.

Evaluate: If you find ways to please your partner and accept each other physically, consider yourself exceptionally lucky and enjoy your relationship. If not, continue with the next strategy.

Test 5: Extreme clarity

Communicate with extreme clarity: "I don't like it when you touch this particular spot, especially when these particular cues are in the environment (the kids are nearby, I am busy, if it's less than an hour after I've returned home from work, if the lights are on)." In a relationship that involves someone on the spectrum, direct, explicit directions are necessary.

Describe what you need the same way you would give directions to someone driving to a new location: "Move your hand to the left two inches." Do not expect each other to know these things intuitively.

Evaluate: If your partner accepts your clear communication and this works to help your partner accept your body (and his or her own) this has worked. If your partner is unreceptive to this feedback, try the next test.

Test 6: Boost positive feedback by a factor of 10

Your partner may make more mistakes than most. Make sure that you give so much positive feedback that he or she "almost feels normal" (my husband's words). Positive comments could be:

"You look so good today."

"I love your body so much."

"I love it when you kiss me."

"Thank you for being with me."

"You make me happy."

"I appreciate you."

"I love the way you interact with me."

"I'm so glad we're together."

"I'm grateful that you are part of my life."

Any similar comments that express appreciation and gratitude may put your partner at ease enough so that he or she ceases to look for flaws.

Evaluate: Sometimes flaw-seeking is the sign of a person needing to know that they are loved and accepted. See if this works. If it does work, your partner will slowly reduce the flaw-seeking and increase the acceptance.

If none of the above strategies work, seek professional help, the equivalent of sending your computer to a repair shop. A professional with experience with your particular make and model (a model with the autism "upgrade") will be able to troubleshoot further.

Most practitioners will request that you rule out medical issues first, so make an appointment with your doctor before seeing other sources of professional help.

WHAT FEELS GOOD TO YOU IN PARTICULAR

Your ability to enjoy sex depends on your ability to be aware of your sensory system's sexual response regardless of being on the spectrum or not. That said, being on the spectrum makes this awareness even more crucial.

For this particular section, the tests are not ranked in linear order since all of them are equally likely to work and there is no progression from one to the next. For this reason, they are listed without an Evaluate step. There is only one evaluation: does sex feel good to you? If yes, then you have succeeded.

For the person with autism, your partner may want you to try one or more of the following:

Explain why you need physical contact to be a certain way

To you, your needs will be obvious. To your partner, these needs will not be obvious because:

- despite being able to read body language and other cues, most partners are not mind-readers

- your needs will be different from the norm. Your partner will not be able to make assumptions based on what worked with other NT partners.

For example, if you explain, "I can't make love to you when you are looking at me," you may end up with a baffled and frustrated partner. Some NTs derive intense pleasure from eye contact during sex.

If you add, "I need you to not look at me since it feels like overload," then your partner can recognize that you both are experiencing it differently. Even better, make it positive: "I am so focused on touching you, feeling you, that I can't also look at you. That would be too intense."

Don't mention it

Another option is that your partner may not want you to mention it. Perhaps it is easier to make adjustments without having conversations about them first. Perhaps turning off the lights and/or lighting a single small candle will communicate love and also meet your need for limited eye contact.

Have a high level of patience

There is a good chance a partner with autism will consider his or her relationship with you to be a grand adventure: scary at times, deeply gratifying at others. There is a chance your partner simply needs more time than others would. Be patient.

Take the long-term view

As you search for what works for you in the bedroom, recognize that most of the literature and available teaching tools are not helpful for a logical mind. Pornography whether photographic or written text can easily confuse the autistic mind. If you are seeing one person while touching another, this is inherently confusing. For example, while an NT can fantasize about Brad Pitt while making love to her husband, to a woman with autism this may seem absurd at worst, illogical at best.

Be a sex scientist

Search for what pleases your partner in the same way in which you would look for your next computer.

If you look at sexual expression throughout history, you will see a far more well-balanced view of how humans have viewed it. One way to get this viewpoint is to visit highly respected museums such as the Museum of Eroticism in Paris, France. If travel is out of the question, consider some of the books in the References section at the end of this book.

Find what works to please your particular sensory system

Remember, sex is not limited to ejaculation and orgasm. It is about physical pleasure (among other things). When you find out what makes your body feel good, make a note (either written or mental).

The best advice I ever received was this: "There are times when sex may be awkward, frustrating, or otherwise unpleasant. Before you say, 'not tonight,' give yourself a chance to warm up. As long as you and your partner have built a foundation of trust and respect, you can tell him what you need and sooner or later you will work past the difficulties and find out that it is *so very worth it!*"

This was particularly crucial advice when considering unusual sensory system needs. For someone with autism, there will be no:

- flirtation (body language missed)
- batting of eyelashes (facial cue missed)
- gentle, suggestive touch (unpleasant when deep pressure is preferred).

Because of this, foreplay may be entirely different.

Perhaps your partner will consider it in logical, technical terms. "Look for the 'on button' (or power switch)."

Here is a visual image of "searching for the 'on button'" in real life: I travel extensively and as a married woman with a husband who also loves traveling and with kids who are often going in different directions, we end up with complex travel schedules. During one trip, I was driving from Utah to California (home) and stopped overnight in Reno, Nevada. When I woke up, it would be only another four or five hours until I would be home. I planned on leaving early the next morning.

We had been apart for more than a week and we missed each other physically. We often texted "I love you" messages on our cell phones. As I crawled into bed that night my husband texted: "We'll be together before you know it."

I forget what I replied, but his next text was, "Knock, knock." Then I heard a knock on the door. He had driven for half the day to meet me on my trek home. If I was an extrovert who liked surprises this would have been enjoyable. But I am not. I am an introvert who loves knowing what is coming. His message made me scared. Immediately my mind was flooded with plans, schedules and repercussions to what he had done.

I knew I should have been flattered and swept off my feet with the romantic nature of his act, which only added guilt onto the pile of mixed-up emotions.

When I opened the door and saw him, I tried very hard to keep my face from showing anger. I needed a minute to think. He began kissing me and during that minute he searched for that "on button," kissing and touching.

If you would have told me then, "In 30 seconds you will be responding to his advances," I would not have believed you, but sexual response is a powerful thing. In a surprisingly short amount of time I was thrilled to respond and we had a tremendously satisfying, memorable night together.

Summary/Maintenance

Knowing how your body will react to certain stimuli is a way of writing your own user manual for your own body. Any good computer user manual tells you how your computer should respond so that you can tell if it is working properly. In this manual one of the most important messages is: sex is supposed to feel good. If not, you are doing it wrong.

CHAPTER 12

Troubleshooting Perfection, Aiming for Imperfection, and Making Your Life Lighter

This chapter explores a few of the topsy-turvy, doesn't-make-sense aspects of relationships. There are three main sections: troubleshooting perfection, aiming for imperfection, and making your life lighter.

Troubleshooting perfection

Logic indicates that if you problem-solve enough, soon you may reach a point where there are no more problems. That is how it is in troubleshooting—you fix the bugs in the software until you reach a point where it is just not worth it to touch the code anymore. The software is good enough. Similarly, there is a point in relationships where things are good enough.

Relationships are naturally flawed, in the same way that software, a garden, or a project is flawed; there is always more to do, more to improve.

___

IDENTIFY: MY PARTNER WITH AUTISM EXPECTS ME TO BE PERFECT: I AM NOT

Test 1: Define "expectation"

I am fascinated by the concept of perfectionism. Perfection is the most unattainable delusion, yet we strive for it. Why?

Perfection is flawlessness. What, however, is a flaw? A flaw is subjective. The definition of perfection can change from person to person and even from day to day within the same person's belief system. The definition of "perfect" can change. It is an opinion.

For someone with theory of mind issues, comprehending subjective terms is nearly impossible. Add to that the tendency to see the world in binary terms and perfectionism may become an issue in your relationship. It may be easier to let the perfectionism issue rest and instead work on your expectations of each other.

Together, as a couple, work to define what you expect in each other, yourself, and your mutual relationship. The list will probably contain items such as, "Takes good care of his or her body. Exercises regularly." Such line items allow for flaws, but give a general guideline. Write them down so that you can use this list later for reference, to adjust when one or both of you get off-track.

Evaluate: It is likely that defining and setting your expectations will be sufficient in eliminating the negative consequences of perfectionism, but if you need more, see Test 2.

Test 2: Communicate how you define perfection

After you understand your own personal view of perfection, communicate that to your partner. My view of perfection is: a life well-lived, few (or no) regrets, evidence of happiness, and a sense of peace with one's way of being. You will have your own unique definition of perfection. Your view will be influenced by your environment, your upbringing, your culture, and your personal views.

Here is one personal example: when I lived near Hollywood, I saw a woman one day who looked perfect according to current fashion. Her hair was perfect. Her clothes were perfect. She had probably had several face lifts, a breast augmentation, perhaps a rib or two removed, and her body was the shape that was the pinnacle of Hollywood standards at the time. Any wrinkles she may have had on her face had been smoothed over like a new cement pavement. As I walked past her, I thought, "Technically she is perfect, but wow, I'm glad that's not how I define perfection."

I was contrasting this perfect surgically altered Californian blonde to a vision of perfection I had seen many years earlier in North Eastern France. One chilly winter day I went running, training for a marathon. I saw an old woman, bent a little at the shoulders, her soft wispy hair falling to her shoulders. She had a broom in her hand and was wearing a ragged old apron, a gray work dress, and utilitarian shoes. Sounds beautiful? Perhaps not to you, but to me, in that moment, she was the image of a life well-lived. Her smile radiated confidence, peace, and love. Her skin was soft and radiant, sun-kissed from days working out in a large garden. Her smile was well-worn. She had many wrinkles testifying to years of smiling and laughing.

Her broom could have been displayed in an art museum. The handle had been worn smooth over the years. It is hard to describe, but she was holding the broom at an aesthetically pleasing angle. It seemed to indicate that she had lived a life of service to others, making their world, and her own, more beautiful. Later that evening, when I tasted her cooking, it was confirmed. She was perfection. She was flawless in a unique type of way. She was satisfied. She wanted for nothing. She had lived a good life, no regrets, no flaw.

Perfection is an opinion. A common phrase is, "Beauty is in the eye of the beholder," but it also holds true that, "Perfection is in the eye of the beholder." So, when you find a partner, you can choose to see them as perfect or you can see their unique traits as flaws. It is a choice; it is an opinion.

Evaluate: If you and/or your partner are able to see each other as perfect, or at least as good enough, then you have succeeded. If you and/or your partner still expect perfection but see flaws, continue to Test 3.

Test 3: Accept yourself and your partner as is
Ignore the rest.

Evaluate: Acceptance of reality is usually the final step, the point at which you stop trying to fix it. It is crucial that you learn to ignore the rest. If your partner continues to be critical (and you still want to live with your partner) then putting up a mental barrier against the criticisms is the best way to protect your sense of self-worth in the long run.

IDENTIFY: MY PARTNER WANTS ME TO SOLVE ALL MY PROBLEMS RIGHT NOW

In an effort to achieve the perfection for which we are all supposed to be aiming, your partner may assume that you should be solving all of your problems right now.

Test 1: Parse out the details

Show your partner that you are sincere about taking her opinions seriously and that you are equally serious about wanting to live a happy, healthy life with her. Ask her for a list of things that need to be changed. It may be scary to ask for this list.

Evaluate: It is probably that when your partner writes out this list, she will see how unreasonable, and perhaps even undesirable, the demands are. Seeing all the requested traits in one list may show her that what she thought she wanted wasn't actually what she wanted. It is similar to "letting the genie out of the bottle," which refers to the Arabian myth about genies who could grant wishes which gave you *exactly* what you asked for, but which, inevitably, was not what you needed.

Your partner may believe that she wants one type of person when in truth what she really wanted was what she got—you. If writing a list exposes this truth, then this test worked. If not, proceed to Test 2.

Test 2: One thing at a time

If you have a logical brain that can focus intensely on one problem at a time, use that to your advantage. Pick one, and only one, problem with your relationship and have that be the only problem. Take the approach, "The other problems can wait," or, "I'll work on them after we are done figuring out _____."

For example, imagine that you are in a relationship with someone who has too many cats, hums incessantly while walking around the house, dresses poorly, forgets to shower more than once or twice a week, is easily offended, does not give you eye contact, does not want to go out with you as often as you want to go out, and who needs to be more receptive to your requests during sexual encounters. Choose only one of the things that bother you, then:

1. determine whether or not it is something you wish to change in yourself

2. make that change

3. set a date on your calendar to check back in a week or longer to see if the change is fully implemented; if it is, choose a second item off the list

4. repeat.

Evaluate: For this to work, you need to be patient. You should see regular, consistent improvement. If you do not, try Test 3.

Test 3: Flip flaws

What you see in your partner may be:

Positive: A quirk, a lovable trait.

Negative: A flaw, an annoying habit, something that needs to be fixed.

Here are a few examples of how something good can be bad and something bad can be good.

Your partner dresses nicely:

Negative: You are annoyed at the expense and time spent maintaining appearances especially when just staying home or going to the grocery store.

Positive: You appreciate that your partner works hard to look good for you.

Your partner dresses in sweatpants and t-shirts most days:

Negative: You are disappointed that your partner has "let himself go." You worry that a beer belly and general slobbish behavior is next.

Positive: You are grateful that the clothing budget is low and appreciate seeing your partner relaxed and comfortable.

Evaluate: If you can successfully flip flaws to something positive and lovable, then you have succeeded. If not, try the final Test.

Test 4: Ignore it

This may be a controversial but:

1. It is a societal norm for people to want others to fix everything about everyone right now.

2. It is not possible, but for some odd reason, people are still frustrated that they cannot do it.

The only options you have are either 1) frustration at the impossibility of perfection, or 2) acceptance/ignore it. It is better for your own health and the health of the relationship to accept the imperfections.

Evaluate: You can tell that this is not working if there are negative consequences such as your partner's increasing frustration or other negative consequences. If the there are no negative consequences to ignoring it, then this works.

Aiming for imperfection

The easiest way to deal with the negative consequences of perfection is to aim for imperfection; embrace the unique and quirky nature of being human. See flaws as personality traits and mistakes as learning opportunities.

IDENTIFY: MY PARTNER WITH AUTISM HAS A NEGATIVE VIEW OF ME/LOOKS DOWN ON ME/SEES ME AS "BAD"

Test 1: Use logic to your advantage

Look at it logically. In a binary world, you are either perfect or not. You are probably imperfect. You are good. Imperfect is good.

Evaluate: This test works if the logical view helps you to:

1. relax, accept (or dismiss) your partner's binary view, and

2. not let that view influence how you see yourself.

If not, see Test 2.

Test 2: Explain

Either verbally (if your partner with autism is a verbal/auditory person) or written (if your partner with autism is a visual person) explain that, "I am both good and bad, depending on the day. Love is a third factor, a neutral factor, independent of good or bad. Can you love me whether I am good or bad, regardless?"

Evaluate: If the explanation helps your partner to appreciate love as an unconditional expression, you have succeeded. If not, see Test 3.

Test 3: Relate

It might be impossible to explain that you, as an "object" in your partner's life, can be both good and bad. If so, find something in your partner's world that he or she is currently not judging. Perhaps he or she does not judge the cat. Explain that you are like the cat—you are not bad due to imperfection. You are good just because you are you.

Evaluate: If you notice your partner with autism treating you with more affection, do not be surprised. Voice the cat analogy and you may find yourself being petted. If not, see Test 4.

Test 4: Learn to forgive

There are serious long-term consequences of living with someone who has a negative view of you. If your partner keeps a negative view of you but you still want to live with him or her, then the quickest route to a healthy (or not-so-unhealthy) relationship is to forgive your partner for this misjudgment of you. Every day, forgive your partner for seeing you as an imperfect, "bad" person. This allows you to distance yourself fully from the judgment and get on with your life.

Evaluate: The end goal is to maintain your own self-respect while helping your partner to see that you are not bad, just human.

Making your life lighter

I am hoping that you will do a little experiment with me. Think of the things that you have to do, the people with whom you live with or interact, in terms of weight. This is a simple equation: if you have only one easy task to complete today, your load is light. If you have dozens of difficult, spine-crushing tasks such as a meeting with your boss or a difficult discussion with someone you don't understand, your daily load is heavy.

The weight concept applies to our relationships. If the person with whom you interact is easy to get along with, always forgiving, and tends to support you in helpful ways, then your relationship is generally light. If your partner is difficult, needy, takes a large portion of your time, then your relationship is mentally heavy for you.

The general assumption is that it does not feel good to be crushed by too much weight.

This is a visual example of how this experience of weight became real for us: as previously mentioned, on 4 November 2009, my husband went to work and was told that all the engineers in the company were being laid off so that the company could, "show a profit by the end of the year."

His job had always felt like a heavy weight. It drained him daily, pushing him to his limits and beyond. The loss of the job should have been a relief, lifting the weight completely, at least until he found a new job, but ironically the weight only became heavier.

Over the next week, Carl was extremely stressed about being "too busy." There were things to do on our family calendar such as, "Take kids to the park," but the activities were supposed to benefit and supplement our lives, not create more weight. None of them were requirements. Throughout his first week off work he said over and over again, "I'm so busy. I can't do it all. There's just too much to do." He freaked out, a week-long meltdown.

We sat down at the table together and went over every activity. I showed him that they were activities for me and the children. He was not responsible for any of them. He was welcome to participate, but they were "zero weight activities."

Yet, he still felt crushed.

So, I deleted, erased, removed every task, appointment, and fun event off the calendar, stating, "None of this is your responsibility. This is not a weight for you." (I switched all calendar tasks to my own private, hidden, separate calendar.)

This still did not ease the strain he felt, however. He felt crushing weight along with his new joblessness. He had generous severance pay which meant that he had a month off at full pay then several months off at half-pay. He could also get unemployment benefit (which he did) to support the family. There were options, many options.

He still felt financial stress, however. He felt it as a crushing weight. He went into great detail about all the things that were urgent to the point of being deadly: "We won't make it." It felt like he was describing a horror movie instead of real life.

In my mind, I perceived this as a tremendous opportunity for him to see the perceived weight for what it was—a mental perception, not reality. I saw the layoff as a chance for him to take a break, relax, reassess, and be grateful that he no longer had to deal with an employer who had such an extreme disrespect for their engineers, but the fear and crushing weight continued. On a day when he was well rested and had exercised, I asked him to go on a car ride with me. He agreed. I asked the question that was at the root of it all.

Me: *"It looks like you are being crushed under a heavy weight."*

Him: *"Yes."*

Me: *"Can you please describe that weight for me? What is it?"*

He thought for a while as we drove. He could not name it, could not identify what was causing him the level of stress he had been feeling. *In those moments of forced introspection, the weight lifted.*

The weight had been one of those unnameable, illogical, unidentifiable monsters that can sometimes cause us tremendous unnecessary pain.

It was this experience that helped us to quantify what it means to "feel weight" mentally and even physically. When a person feels overloaded, they often slump. The body physically expressed this act of feeling excess weight. The act of carrying too much mental weight can be detrimental to your health. It is well-documented how stress and strain cause disease.

Not all situations will be clear-cut like this one. In most situations, the weight you or your partner is experiencing will be quite real, perhaps crushing, such as the death of a parent or a child, an accident that causes irreparable damage, or a job loss where there is no safety net.

For the most part, however, the weight we feel every day can be lightened by approaching it logically, clearly, and with a sense of, "Is this really worth the stress?" and "Where is this weight coming from?"

Before I mention solutions, please note that it is crucially important to not judge what is a weight for another person and what is not. Point out honest truths about what you can observe in a person's life, but when the person states that something is difficult for him or her, respect it.

Solutions:

1 Identify the weight.

2 Remove the weight one chunk at a time.

3 Assess. Fix. Repeat.

IDENTIFY THE WEIGHT

This is the most powerful, effective, quick way to get from difficulty to relief:

Him: *"I'm stressed. I don't have enough time to do all the things I need to do. It all has to get done right now. I just can't do it all."*

Me: *"Well, what do you need to do immediately?"*

This is a crucial first step. By recognizing what is a real weight and what is not, you can live better, more in control of your own life.

REMOVE THE WEIGHT ONE CHUNK AT A TIME

In the above example, review the list of items your partner is stressed about. In the first pass through the list:

1 eliminate tasks that are nice but not necessary

2 move tasks that do not need to be today to do a "do tomorrow" list

3 identify all tasks on the list that can be done in five minutes or less and complete them one at a time. This may significantly shorten your list, giving a mental boost that allows you to tackle the harder tasks with optimism

4 prioritize the remaining tasks and complete them one at a time, giving yourself a positive reward or a quick break after each one.

Summary/Maintenance

In long-term relationships, especially those where autism is interlaced between you both, it helps to identify what you define as perfection then evaluate what you truly want in a partner and in yourself. The end goal is to live more lightly, happily, and with a deep abiding satisfaction with each other and with yourself.

CHAPTER 13

Troubleshooting Personal Attachment Style

ANXIOUS, AVOIDANT, OR SECURE ATTACHMENT

Researchers generally agree that there are at least three attachment styles that define the dynamics of how we interact.

- *Anxious attachment*: fears abandonment, co-dependent, nervous, anxious that partner will leave.

- *Avoidant attachment*: distant, unattached, withdrawn, avoiding connection with partner.

- *Secure attachment*: safe, happy, confident, secure in one's ability to live happily.

If you wonder which style best defines you, see Levine and Heller (2010), Tatkin and Hendrix (2012), and Lucas (2012).

Most books on attachment styles contain simple self-tests for determining your attachment style. In the most basic sense, if you have an anxious attachment style, you tend to cling to your partner, or in the case of someone with autism, it may be that you *appear* to cling. If you have an avoidant attachment style, you easily and quickly detach, or in the case of someone with autism, you *appear* to be socially detached from your partner or others with whom you live and work.

When researching attachment style and other similar topics, please read with caution since the outward appearance of a person with autism may look like classic avoidant or anxious attachment style, but once you peel back the surface layer and look at a person's motivation, you see something entirely different.

Anxious attachment style through the ASD lens

A person with autism may appear anxious due to needing help with tasks that seem too basic. Some of the following may apply if you or your partner has anxious attachment style:

- The partner may rely on the other to act as a social buffer when in public, thus "clinging" to the partner, hoping he or she won't be left alone to fend for him- or herself socially.

- It may appear as if the person is playing dumb so as to get attention when in truth the questions are honest need-to-know questions.

- The supposedly anxious behaviors may be only a clumsy, ineffective way to relate to the partner.

If the apparent anxious attachment is disability-related then there will be a different motive, and different reasoning, and, in turn, a different reaction will be required. That is why I have covered it here in this book, calculating autism into the equation.

To contrast the differences:

- An NT with anxious attachment style is generally motivated by fear of abandonment. His or her actions may appear clingy, needy, requiring more attention than a non-anxious partner.

- In contrast, a person with autism may appear anxious if he or she misunderstands what is appropriate, misses cues, or misreads boundaries. The outward appearance may appear the same, but the motivation and desired reactions are very different.

Avoidant attachment style through the ASD lens

A person with autism may appear avoidant due to lack of reciprocity, not hearing you, or not "syncing up" with you. This is not purposeful avoidance about which you might read in other books on attachment style. For a person with autism, action is motivated by a lack of understanding instead of a purposeful avoidance.

To illustrate this contrast:

- An NT with avoidant attachment style is scared of forming a relationship because the closer he or she gets, the more it will hurt if things go wrong.

- A person with autism may appear avoidant due to lack of understanding of body language, eye contact, gestures, and other signs of intimacy.

The motivation is so different with both attachment styles that, if autism is not accounted for, misunderstandings will abound. As a general rule, if autism is part of the equation, the dysfunctional anxious or avoidant behaviors are unintentional.

IDENTIFY: MY PARTNER (ASD) IS ANXIOUS/ CLINGY/CONTROLLING/CO-DEPENDENT

Test 1: Is it a misunderstanding?

Check if it is a misunderstanding of how adults are supposed to interact. If your partner grew up with a parent who had anxious attachment, he or she may be interacting in an anxious way simply because it was scripted for him or her. This is a very simple misunderstanding and probably easily fixed, depending on whether habit or logic is stronger for your partner. If habit is strong, it will be hard for your partner to change. If logic is stronger, it will be easier for your partner to switch once he or she understands the problem.

Evaluate: If this clarification helps your partner switch to a more secure way of interacting, it worked. If your partner still cannot see the problem, try Test 2.

Test 2: Role models work

Look for role models who can script for your partner. It can be simple or in-depth. The simple method is casual observation of anxious versus secure behavior: "You know Mark and Kelly? Have you noticed how they interact?" The in-depth method is to watch movies together, read books, or listen to audiobooks together, identifying characters who exhibit anxious behavior and compare it to those exhibiting secure behavior.

Evaluate: If scripting healthy interactions helps your partner adopt a more secure interaction style with you, it worked. If not, try Test 3.

Test 3: Track progress

Choose one dysfunctional behavior at a time and chart progress. Here is a personal example to do with criticism. I kept a notepad with me during the day and tallied up the number of critical comments and critical thoughts I had. I did this several times and saw distinct progress.

Evaluate: If tracking progress results in regular, marked improvement in behavior with a sense of "I can control myself" (as opposed to "She's controlling me, measuring me") then it is working. If not, try Test 4.

Test 4: Acceptance

Many older couples have learned to live with anxious (or avoidant) behaviors, though couples with an anxious partner tend to be more common. This is due to avoidant partners pushing away from the relationship whereas anxious partners cling to the relationship.

If you are linked to an anxious partner or are one yourself, all of the above methods will help take off the rough edges of your anxious behavior. It is unlikely that you will become a fully, naturally secure person, but the closer you get to secure behaviors, the happier and more calm you can be.

Evaluate: The goal is for you both to experience peace and happiness in your relationship. If full acceptance of either your way or your partner's current way of relating helps you feel greater peace and happiness then you have been successful.

IDENTIFY: MY PARTNER (NOT ASD) IS SO ANXIOUS/CLINGY/CONTROLLING/CO-DEPENDENT

Test 1: Is your partner getting what she needs?

Ask your partner to write out a list of what he or she needs from you. Often the anxious person is having "pre-emptive suffering," worrying in advance about things that have not happened yet. Review the list and mark items as either, "Current," or "Pre-emptive." During this exercise, it is probable that your partner will see that worrying about things that have not happened is a miserable way to live.

Evaluate: If bringing awareness to the issues helps make your partner less anxious, great. Make sure you shorten the list by differentiating between problems worth worrying about and those that are not in your control such as the weather, politics, or actions of other people. If this does not reduce anxious behavior, see Test 2.

Test 2: Are you giving sufficient comforting signs of love?

If this is a problem, ask your partner to write a list of the main ways he or she can feel comforted and loved. These might include:

- Tell me you love me.
- Hug me when I leave for work in the morning.
- Give me eye contact for at least two minutes when I get home from work at night.
- Don't burp loudly when I'm around.
- Pick up your things off the floor.

It is likely that every item on the list is triggering a fear of, "My partner doesn't love me." Specifically, an anxious partner may see that you threw your sweater on the floor and assume, "He knows I hate it when he throws his clothes on the floor, so if he is doing this, he must not want to live with me. He obviously would prefer to be single." If you are not an anxious person, this may seem silly, but if you do have anxious attachment style, this is how you think: your mind is on high alert for any signs of your partner leaving you.

Evaluate: Helping your partner with the specific triggers for anxiety will, it is hoped, help to reduce the anxiety, but if not, see Test 3.

Test 3: Misdirection

The previous test may not work if your partner does not connect, "I don't feel loved by my partner," to his or her anxious behavior. For example, he or she may say that he or she is angry at you for one thing, when in truth, he or she needs reassurance of your love. If this is the case, try expressing your love for your partner more often.

A personal example of this is that my husband has learned that when I am upset, usually all he needs to do is throw his arms around me and remind me that he loves me. It puts everything into perspective for me and is surprisingly effective.

Evaluate: If reassurance works, you now have a very simple way to solve most problems. If not, see Test 4.

Test 4: Speak the right language

The previous test may not have worked if you did not express love in a way your partner without autism can hear it. Read *The 5 Love Languages: The Secret to Love That Lasts* by Gary D. Chapman (Chapman 2009). Identify your own love language and ask your partner which love language he or she needs.

Evaluate: If you notice a reduction in anxious behaviors, even a little, after approximately a week, then it is working. Note that it may take a very long time, possibly years before significant progress is made.

Test 5: Acceptance

Your partner may enjoy being anxious, or may have a physiological condition where too many stress hormones are triggering the fear circuitry in the brain so that nothing you do will calm down the anxious behavior. Also, perhaps he or she is still working through issues that are separate from your partnership (but that affect your partnership nonetheless).

Evaluate: Full acceptance of the problem is the last thing you do after you have tried everything else. At that point, you decide whether or not the level of anxious behavior is acceptable to you long-term.

Note that the most common scenario for autism-linked relationships is for the partner with autism to appear avoidant.

The specifics of the autism diagnosis dictate that a person with autism will not relate as easily or as closely with others, but close relationships are still possible! The purpose of this book is to help build those close relationships regardless of behaviors that appear avoidant, regardless of communication issues.

IDENTIFY: MY PARTNER (ASD) APPEARS AVOIDANT AND IT IS BOTHERING ME

Test 1: Explain

Explain what you see your avoidant partner doing and tell your partner what you need. Often a simple To Do list is all it takes to fix a problem. Appendix A contains a sample How to Love list.

Evaluate: If your partner is less avoidant and more interactive with a simple How to Love list, great. If not, or if this seems to "false" to you, see Test 2.

Test 2: Flip your own understanding of avoidant behaviors

Instead of seeing your partner's behaviors as, "My partner doesn't love me," look for the upside. Focus on the good parts of your relationship. Use the autism diagnosis to re-interpret your partner's behaviors. A prime example could be when your partner walks through the door at the end of the day and goes straight to another room without saying "hello," remind yourself that your partner, "is in mass overload and is aware that if he or she talks to me now, it may easily become an unpleasant experience. She is taking care of herself, decompressing so that we can interact in a loving way later."

If this test looks promising for you, but you need more support, read *The Story of You*, by Steve Chandler (2006) listed in the References section. It will help you to see how easily and effortlessly beliefs can be changed for the better.

Evaluate: If changing your opinion helps you feel loved even when your partner is doing things that appear avoidant, great; it worked! If not, see Test 3.

Test 3: Identify expectations

You may see a How to Love list as fake. You may not want to have to say to your partner, "Kiss me when you come home at night." Note that this type of expectation is the downfall of many could-have-been-great relationships. Having unrealistic expectations is a mistake, even in the NT realm. Identify your expectations and purposefully eliminate them.

Evaluate: The problem is only solved when both of you feel secure in your relationship. If expectations and avoidant behaviors are still causing problems for your relationship, keep working on it and try Test 4.

Test 4: State choices

Your partner may see a How to Love list as "bossing me around." If so, explain the situation in a binary, black and white, logical way. "I don't feel like we are partners because we don't act like partners. If you want to start acting like my partner, great. If you want to know what it means to be my partner, please let me know. If not, then I will be moving on."

The other option is to be angry, upset, nag, yell or respond by withdrawing into avoidant behavior yourself. I do not recommend it as a possible solution to the problem, though it is what many people do (and I have done it a few times myself).

Instead, after doing what you can to inform your partner of what you need, respect your partner's choice.

Evaluate: Giving your partner a choice will work one way or the other, even if your partner chooses not to do anything, silence means, "I choose to continue my avoidant behavior." At this point you make your own choice and either stay with the avoidant partner or separate/divorce and move on.

IDENTIFY: MY PARTNER (NOT ASD) IS AVOIDANT AND IT IS BOTHERING ME

Test 1: Check your radar

Perhaps your partner is telling you that he or she loves you but you are not picking up on the signals. Read up about signals of love in Appendix B.

Evaluate: If increasing your awareness of the signals which your partner is sending you that he or she loves you works, great. If not, see Test 2.

Test 2: Is this the right partner for me?

A person with an avoidant attachment style may marry a person with autism because it is a good match; someone who appears avoidant being married to someone who actually is avoidant. If so, ask yourself if this relationship works for you. If you want something different, ask.

Evaluate: If asking for what you need works, great. If not and your partner still chooses to be avoidant—and that bothers you—then you need to choose whether or not to live with it.

Summary/Maintenance

The purpose of studying the different attachment styles is to use the knowledge of your style to improve your relationship. The information you will find in other books about how to deal with avoidant/anxious behavior, however, may actually be detrimental if you do not take the specifics of autism into account. For this reason, read carefully and remember to be compassionate and generous with each other.

According to most researchers, the ideal relationship is secure/secure, but, with the autism diagnosis you may end up as a blissfully happy avoidant/avoidant couple. (They are such a small percentage of the population that they are often given a less than 1 percent ranking.)

You may end up as an anxious/anxious couple, extremely close to each other, assisting each other with many basic everyday needs. Some may perceive it as a mutually co-dependent relationship.

Most couples are avoidant/anxious with one partner holding on while the other partner pulls away. It is the most common relationship pattern. In any case, figure out how you are wired and how your partner is wired. You may find further help in books such as *Wired for Love: How Understanding Your Partner's Brain and Attachment Style Can Help You Defuse Conflict and Build a Secure Relationship* by Tatkin and Hendrix (2012).

The goal is to:

1. first identify your own attachment style then your partner's style

2. interpret that style within the framework of your ASD-linked relationship

3. find solutions for your problems based on how you perceive the relationship and each other (your attachment style).

Keep your eyes on the prize. The end goal is happiness and fulfillment for both of you.

CHAPTER 14

Troubleshooting Reciprocity

TIPS AND TRICKS TO CREATE SUPPORT, APPRECIATION, AND RESPECT IN YOUR RELATIONSHIP

Five generally accepted aspects of healthy, mindful relationships are as follows, with ASD complications in parenthesis:

1. *Knowing and being known*: seeking to understand the partner (mindblindness can block this understanding).

2. *Making positive attributions for behaviors*: giving the benefit of the doubt (misunderstanding motive can block this attribution).

3. *Accepting and respecting*: empathy and social skills (empathy is hard-won for those on the spectrum).

4. *Maintaining reciprocity*: active, spontaneous participation in the relationship (participation will not come naturally and may need to be prompted).

5. *Persisting in mindfulness of your partner* (relationships take more work for those on the spectrum, making persistence a much tougher accomplishment).

When I showed this list to my husband, he read it and muttered, "Oh crumbs. I'm in trouble, aren't I? How am I going to keep track of all this?" His comment prompted a new theory: keeping score trains reciprocity.

Note that "keeping score" in a relationship is generally regarded as a bad thing. You are supposed to give freely and fully in a relationship. Many people say that they aren't keeping score, but they are, even if subconsciously. Generally people are aware of how much they have done for another person versus how much that person has done for them.

We cannot make a generalization about whether those on the spectrum are more likely to keep score than those who are not because:

- there may be an affinity for numbers and logical accounting that causes the person with autism to keep score, or

- there may be a lack of awareness concerning reciprocity that makes keeping score seem odd or useless.

In an NT relationship, keeping score is seen as a universally bad thing. Tracking what you have done for your partner in comparison to what your partner has done for you is seen as crass, unfeeling, rude, stingy, and antithetical to intimate love.

In an ASD-linked relationship, keeping score may achieve an opposite result. It may be the most loving, respectful way to train and maintain reciprocal relations. Keeping score can be used in a hurtful way, specifically using the list to say, "I am working so much harder than you are." Perhaps, however, that comment may be helpful if the situation is terribly imbalanced. I believe that keeping score may be an exceptionally useful tool in creating and maintaining long-term relationships which involve autism. It prompts reciprocal action that otherwise would not occur naturally.

Rules for keeping score

1 Use the results of your scorecard to:

- motivate yourself to give more, and

- give appreciation to your partner for what he has given.

2 Do not share these results with your partner or others in a way that shames your partner (or yourself). "I am doing so much and he or she is doing almost nothing," is an example of a shaming comment.

3 Remember that the purpose of score-keeping is to show the give-and-take of the relationship.

4 Focus on what you have given first. Focus on the good things your partner has given second. Do not give attention to what either of you is lacking.

The number of ways to train reciprocity in an adult relationship could fill a whole book so I include only a few ideas of keeping score.

- *Make a daily gratitude list/accomplishment list.* I do this in a diary which I purchased that has a single page for each day of the year. On each page I write those things for which I am grateful. Invariably it includes what my partner has done for me and what I have done for him. For example, "I am grateful that my husband did the dishes so that we could have time for intimacy tonight," and "I am grateful that I had time to clean out his car. I found lollipops on the back seat so now I know why the kids' pants have been sticky."

- *Make an actual tally of compliments.* Do this only if you have a hard time remembering to compliment your partner, but don't go overboard. If you give too many compliments they can seem false. For example, set yourself a goal: I will notice five good things about my partner tonight and tell my partner about them verbally or in writing.

- *Tie your good deeds to rewards.* Imagine that you really dislike doing certain things for your partner. Perhaps it is not logical to you that you should have to do them or perhaps you find the tasks unappealing. Give yourself a reward for every good thing you do. If you take out the trash so that your partner doesn't have to, then reward yourself by playing your favorite game for 30 minutes. I do this too. If I do a difficult task that benefits my partner (and usually me too) then I play a short game afterwards, usually Sudoku since I love numbers. Train your brain to like doing things for your partner. It will be easy to keep track since it will be easier to remember the number of rewards you have given yourself.

IDENTIFY: MY PARTNER IS NOT MOTIVATED TO BE RECIPROCAL

Test 1: Check for understanding

Check to see if the term "reciprocate" means anything to your partner. If your partner has no context for it, draw comparisons from his or her daily experience such as, "You did the dishes last night so I made breakfast this morning. You did something nice so I reciprocated."

Evaluate: If your partner grasps the concept of reciprocation, skip to Test 3. Understanding reciprocal action is a first step, not a final solution. If your partner does not understand reciprocal action yet, continue to Test 2.

Test 2: Give the geeky explanation

Refer to concepts in physics, mathematics, and other areas of study that may make sense to your partner.

- In *electromagnetism*, reciprocity refers to many different theorems such as Lorentz reciprocity, Rayleigh-Carson reciprocity, Green's reciprocity and many others involving the flow of electrical currents. In fact, reciprocity and electromagnetism are synonymous.

- In *engineering*, reciprocity is used to analyze structures in regards to complex load conditions.

- In *network theory*, reciprocity describes a theorem about how passive networks transfer content.

- In *mathematics*, reciprocity law covers quadratic reciprocity, cubic reciprocity, quartic reciprocity, reciprocal square root, reciprocal polynomials, and many others including Hermite reciprocity, Frobenius reciprocity, and Stanley's reciprocity theorem.

- In *photography*, reciprocity refers to the correlation between the intensity of the light and duration of the exposure.

- *In contract law*, reciprocity is also known as mutual assent.

Evaluate: If viewing the concept of reciprocity from a geeky angle helps define the concept for your partner, then this has worked. If it has not, move on to Test 3 regardless.

Test 3: Train your partner to appreciate reciprocal interaction as something that feels good

Over the years I have sent my husband emails and written notes similar to the following note:

I appreciate you today because:

1. You made an amazing breakfast for the kids, breakfast tacos, everyone's favorite.

2. You hugged me when I had a headache.

3. You did your work without a single complaint.

4. You stayed home in the evening instead of going out with buddies like my friend's husbands do.

5. You put on my favorite TV show for me to watch while I made dinner.

6. You took care of your body by taking a nap in the late afternoon and by putting in your headphones so that the kids' sounds did not drain you in the evening.

7. You went running, got your exercise this morning.

Sending your partner lists like these has significant positive effect:

- It trains your partner to link the act of giving with the sensation of being appreciated.

- It highlights reciprocal interaction, shining a bright spotlight on how important these actions are, making it more likely that your partner will do them again in the future.

- It serves as a sort of journal, preserving the happy memories of your marriage, an extremely important thing to do for your own long-term health (among other reasons).

Because these notes feel good to your partner, they cause a surge of serotonin and other feel-good hormones when he or she reads them. My husband has written me notes over the years, not list style, but his own style. I carry my favorite in my work backpack along with my laptop and other supplies. It says simply: "You are awesome," on a square piece of pink notepaper.

This note is particularly meaningful because I can see from his handwriting that he is relaxed, confident, and happy. One's writing often reflects one's mood and when I see his penmanship on this note I remember that it was written after a long weekend when we were home alone, the kids off to camps and friends' homes. I remember the sexual intimacy we shared, sleeping late, relaxing in each other's arms in that state of blissed-out near-sleep that is terrifically rejuvenating for one's body and mind.

Evaluate: If you can train each other to give reciprocally and you both find it satisfying enough most of the time, then this is sufficient. If not, refer to Test 4.

Test 4: Be self-centered

This test shows definitively that this book is written for a non-NT audience! A book on relationships for the general population would not advocate being self-centered, especially within the context of desired reciprocity. Within the community of people dealing with autism, however, there are certain situations and times when unique against-the-grain solutions are most appropriate.

To "be self-centered," redraw the boundaries. Instead of seeing "You" and "Me," see, "Me," and "World." This way, you put less pressure on your partner to provide what you need. If you can get your needs met by either your partner or the world (other people), then when your needs are not met by your partner, you are not limited to your partner being the only solution.

Imagine that you need more support for your work. Perhaps you are working hard, have hectic mornings, exhausting days, and too much work when you come home at night. Arlie Hockschild and Anne Machung, authors of *The Second Shift* (1997), wrote a classic work explaining this dynamic. They describe how many women (though it could just as easily be men) work double-time with a day job then when they get home, work a second job caring for home, family and, if there is time, self.

If you require your partner to meet your needs, you will probably be sorely disappointed, regardless of your partner being on the spectrum, NT, or other. If your frame of reference is, "Me," and, "World," when you have a problems, you may reach out to a wide variety of resources.

In the example above, solutions might come quickly in the form of asking parents or friends for help with carpooling, combining resources such as a dinner-share (five families each make one large dinner only once per week), using after-school childcare, or streamlining some of the more difficult tasks. Instead of assuming your partner with autism will watch the kids after school while you work late, consider asking a teenager to watch the kids, or doing the kids' homework with them. Instead of asking your partner to do the grocery shopping, have it delivered or pay the elderly person next door to get your groceries for you.

Instead of assuming your partner needs to fill every need, see your partner as only one part of a large support structure you have in your life. It is far more stable, less stressful, and more respectful to your partner.

Evaluate: If you find that being self-centered helps take pressure off the relationship then this has worked. If not, try the next test.

Test 5: Adjust your attitude

Adopt the following motto:

> *Expect nothing;*
> *Appreciate everything.*
> *Be easy to surprise*
> *And impossible to disappoint.*
>
> (Anonymous)

It is particularly hard for logical people to see the power of adjusting your attitude. It may help to consider an attitude adjustment as a lever or valve you adjust on the complex control panel of your relationship. Adjust expectations to 0. Set appreciation to full on. Sometimes adjusting your attitude makes all the difference.

Evaluate: If adjusting your expectations down to 0 does not ease your frustration over lack of reciprocity, perhaps there is some other issue causing the problems. Go back to the beginning and verify the main problem.

Habits of reciprocity

The basics of reciprocity are well covered in other books on autism, so I will cover only three actions (habits) that relate directly to adult long-term relationships:

- support
- appreciation
- respect.

The overarching principle is that you can create habits of reciprocity.

HABITS OF SUPPORT

The concept of "support" in a long-term relationship is one of the most fought-over topics. Who does the dishes? Who earns the money and how much? Who manages the money? Is he doing his fair share? Is she?

Support means:

- to bear or hold up

- to maintain by supplying necessary things

- to sustain or withstand without giving way.

There is little emotional charge to the act of supporting one another, yet in many NT relationships, the topic of mutual support carries an explosive emotional charge.

Perhaps autism can serve you well if you lean on the tendency to interact with less emotion, love routine, appreciate clear rules, and be loyal. Use these traits to benefit your relationship; get into the habit of supporting each other.

Examples:

- Choose a few favorite tasks and make them routine. Make doing the dishes or paying the bills part of your routine.

- Divide up the financial responsibilities with an unemotional, logical approach, exactly what is appropriate in handling family finance.

- Be reliable. Use your love of routine to create a sense of stability in your relationship.

HABITS OF APPRECIATION

Anyone who is even marginally on the spectrum will have a hard time with appreciation. It is simply hard to remember to appreciate someone. Even if you are the most gregarious person alive, you may take others for granted.

Appreciation is cumulative. NTs would say, "The more you give, the more you get," but we need to adjust that for those on the spectrum to read, "The more you give, the more you remember to give." Training oneself or one's partner to appreciate each other is central, but so easy to overlook.

Perhaps set a date once or twice a year, at the winter and summer solstice or some other memorable time of year, to reset your ability to appreciate each other. Put it on your calendar: Appreciation Reboot. Spend an hour or two together doing the following:

1 Make a list of the things you appreciate most about your partner.

2 Make a list of the ways you can best express that appreciation: verbally, in writing, by doing the same act in return, by doing some other act that means a lot to your partner such as kissing him or her on the neck whenever he or she does the dishes or giving your partner a tight squeeze whenever he or she remembers to hang up his or her coat.

Whatever you do, make and build habits of appreciation so you do not end up like so many couples do several years into their relationship realizing suddenly that they are taking each other for granted.

HABITS OF RESPECT

In some cultures respect is given and even required, at least in public. In other cultures, respect is rarely given. Regardless of your culture, healthy relationships rest on a healthy respect for each other.

Since respect is such a large subject, I will include only my favorite top three that are particularly important in ASD-linked relationships:

1 Respect/remember your partner as he or she is, not as you wish him or her to be. Do whatever it takes to make sure that you maintain the delicate balance between supporting your partner, encouraging him or her to succeed, and accepting him or her as he or she is. This will be an every day act of respect.

2 Stop disrespectful comments before they leave your mouth. There are several ways to stop them:

- Get in the habit of pausing briefly before saying anything. Making rash comments is a habit. You can train yourself to pause, evaluate, and adjust.

- Pretend that other people are listening, if that helps you to not make disrespectful comments.

- Give yourself physical feedback such as literally biting your tongue when you want to say something disrespectful.

3 Build habits of support, appreciation, and respect. You will find these habits create an environment of love and enjoyable intimacy.

Summary/Maintenance

What doesn't come naturally can be trained. Most of what we do day-to-day is trained anyway, so why not reciprocity? We were trained to write, talk, even potty-trained. We were trained professionally, too. Despite the common stereotype that reciprocal interaction should come naturally, training is a good thing. It enhances your abilities and enhances your life.

As I once told my husband on a day when he felt badly about not realizing that he needed to reciprocate, "Just because you have autism doesn't mean that you are unique in forgetting to reciprocate. It is ok. It is simply something that is learned, practiced, then—if I do my part—it is appreciated."

PART 4

TROUBLESHOOTING BIG PROBLEMS

CHAPTER 15

Troubleshooting Blame and Avoidance

If you like binary thinking, black and white, there is a simple technique you can use during any conversation (or argument) with your partner.

How to defuse blame

Ask yourself: "Do I want to be right or do I want to be married?"

If you sense your partner is motivated by a desire to be right, you have two choices:

- Let your partner be right. It is the easiest option by far.

- Ask your partner: "What are you fighting for? Are you fighting to be right or are you fighting for us?" It adjusts perception so that you can both get back to solving problems.

Personally, I could not care less whether or not I am wrong in an argument. I care far more about solving problems. Blame and finger pointing do not bother me, but they do waste time. So, when my partner feels the need to be right, I let him be right. Here is one example that I actually taped from a recent difficult discussion after a long day:

Me: *"You're right. You're 100 percent right. It's my fault, all my fault. I'm the one who made us late. I'm the one who caused the problems. I'm the one who made us go in the first place. It's all my fault."*

Him: *(deep breath, shoulders relax, brow unfurrows) "Ok, um, thanks. So, do we still need to fix this?"*

Admitting fault often defuses tension for the person who is in blame mode. The blaming partner no longer has anything to fight over. It is possibly the most stress-relieving troubleshooting tactic I know.

How to defuse avoidance

When discussing something, even if it seems innocuous to you, and the conversation goes awry, keep one main, overarching question in your mind: "Are we talking about the core issue or did we get distracted?"

When someone is presented with an issue which they do not want to deal with, they may wriggle away from the problem in the same way that a trapped animal wriggles away from its captor. It is natural to not want to deal with tough problems. For someone who is not a social butterfly, discussions may be unpleasant. For some it may be akin to dumping the trash, doing the dishes or washing the laundry. It is not fun, but it has to be done.

Fortunately, if you can keep yourself from running away from the problem, you can find fun in it (or at least relief) and you can get it done quickly.

Problems occur when you lose sight of what you are trying to accomplish. Here is one example. Names have been changed.

> One afternoon Karyn wanted to talk with her husband about problems they were having with who-does-what around the home. She picked one specific problem and asked, "Can we talk about how frequently the garbage is being taken out?" Her husband Jim's response was a classic avoidance technique that used to work every time with her. It is called "The Kiss Up."
>
> Jim replied with, "Sure, but first, I want to make dinner for you. What are you craving?" Both of them knew that he had no intent to talk about it later. He wanted it to be forgotten. If he offered a generous gift, perhaps Karyn would be bribed into temporarily forgetting about solving the issue.
>
> Typically Karyn would give a dysfunctional reply in response to the dysfunctional effort to avoid the problem. Most often she fell for the distraction and let the problem fester; but the problem always came back to bite them in larger, more potent ways later.
>
> Worse, Karyn would force the issue, and when she did it always played out as her being the villain, the nasty person talking about

negative, contentious things while Jim is just the poor husband trying to make a nice meal for his wife.

Karyn: *"Can we please solve the garbage problem first?"*

Jim: *"So, you don't want dinner? I'm just trying to be nice and make you dinner after a long day. What's so wrong with that?"*

After which he storms out, getting to avoid the problem *and* not make dinner. It is a handy technique.

In the vast landscape of human communication there are many, many ways to avoid talking about an issue. I have included an example with each avoidance tactic so that you can see the shape that these distractions can take. Once you can see them clearly, you can better identify and eliminate them.

I have also given each avoidance tactic a name. It may sound corny, but after so many years of identifying and seeing avoidance techniques in action in my own marriage, it seemed more fun, playful, and ice-breaking to give them names, as if they were plays that a quarterback calls to fool the offense. When things are difficult, a bit of levity is often good.

THE KISS UP

Partner A: *"Can we talk about how frequently the garbage is being taken out?"*

Partner B: *"Sure, but first, I want to make dinner for you. What are you craving?"* (The intent is to forget the original question.)

Why this is harmful to a relationship
It does not solve anything, just postpones the resolution of the original problem. Also, when Partner B is "just trying to be nice," in the avoidance of a problem, Partner A is forced into only two options: Option 1 is to join in the avoidance of the problem, allowing the avoidant partner to hide under a false shield of nicety. Option 2 is to force the issue, thus becoming the villain, disallowing the supposedly kind, generous partner to do something "good" and force that partner into a contentious problem because he or she is "just trying to be nice."

The fallout

It creates a good guy/bad guy dynamic that makes both of you feel bad in the end. Partner A wants to solve a problem. Partner B does not want to deal with it so he or she offers a generous reward in exchange for co-avoidance of the problem. There is a tremendous benefit to Partner B for using the Kiss Up technique. The end result can be Partner B stomping out, "I was only trying to be nice!" thus avoiding the original question and the promised reward of having dinner made.

The solution

Create a catch phrase that will help pull your partner out of this dynamic. This phrase will probably be quite difficult to find since this technique can so easily blind one or both partners. It needs to be something that will break the spell, break the habit. It may work to simply call it what it is, "Hey, are you trying to Kiss Up?"

THE DISMISS

Partner A: *"I am concerned about how much money you spent last month."*

Partner B: *"Oh, it's not a problem. Don't worry about it."*

Why this is harmful to a relationship

Dismissing a concern is more detrimental than many realize. Dismissing is to abolish, banish, brush off, cast off, detach, discard, dispense with, dissolve, drive out, expel, force out, lock out, push back, repel, shed, sweep away, and passively reject what your partner has said. All of those actions are incompatible with love. The Dismiss is possibly one of the more damaging avoidance techniques and most frequently used. The Dismiss is so easy to do.

The fallout

When the topic is dismissed, the end result is a partner who has been told his or her opinion is worth nothing, his or her concerns are invalid, not even worth the most basic, "I hear you," recognition. Not only is the concern still unsolved, but a clear message of rejection has been conveyed. A partner who uses the Dismiss too often will end up either with a completely demoralized partner or no partner at all.

The solution

In order to have the Dismiss become a thing of the past, both of you need to trust that your partner will not waste your time by making frivolous comments. If your partner wants to talk to him- or herself, make sure that you both understand and agree that this does not require your attention. Agree that any direct comment to you (comments that need a response from you) will be prefaced by your name. If your partner wants to chatter at you without needing a response, make your own ground rules for what works for both of you in that situation.

If chattering and mumbling are difficult for you (in our home chattering is not allowed in open shared spaces) agree with your partner that you will only bring valid concerns to each other. If your partner wants to complain, he or she can go online and complain there or call someone on the phone or write in a journal. For ideas on how to minimize complaining see Chapter 22, "Troubleshooting Complaints: Toxicity in Relationships."

Once you both understand and trust that all of your partner's comments are worthy of your attention and not just complaining, chattering, or mumbling, you can safely assume that whatever words your partner says are legitimate and need your attention.

THE SUBJECT CHANGE

Partner A: *"I need to know what you want to do about the backyard. It is so messy back there."*

Partner B: *"Did you hear what happened on the news today?"*

Warning! Be careful with this one. Your partner's response may in fact be an answer to your concern, but possibly appear random and unrelated at first. There may be simple theory of mind issues at play.

In this particular example, perhaps Partner B heard on the news that there is an incoming storm which may naturally water the backyard sufficiently for you to plant grass next week thus answering your question of what to do about the backyard. You will not know until you hear the rest of your partner's thoughts. In order to keep conversations on track, you can ask a follow-up question with a yes or no answer, "Was there something on the news related to our backyard?"

The key is to verify first that your partner actually did a Subject Change with the intent to avoid the initial question.

Why this is harmful to a relationship

A Subject Change distracts, wasting time and energy. It does not answer the question. Unanswered questions fester. They create mental weight. You may forget it consciously, but the incomplete communication between the two of you will probably stay in your memory banks, using up precious space until it is resolved. As David Allen of *Getting Things Done* (2002) often describes, any unresolved issues will be stored in your mind as incomplete tasks on your too-long mental To Do list.

The fallout

Using the Subject Change technique too often can make your partner feel as if he or she is loony. After a while your partner will not mention any problems to you since it only makes him or her feel as if his or her comments are floating off into the ether.

The solution

When a partner uses the Subject Change technique, the easiest and most effective solution may be just to call his or her bluff. Ask, "Did you just change the subject?" or the softer version, "I think you just changed the subject." There is no need to get an admission of wrong-doing, just call your partner's bluff and re-ask the question.

If your partner forces the Subject Change, write down the question you asked originally and say, "Ok, I will give you up to five minutes to discuss your question before mine. After that, I will ask my question again and expect you to show me the same respect I am showing you now." In this way you can role model what it looks like to respond directly and accurately to a person's comment, question, or concern.

If you don't have enough time for this and do not have the luxury of role modeling at that particular time, you can simply repeat the question. Be deaf and blind to the Subject Change. Repeat the original question in a kind and gentle voice as many times as it takes for your partner to realize that you will not fall for the Subject Change trick. The second time you repeat the question, add a kind smile. The third time you can repeat it in a bored voice. The fourth time as you repeat the question, blow him a kiss. The fifth time, wink at him that knowing wink that says, "I love you and I'm not going to take the bait." If your partner cannot read facial expressions or you cannot make them accurately, feel free to say it directly. There is a good chance that sooner or later your partner will respect your tenacity and simply answer your original question.

THE FINGER POINT

Partner A: *"I have a problem with you leaving the towels on the floor in the bathroom."*

Partner B: *"Well, did you remember to put the garbage out last night?"*

Why this is harmful to a relationship
It is a dismissal of the partner's concern. It seems innocuous, but in short, you have said, "Your concern is so irrelevant to me that I did not even bother to listen." To make it even more damaging, it immediately doubles the number of problems that need solutions: the initial problem plus the one you mentioned.

The fallout
It is punitive. By bringing up a secondary problem Partner B communicates, "If you dare bring up any issues I will just bring up more issues to one-up you." It can be devastating to compete in the "Who is worst?" game.

The solution
Give an immediate and full apology, role modeling the type of interaction you would like with your partner. For example, "Oh no, I am so sorry. I did forget to put the garbage out last night. I am going to set a reminder on my calendar so I do not forget next week. Now, how about the towels on the bathroom floor?"

In this situation, simply repeating the original problem (a strategy that works in other scenarios) does not work in the Finger Point. The Finger Point is the perfect time to show your partner what you really want—a quick solution to a simple problem.

THE BLAME SLAP

Partner A: *"I need to talk with you about how loud you have been playing your music lately."*

Partner B: *"Well, if you wanted it changed, you should have told me a long time ago. I can't do anything about it if you don't tell me."*

Why this is harmful to a relationship

The Blame Slap is a defensive maneuver that allows the defensive, avoidant partner to be just as angry at you as you (supposedly) are at him or her. The problem with the Blame Slap is that the initial comment probably was not meant to blame, just to solve an issue that will make your relationship better.

The fallout

The Blame Slap avoids the initial issue and escalates the conversation. If the conversation started out as an innocuous question, the Blame Slap turns it into a fight. It is the verbal equivalent of saying, "Put your dukes up!" (put your fists up to protect your face from a hit). It is difficult to regain a positive conversation once the Blame Slap has occurred.

The solution

The Blame Slap could be a big red flag indicating that your partner is not feeling safe. Your partner is acting much like a cornered cat taking a swipe at your face. The best response is to move out of the way of the claws. When people are angry or scared, the part of their brain with which they solve problems is shut down. The most helpful solution is to remind them that you love them and will wait until a better time to address the issue in question.

THE DOUBLE-WHAMMY BLAME AND POINT

This is the combination of two techniques: the Blame Slap and the Finger Point. It is head-spinning, highly effective, and an extremely hurtful way of interacting.

Partner A: *"I need to talk with you about how you use too much perfume."*

Partner B: *"You're one to complain! You don't use any and you smell bad. I can't even remember the last time you took a shower."*

It may sound ridiculous and unbelievable in print, but listen to a few dysfunctional conversations and you will be surprised at how easy it is for a partner to get defensive and do whatever it takes to lift the blame off him- or herself and onto anyone or anything else.

Why this is harmful to a relationship

The Blame and Point dismisses the partner's valid concern and creates an atmosphere of blame. Within an atmosphere of blame, problems cannot be solved. This particular example (sensory issue, olfactory response to certain smells) is obviously an issue that will need to be solved sooner or later if you plan on being near each other. Postponing a solution-based conversation only hurts both people longer and deeper.

The fallout

The Blame and Point may cause the partner who brought up the initial question to give up trying since there is very little possibility of successfully recovering from a double-whammy. If valid concerns are not addressed, after a while, the relationship becomes toxic or falls apart.

The solution

Solve problems early and often. Solve them while they are small. If your partner does the Blame and Point, one potential solution is to respond gently with, "Let's stick to one issue at a time and please know that all I care about is the health of our relationship."

THE COOL CAT

The classic aloof superiority that often accompanies autism can make healthy conversation difficult, but out of all the avoidance options listed it is the least damaging, relatively speaking.

Partner A: *"I need to talk with you about the event that's coming up this weekend."*

Partner B: *"Um. Sure. Whatever."*

Why this is harmful to a relationship

It tells your partner that you are only mildly interested in his or her life. On the list of things that interests you, he or she is barely on the list. This can be demoralizing and erode the sense of love and connection between you. That sense of connection is hard enough to establish in the first place. Be gentle with it.

The fallout

A slow and imperceptible erosion of the relationship will occur. Partner A will have the sense of "Partner B doesn't care about me much. I wonder if he or she even wants to be with me?" It creates doubt in a type of relationship that relies heavily on a solid mutual trust.

The solution

The Cool Cat may be occurring out of simple ignorance. If your partner has autism he or she may not realize that you need him or her to be interested in your life. Clarify ground rules such as, "If you want to be with me, you need to show interest in my life." There is a good chance that your partner is, or at least will be, honestly and genuinely interested once he or she hears about the cool things that you do. Sometimes you just need to flip this switch on in your partner's mind.

THE TOO BUSY OVERLOAD

> **Partner A:** *"We really need to talk about whether or not we are going to have a baby."*

> **Partner B:** *"Oh, can we talk about that later? I'm busy."*

Have you heard your partner say often, "I can't deal with this right now"? It can mean many things:

- Your partner is truly overloaded.

- Your partner is using a false sense of busyness to avoid dealing with problems that need to be solved.

- Your partner has put you and your concerns low enough on his or her priority list that the basic relationship concerns will be neglected on a regular basis.

- Your partner needs help with executive function skills—he or she does not have the ability to prioritize and therefore does not have the ability to control keeping you as a high priority.

Why this is harmful to a relationship

Sooner or later your partner will get a sense that you are too busy to be in a relationship at all. The busy partner may not even notice that the relationship is deteriorating since the state of being too busy can be blinding.

The fallout

All relationships need time and attention. If one partner does not have sufficient time to solve basic problems in the relationship, the relationship will either become dysfunctional or end.

The solution

There are no simple solutions to the Too Busy Overload. There are many bad ways to handle it. For example, in the case of whether or not have a child, the logical consequence is to end the relationship if the issue of childbirth cannot be addressed. This is a very serious consequence and it is likely that the person avoiding the issue is not fully aware of why he or she is avoiding the issue.

Seeing a counselor or therapist can assist in gently helping your partner to recognize that the sense of busyness in his or her life has been created to act as a buffer against difficult choices.

THE GOLD STAR

Autistic or not, your partner (or you) may need positive recognition, a daily gold star, in order to feel appreciated and loved. This need may interfere in the problem-solving process.

Partner A: *"Can we please review our tax statement now?"*

Partner B: *"Did you see how I did the dishes and the laundry today?"*

It sounds like a childish reaction when reading it on paper, but if you hear it in real life you may recognize that we all do this from time to time when we need a verbal confirmation that we are doing good things.

Why this is harmful to a relationship

The Gold Star is harmful in a way that is opposite of all previous avoidance tactics. In this scenario it is Partner A who needs to create the solution. Partner A needs to give the vital compliment so that Partner B can be soothed enough to hear his or her partner's question. It is only a minor inconvenience for Partner A, but it can be harmful to Partner B if his or her need for praise is dismissed.

The fallout

If Partner A does not recognize that Partner B is in need of validation, then Partner B will probably feel dismissed and unappreciated. It is likely that Partner B will find ways to get recognition some other way, even if by bad behavior.

The solution

Give a compliment! Compliment freely, often, and honestly.

If the need for kudos is too frequent or too intense, perhaps talk about that as a separate issue. Perhaps there are aspects of your partner's life that can be adjusted so that your partner's sense of confidence is not so delicate.

How to find the starting point for a conversation

Avoidance and denial in their many different forms may become habits if poor communication patterns are established between you and your partner. Perhaps the best way to eliminate these habits is to go back to the starting point and try to understand what is happening in a conversation for someone with autism.

There are three sequential steps that can occur when conversing with someone who has autism. A lack of information (first step) leads to a surplus of variables (second step), which creates a lack of safety for the person with autism (third step). In greater detail, the steps look like this:

1. *A lack of information.* Conversation for someone with autism contains massive amounts of information that is not being transferred to the listener. Body language, gestures, tone of voice, all of it may feel meaningful when you say it, but lose significant meaning mid-air as it is conveyed to the partner with autism.

2 *A surplus of variables.* When there are too many unknowns in any particular exchange, it feels dangerous to engage in it. Conversation, no matter how intuitive it may sound, can very easily trigger a rush of adrenaline and fear in the partner with autism.

3 *A lack of safety.* As long as the partner with autism does not feel safe, he or she is going to focus on his or her own safety, not on the content of the communication. A person cannot discuss things logically when the fear portion of his or her brain is activated.

In any conversation, the first task is to verify that both partners feel safe. To create a safe environment for the discussion, you can take a step back from the discussion and verify that you both agree about the Rules of Engagement. Verify the parameters for how to conduct yourselves during discussions with each other. This is called a meta-discussion as described in Chapter 9, "Troubleshooting Communication: Meta-Discussions."

Summary/Maintenance

Avoidance techniques are a waste of time and can do damage to the relationship. Recognize them for what they are. Skip any blaming or time-wasting conversations. Recognize that we all try to avoid problems, then move on as compassionately and respectfully as you can.

Conversations can be difficult even for the most skilled socialites, for those who see and interpret every facial expression, hand gesture, and expression of body language. Misunderstandings can occur even with those who can hear the interlaced messages in tone of voice, word choice, and semantics, understanding sarcasm, metaphors, and analogies. Having natural abilities in these areas only makes conversations easier, but it does not necessarily make one better at finding solutions to problems in relationships.

In my view, people who have to work extra hard to acquire a skill can often have a stronger, more valuable sense of accomplishment. Personally, I know that when my husband and I directly address a problem and solve it quickly, I feel a sense of elation and success and he, in his logical autistic brain, feels a sense of pride and accomplishment.

CHAPTER 16

Troubleshooting Monogamy and Faithfulness

Positive psychologists use the term "flourishing relationships" to describe relationships that are not merely happy, but instead characterized by intimacy, growth, and resilience. Flourishing relationships are often described using bullet points that do not translate well to an ASD-linked relationship, but perhaps with slight adjustments, can also fit the unique type of relationship.

A flourishing ASD-linked relationship may be characterized by:

- *Intimacy*: Physically pleasing interactions are important, no matter how unique or adjusted they are to sensory needs. Just as people chastized Temple Grandin for her modified cow press, people may chastize you for your unique sensory needs. The goal is to find a partner who loves and appreciates your sensory system and is able to help you brainstorm for ways to enjoy the more pleasurable physical sensations.

  Note that there are other aspects to intimacy that are purposefully left out. In an NT definition of intimacy there would be a sharing of private details and other acts that are less meaningful in an ASD-linked relationship.

- *Growth*: People with autism often mature more slowly than NTs. They are sometimes referred to as "late bloomers." Because of this prolonged growth period, people with autism may excel at the growth aspect of a flourishing relationship. It is to be hoped that you and your partner recognize that the longer you are together, the more growth you will see in each other.

- *Resilience*: If your partner with autism is prone to meltdowns, "resilience" will probably not be on his or her list of strengths. While someone with autism may be particularly sensitive to sights, sounds, and input that would not bother others, there are also aspects of relationships that are non-issues. The goal with any relationship is to build resilience and within your own quirky dynamic; you can do that, especially by developing highly effective troubleshooting strategies together.

Monogamy

Monogamy means having only one mate.

In modern society, monogamy is seen as old-fashioned, uncool, and perhaps even unwise. In movies and modern culture you hear strong messages about how important it is to have more than one partner. Yet, with respect to autism, there are many good reasons for monogamy:

- Monogamy is logical.

- Training one person to interact with you in intimate physical encounters can be a lot of work. Training other partners seems like unnecessary work.

- Monogamy is the quickest route to predictable, comforting routine. Note that I am not suggesting that sex should be routine! Just the opposite. If you have comforting routine in your daily life with only one partner, it is more likely that you will have energy for being more sexually alive with that one partner.

- From a medical perspective, monogamy makes sense. Diseases are spread by people having multiple partners. Monogamy serves to protect you from disease.

- If you dislike change, lifetime monogamy makes sense. Note that monogamy can refer to having one partner for life or having only one partner at a time for long periods of time.

- Reaching out to form a partnership is not a natural or comfortable act for someone with autism. Having to do that more than once may be a cumbersome, unnecessary task.

FORMING AGREEMENTS: THE RULES OF ENGAGEMENT

The best, most important gift you can give your partner with autism is a set of clearly defined Rules of Engagement, especially if they are binary: All ON or All OFF.

These rules should cover details such as "No kissing other people," but with specifications that would not be necessary in NT agreements. Your partner is allowed to kiss a family member on the cheek, yet, kissing a co-worker would not be appropriate. Be clear and concise. Eliminate assumptions.

CHEATING BY ACCIDENT: AN ASD RISK

In our marriage we have the agreement of complete fidelity. It is a simple binary "off" switch. Yet, we still get into sticky situations. One example: We rent out the lower level of our home in California and sometimes have to do maintenance on it. One day Carl went downstairs to the renter's unit to check wiring. Since there was an air vent near where I was folding laundry I could hear his conversation with the renter.

The renter was a single woman, a professor at a nearby university who often had men over. I could hear her flirting: the tale-tell signs of the lilt in her voice, the sound of her tossing her head to the side as she coyly laughed, all of it. I knew the art of flirting and she was flirting no-holds-barred.

The problem was that before my husband went downstairs I had asked him to, "Please be nice. Be friendly with her." He was not flirting back, but he was being friendly, just as I had requested. Unfortunately this was giving her the impression that he was receptive to the overtures.

After about ten minutes I could tell that she was increasing her flirtations and would not stop. I texted my husband on his cell phone.

Me: *She's flirting with u.*

Him: *Orly? (which means "Oh, really?")*

Me: *Yes. Get out.*

I heard him make an excuse and quickly finish the fix. Crisis averted.

When he came back upstairs he was not entirely sure what had happened. He was flattered that a woman had flirted with him and asked several times, "Are you sure she was flirting with me?" He thought he was just following through on directions to "be friendly." He was a little embarrassed, felt complimented that a woman would find him flirtation-worthy (of course), and quite confused.

I tried to explain what it looks like when a woman flirts, role modeled what she had done, but in our case, as it had not worked

20 years ago when we were dating, flirting still did not register with him. In college, even when I tried the most outrageously suggestive flirting, he missed it entirely. We still laugh about it. I once even tried on some lingerie in front of him. "So, my friend got this little black teddy and I was thinking of getting one like it. What do you think? How does it look?"

He looked up from his book and said, "It looks good," which he knew was a neutral response. He had a "No sex until marriage" off switch and literally could not see the lingerie or the woman in it.

He then went back to studying. There are not many college men who would have had a similar response. I tried again, "What about from this angle?" Same response. Flirting most definitely did not work with this man with autism.

Faithfulness

If you find someone you love and want to spend more time with, create a clear set of rules. This cannot be overstated. The rules will seem ridiculously over-specific to you if you are NT, but for a person with autism, even the most specific is not error-free. That's one side of the equation.

The other side of the equation is probably not what you anticipated. There is a dynamic in an ASD/NT relationship that probably goes under the radar. The dynamic goes like this:

- The partner with autism is loyal, unfailingly loyal.

- Due to communication difficulties, the partner with autism does not communicate that dedication to fidelity.

- The NT partner perceives that the partner with autism is not fully committed to the relationship and perceives infidelity.

- The NT partner is at high risk of infidelity due to lack of connection to the partner with autism.

This dynamic will not be visible to those who do not fully grasp the ASD way of being. The fact that the partner with autism is fully committed but not effectively communicating that commitment is unthinkable to those not on the spectrum.

The saying, "Your actions speak louder than your words," is ingrained in our social psyche. If the person with autism acts in a way that seems disconnected, then no matter what he or she says, he or she will be perceived as disconnected.

While it would be wonderful to shift societal thinking en masse, it is more realistic to fix this within your own relationship. There are two things you can do to shift this dynamic out of the danger cheating zone and into the preferred zone of fidelity.

For the NT partner: remind yourself constantly that your partner is in fact fully devoted to you. Personally, I was not able to keep this fact front and center through willpower alone. I had to create visual aids to help. I took a photo of us and had it enlarged, then purchased a large frame. The photo is so impressively large that every time I see it, it solidifies in my mind, "He is faithful." It helps overcome the lack of messages confirming faithfulness.

For the partner with autism: work to communicate faithfulness. A few NT ways of communicating your loyalty that may not make sense to you but will probably work well for your partner:

- Write love notes and leave them scattered in places where your NT partner will see them.

- Say, "I love you," or "I am glad you are my partner," or other similar message regularly. It won't make sense to do so since you have said the message before and have done nothing to negate it, but saying it regularly is needed for the NT mind.

- Do things that communicate loyalty and connection. Remember birthdays and holidays. Email, text, chat, call, or talk regularly with your partner. Work hard to find ways to enjoy physical touch in a mutually pleasing way.

- Remember that your partner probably has an on/off switch like you do, but it flips on and off for irrational, illogical reasons. Always assume that you need to reset the switch.

Summary/Maintenance

Every couple decides their level of physical loyalty to each other. In an ASD-linked relationship, it is far simpler and more sustainable to vote for monogamy, absolute loyalty to each other. It eliminates variables in a highly complex social realm.

CHAPTER 17

Troubleshooting Existence Together

INSIDE THE HOME

It is surprising how many people are uncomfortable and unhappy in their own homes. As children, we had little power over the quality of our home life but as adults, we have power over where and how we live.

In troubleshooting unhappiness at home, there are many levels of fixability. The top types are:

- physical change over which you have control

- physical change someone else can agreeably fix

- attitude change, personal

- attitude change, your partner or other person.

Take the example of a too-small apartment or home.

Physical change over which you have control

1. Your first fix may be to check if there are less expensive, larger living options within your reach.

2. See if there is a way to expand your current dwelling, perhaps by setting up space for yourself in the garage or building a little office building in the back yard or by building out the attic.

3. See if you can clear out some of the existing stuff to make room for the space you need. For example, perhaps you can get rid of couches no one sits on or a table no one uses to make more space for what you do need.

Physical change someone else can agreeably fix

1. See if your partner would clear out some of his or her clutter. Offer solutions for storing it neatly elsewhere.

2. See if you can have a builder extend the home with a porch or add-on that might work.

3. See if you can do a split-living arrangement such as living in different homes, different apartments, or separate rooms in the same house.

Attitude change, personal

1. Check to see if this change is truly necessary. Perhaps the discomfort stems from hearing others say that they need more space. Perhaps you have not objectively evaluated whether or not it actually bothers you. If you hear others saying that they wish they had a bigger, nicer house, you may begin to believe you want the same thing. Do not let others script for you on these matters.

2. Read about people who live in different environments. There is nothing like a little virtual traveling to widen one's experience. For example, our 20-year-old son is in Brazil. He recently sent us a picture of a friend there, a well-respected working man in his forties who lives in a home built from dirt and leaves. It is a glorified dirt tent. The man is perfectly happy; he believes he has plenty of space and all the supplies he needs. Now our son realizes that one's level of wealth is a matter of opinion. Once you read about people (or better, meet people) in other situations, it helps you to reevaluate your own living conditions. It helps you to see that you have the option of being satisfied in your current environment.

3. Make a list of Uncomfortable Things (explained in the next section of this chapter) and evaluate with each one: "Would I really be happier if this was changed?" Say one of your discomforts is, "too noisy," yet you have young children. Ask yourself: "Would I really be happier without the children?" Many parents, especially when tired, would say, "Yes!" It is not, however, a sincere item on the Uncomfortable Things list. If your children were taken from you, you would probably fight

to get them back. In order to determine the validity of each of these items on your list, ask yourself: "What would life be like if this discomfort was fixed the way I want it to be fixed?" Cross off the items that cause discomfort, but are, what my husband calls, "the good kind of pain."

4) If all else fails, read about extreme mental control that monks and yogis use. For example, perhaps an item on your Uncomfortable Things list is, "Caring for my dying father." If you cannot afford to put him in a nursing home and no other family member will take care of him, then you do not have many options. You can do all of the following suggestions above, possibly see some improvements, but will still be left with a too-heavy amount of discomfort at the end. Read about how to handle extreme discomfort. It is the troubleshooting equivalent of a mental reboot. It resets your attitude.

Attitude change, your partner or other person

Unfortunately, you cannot change other people's views of you. Just know that people often see something other than whom you are. They see versions of you based on their interpretation of how you have behaved previously.

That said, you have tremendous power to facilitate a person's change of opinion. If someone, especially your partner, is misjudging you based on previous behavior, a few things you can say are:

"That's what I used to think, too, but I've changed."

"I'm so glad it's not like that anymore. I've learned to handle it better."

"I remember when I was like that. I'm relieved to have matured beyond it."

"I've changed. Have you noticed? It sure feels good!"

The four problem-solving methods just listed can be used for any problem. Simply look first at what you can do, second at what your partner can do, and third at an attitude change within yourself, and fourth assist in the attitude change of others. We call it "The Sophisticated Four" since it usually yields a dozen potential solutions.

IDENTIFY: I AM NOT COMFORTABLE AT HOME

Test 1: Make it clear in a list

Write out a list of the things that make you uncomfortable. For example, "It's too noisy," or "It's dirty." Order the list by which discomforts make you most uncomfortable, then start at the top. There may be some you cannot solve. If you come across one that appears to be unfixable, skip to the next item on the list.

Evaluate: If using the list to eliminate discomforts works, fantastic. If not, try Test 2.

Test 2: Define comfort

There is a chance that even the most perfect environment will be uncomfortable. Check to see if there is any place or time when you truly are comfortable. Try to mimic that environment in your home, if possible.

Evaluate: You will know that you have been successful when you are able to feel comfortable in your space. If you have still not achieved a comfortable environment, see Test 3.

Test 3: Keep researching

Review the rest of this book in its entirety. Perhaps there are other factors making you uncomfortable that you have not yet identified. If there are ongoing problems with your partner, they could be clouding your day in ways that are hard to identify.

Evaluate: The one place that you should feel comfortable is your own home. If you do not, keep trying until you find a way to make your home a place where you can relax and unwind.

IDENTIFY: I DO NOT HAVE ENOUGH MONEY TO FIX THE PROBLEMS

Test 1: Financial restraints are definitely a tough issue

Having weak executive function makes it even harder to work around a lack of financial resources. Recognize that it is difficult and give yourself credit for how hard you are working to fix your problems.

Evaluate: Sometimes the only solution you need is appreciation of the problem in its fullness. Sometimes that recognition leads to new solutions. However, if not, see Test 2.

Test 2: Make a friend who is creative with finances

Sometimes the best solutions to one's problems are the least expensive, yet it takes a bit of creative brainstorming to see solutions.

Financial stability is a crucial factor in any adult's life. Find a trusted friend who can recommend potential adjustments. Note that if you are autistic you may be gullible. Never give money to another person unless you have verified that it is the correct thing to do (such as giving money to a cashier from whom you are purchasing something). The best way to protect against gullibility is to use your inborn ability for logic. Always look at the numbers. Make sure the budget adds up.

Evaluate: If you are able to make budgetary adjustments that get you into your preferred comfort zone, great. If not, see Test 3.

Test 3: Adjust your expectations

There are multi-millionaires who are unhappy with their financial situations and there are people who make very little who are perfectly happy with having "enough."

The easiest way to be happy is to figure out how much you make every month, and set that point as "enough."

While traveling for business, I often take side-trips to explore. In New Zealand in particular I found that there were people from various countries traveling the countryside. They had lived on minimum wage or a low wage for years, saving aside a little bit each week, then taking a three-month, six-month or even longer trek through various countries. I am not advocating that people with autism go couch-surfing or do global travel, only noticing that funds, no matter how tight, can be set aside for purposes that are most important to you.

Note what is missing from this section—I am not suggesting that you work harder to earn more money. That is unlikely to be a good solution. It is important to work hard and earn the best salary or wages you can earn, but when there are financial troubles, often working harder only masks the leaks that are draining funds. Working longer hours can also cause mental and physical strain that can cause an unnecessary downward spiral.

Evaluate: If you can adjust your expectations to the point that you can be happy with your finances, great. If not, seek help from a financial advisor. Sometimes financial assistance is free through city or county government sources depending on your country's available services.

IDENTIFY: MY PARTNER IS DISORGANIZED AND IS TRYING TO FIX IT SINCE IT IS HURTING BOTH OF US

Test 1: The quick fix

When a person seems mentally disorganized, sometimes the simplest solution is to clean the house. When you or your partner feels a sense of disorganized thought, sensory overload or other distracting sensation, take a few minutes to clean up the room you are in.

Evaluate: If you feel a greater sense of peace and order, great. If not, try Test 2.

Test 2: The harder fix

Physical order and mental order often reflect each other. The next Identify contains a complete list of how to deal with a physically messy environment, but here is a short description of a few things you can do to quickly test whether or not a cleaner environment will result in better mental clarity.

- Set a timer. You can do nearly anything for five minutes. Clean for just five minutes. That is often enough to motivate you to do five more minutes of cleaning later.

- Start in one small, teeny space. Trying to clean a whole room is far too overwhelming. Find one little spot, a tabletop or corner, and clean that spot first, then move on to another.

- Give yourself a reward. If you simply cannot get up the energy to do the task, offer yourself a sweet treat or a rare indulgence to get something done. A bite of candy can sometimes be plenty to help your brain connect "clean" with "good."

Evaluate: If you were able to clean up and it helped with mental order, great. If not, see Test 3.

Test 3: Professional fix

If the simple environmental clean-up does not work:

- Check out some books on mental clarity and ADD/ADHD.

- Contact a doctor, medical provider, therapist, or other clinician who can assist.

Evaluate: If the professional approach works, great. If not, refer back to Tests 1 and 2. There is a chance that a person with the autism and ADD/ADHD mix thrives best in a constant state of chaos. There may be no good way to "fix" it. If reevaluating Tests 1 and 2 still yields no result, see Test 4.

Test 4: Hire support

There is a chance that your own personal fixes to create mental clarity out of physical cleanliness may have failed due to the tasks being too difficult. This has been the case for us in several areas. For issues that are insurmountable, hire help. The cost may seem extreme and may actually be impossible if funds are severely limited, but do consider:

- A housecleaner is cheaper than a divorce lawyer.

- A handyman is cheaper than the sick days you had to take due to fights: lowered immunity following the stress of an argument can lead to having to take time off work to recover.

- A gardener to keep the yard in shape is cheaper than having the whole thing redone due to mass overgrowth. (This may not be the case in all areas, but for us in California it was $25/month for maintenance versus $2,000/year to have the entire thing redone when we let it get into disrepair.)

Evaluate: If you are able to hire help and it makes a difference, great. If not, see Test 5.

Test 5: See the greener grass

If all of the previous fixes do not work, you may need to test for yourself whether or not the solutions you think you want are actually the best choice. Try one of the following:

- Watch shows about people who are uncomfortably absorbed in cleanliness, especially on a debilitating level.

- Consider what your life would be like if the problem was fixed. Typically, people think that they want to live with someone who does things exactly how they want them done, but if that wish is granted, the unhappiness can be far worse than the initial complaint.

- Consider, "How would it feel if I got what I wanted?"

Personally I have some people in my life who are both ultra-organized and some who are chaotic. The ultra-organized will see a crumb on the floor and reach down to pick it up. The chaotic have floors so messy that it is hard to find a place to step to get from one side of the room to the other. Both help me appreciate the other and remind me to respect differences. In all cases that I have seen, a clean environment equals both physical and mental organization.

Evaluate: If considering the alternatives is sufficient, then great, problem solved. If not, see Test 6.

Test 6: Acceptance

This is always the last step. Ask yourself if you are willing to accept the behavior, recognizing that no one is perfect and sometimes in hindsight these problems seem like adorable quirks.

Evaluate: If you can fully accept that your partner is trying his or her best, then you have been successful. You will know you have fully accepted this if you only rarely feel frustrated.

IDENTIFY: MY PARTNER (ON THE SPECTRUM OR NOT) IS MESSY

Test I: Make a pile

In a non-ASD-linked relationship, the suggestion is usually to have a conversation about it, but in an ASD-linked relationship, conversations often have far less meaning since cues are missed. Action-based solutions will probably prove more helpful. When you pick up one of your partner's items off the floor, put it in a pile on his or her side of the bed so that your partner cannot sleep at night without dealing with the pile first.

Evaluate: There is a good chance that your partner will simply push the pile onto the floor, but since this is the most respectful method, at least try it first. If it does not work, do not be surprised and then try Test 2.

Test 2: In bag or box

Collect all the messy items into a box or bag hidden in a closet or other out-of-the-way spot. At the end of the week, tell your partner that you have something to show him or her. Bring out the bag and empty out all the things that you have picked up during the week.

Evaluate: If seeing the sheer volume of misplaced stuff solves the problem, great. Keep doing this method since it saves you time in the long run as you only have to pick up each item one time per week. If this method leaves you feeling imposed upon, try Test 3.

Test 3: Love, Like, Blech

The previous Test may not work if the volume of items is simply overwhelming rather than motivating. With all of the accumulated items in one spot, do a Love, Like, Blech sort. Get three boxes or containers ahead of time and tape a paper sign on each box. Put all must-keep items in the Love box; all should-keep items in the Like box; and all can-discard items in the Blech box.

When the last item is tossed into one of the boxes, immediately close up the Blech box and put it in the garage or other location to go to the garbage or to be donated.

Next, take items out of the Love box one by one, finding a good location for each item. If the item does not currently have a place where it belongs, then decide together where that item should be located. For example, decide that all pens and pencils should go in a particular drawer. The goal is to remove all excuses of, "I didn't know where to put it."

By this time, your partner will probably be mentally exhausted. Close up the Like box and put it in the closet or other out-of-the-way location. At a later time, when you feel rested, go through the box and throw away as many items as you can, leaving only the best, most useful and valuable items to use.

Evaluate: If an occasional Love, Like, Blech session helps keep your home cleaner, this has worked. If the sorting causes fights, then it has not. See the Test 4.

Test 4: Pack it away

If your partner is showing no signs of cleaning up his or her messes, get several cardboard boxes and put them in the basement or other out of the way location. Dump everything that is: 1) making a mess in your shared space, and 2) not yours into this box. This is the method I use in my marriage. Since my husband prides himself on owning very few things and on being neat, he was quite surprised to find that he had several boxes full of miscellaneous junk. He was not aware that he had brought so many items into the home, and had then assumed that they would be taken care of for him.

Evaluate: This strategy allows you to have the home the way you like it, plus it is likely that the items will never come out of the box and back into circulation in the home. If your partner still drags too many messy things into the home, try Test 5.

Test 5: Imagine what it would be like if your partner was no longer there

Would you miss the pile of magazines in the corner by his or her favorite chair? Would you miss the crumbs on the counter that he or she left after making you breakfast?

Evaluate: When the messiness is bothering you, consider if you would be so bothered if your partner was gone. If you would, this is probably enough to dampen the frustration over messes. If this does not comfort you, see Test 6.

Test 6: Divide the room

Use an adult version of a piece of tape across the room. Make sure both of you know, "This is my area; that is your area. Don't mess up my space."

Evaluate: This should work for placement of items, but will not fix messes that are still within your visual field (but on the other side of the line). If the mess still bothers you, try Test 7.

Test 7: Try living in separate homes

It is not uncommon for married adults to live apart for various reasons: work, family, various living conditions. It may cause people to ask questions if you do not have a socially acceptable excuse for living separately, but it might be the best solution of all.

Evaluate: If living in separate homes creates a greater level of peace and happiness for both of you, then this strategy has been successful.

Living apart

Couples of every variety work together to figure out how to organize their living arrangement.

For us, we found that we do best with regular changes in environment. When we were first married, we moved approximately every six months for the first three years. Then we slowed down a bit and moved only once every one to three years, never staying longer than three years in one place. This worked for us.

I mention this only as an illustration of a unique, unusual living arrangement. I am not suggesting it as a recommended option for ASD-linked couples.

We recognized that this type of movement worked for us. In our late thirties, early forties, we began transitioning our career trajectory to jobs that are location independent. This means that we have the choice of where to live. Many location independent people are known as "knowledge workers": programmers, writers, freelancers who can choose their geographic location.

Now, we travel extensively, always on a budget. As an example of our autistic way of living, here is a glimpse of where we have been living the last few months. While writing this chapter, I am in New Zealand (NZ) in a home near Wellington, a block from Mount Victoria, an amazing forest where scenes from *The Hobbit* were filmed. We spent the last two months together in NZ, then Carl flew back to the US (at the end of his three-month visitor visa). He spent two weeks in California at our home which we rent out when we are not there, making travel more affordable. Carl spent one week in Utah with our college-age son while our son was on a college break. Carl will then fly to Hong Kong for one week for work, then back to NZ for three months. When he arrives in NZ, he will have two days together with me and our children, then the children and I head back to the US for a month. For a full month Carl will be entirely alone, on his own, using the time to complete some programming projects in complete silence, uninterrupted for weeks at a time.

It sounds complicated, but we seem to be happiest as a couple and as individuals in this type of schedule. For someone with autism who craves stability and routine, this type of schedule could be disabling. As one friend of ours who has autism says, "That sounds like hell." To him, every aspect of our nomadic lifestyle is repulsive. He wants his regular home with his regular stuff. He finds happiness in routine and that is ok. Everyone needs to figure out what works for their physical, emotional, and intellectual needs.

The goal is to find what makes *you* happy and build a life that works for *you* whether it falls within the realm of social norms or not.

Be aware that NTs assume that couples want to live together. Do not challenge this assumption. It makes them uncomfortable to think of a married couple wanting to live apart. It can be threatening to an NT to think of a married couple as living separately.

In our experience, it is easiest to blame our work for our being apart. Here are a few socially acceptable excuses we have used for living apart:

"I need to research autism for a book and a university in _____ is doing research in which I'm interested. I'm hoping to connect with some of the professors and researchers, so I'm just heading there for a few weeks."

"I've always wanted to show my kids what it's like to live on a farm, so I'm going to take the kids to a WWOF (World Wide Organic Farm) in New Zealand."

"I'm going to visit family."

In my experience, it is significantly easier to say, "My husband is on a business trip." No one asks questions and everyone is happy.

Summary/Maintenance

Something interesting happens once you get your own home as an adult. Most people find that they want a bigger apartment/bigger house, a nicer kitchen, a bigger living room, another bedroom that could be turned into an office. I have talked with people in homes that are larger than 4,500 square feet/418 square meter and found the people in the home wish it was bigger, or wish that they had an extra room or two, or wish that they had a swimming pool or basketball court in the back yard. I've talked with people who had nine couches in their home and still bemoan the fact that they need another couch in another sitting room.

Unless you are starving or sleeping on the streets, you probably have "enough."

The trick is to work with that space until you find your own unique blend of comfort. Perhaps your idea of comfort is a window seat where you can sit with the afternoon sun warming your back while you read a great book. Perhaps you do not have the funds for this so your window is actually a wall, your seat is actually a pillow on the floor, the warmth that should come from the sun comes from an extra blanket around your shoulders, and your book is from the library. You can be just as happy with the accommodations. Happiness is quite often a choice we make: not always, but often.

The place you go home to at night should be your refuge, your safe place, your home. Make it a good one.

CHAPTER 18

Troubleshooting in the Wild

OUTSIDE THE HOME

One Sunday afternoon my husband and I took our children to the San Francisco Museum of Modern Art. These outings are overwhelming, but Carl did it as a favor to me.

In one part of the exhibit was a 13 feet/4 meter tall painting of mass chaos: lines, squiggles, splashes, shades of every color. There was no order, no purpose, no message, only aimless, overwhelming confusion.

He said, "That's what it feels like inside my brain."

I gasped. Self-awareness is rare and unprompted introspection is even more rare. I was surprised to hear his comment. I did not reply but felt a pain in my gut, a sharp internal pain as I realized how chaotic and unpleasant the world must be when the brain does not organize itself to recognize certain patterns.

In sharp contrast, my favorite artist is Mark Rothko, a painter who used simple, easy, large blocks of single colors. That is what my mind feels like. Well-organized, not overcrowded, just enough room for all my favorite colors. Some would say "simple," I would say "organized."

When a brain is wired for social interaction, it seems simple, purposeful, and enjoyable. When a brain is wired for things other than social interaction (the definition of autism), those same interactions are confusing and seemingly chaotic.

As an ASD-linked couple, public experiences may be the root source of marital/relationship strife.

IDENTIFY: I (PERSON WITH AUTISM) AM GRUMPY AND UNPLEASANT TO BE WITH

Test 1: Find the cause

Simply the act of being in public can be unpleasant. Ask yourself, "Was there external input that is making me feel bad?"

Evaluate: If finding the cause allows you to correct the problem, great. If not, see Test 2.

Test 2: Chart time

For a week, track how many hours you spend in public. You may be surprised at how many hours you have to interface socially. Or you may find that it is actually very little time and that you have less to worry about than you thought.

Evaluate: If seeing the number of hours gives you the information you need to fix the problem, great. If you are still experiencing significant distress over time out in public, see Test 3.

Test 3: Trim down the social time

If you find that you are spending too much time in public, find ways to trim down that exposure. Any time that you are interacting with other people in public may be draining you without you knowing it: grocery shopping, work, getting your exercise by walking or running in public areas, and even commuting, any time that you can see another person.

Evaluate: If trimming down the social time works to help you be in a better mood day-to-day, great. If not, you may need the approach of Test 4.

Test 4: Build tolerance

If you cannot minimize your daily social exposure sufficiently, consider building your tolerance for it. Consider it "social weight lifting."

Evaluate: Giving yourself credit for the effort it takes will probably help you to be kinder to yourself and less grumpy; but if not, see Test 5.

Test 5: Block it

If you cannot avoid it, cannot tolerate it, and cannot learn to like it, then consider learning strategies that help you block the input. A few creative examples:

- See the people around you as MineCraft (game) characters or any other computer characters. If you like games, this may work well.

- See them as if in a movie. In many movies, a character takes on superhuman powers. See yourself jumping from block to block rather than walking through a sea of people. See yourself as if in *The Matrix* or as if in *Sucker Punch* or any of the other movies where reality is actually not real. This may soften the impact that social noise has on your body and mind.

- See blocks of color rather than details. For some people with autism, there are too many visual details in the world, making it overwhelming. Choose one color for the day and see only that color (except when driving and you need to see colors on the stoplights). Training your eye to dismiss details can be relaxing.

- See only the path ahead of you. Block out other details. Unless you are driving or otherwise need to be aware of the environment, it might help with overload if you focus on visualizing your path and only your own path.

The desired end result is a fulfilling, happy life where grumpiness is rare. If you find yourself feeling grumpy on a regular basis, it may be your body trying to tell you that it is annoyed by something. Pay attention to your body's cues, solve the annoyances and live a happier life.

Evaluate: If none of the above strategies work and grumpiness is still a problem in your relationship, perhaps seek out counseling or a medical evaluation or both.

IDENTIFY: I ENJOY GOING OUT IN PUBLIC; MY PARTNER DOES NOT

Test I: Be specific

It may be that your partner does not like going out as much as you, not that there is a stark black and white difference. List the number of hours you went out last week. Determine what is a healthy balance for each of you.

Evaluate: You may see the number of hours out in public and say, "Actually we didn't go out that much," or "We went out so much!" If seeing the specifics helps, great. If not, see Test 2.

Test 2: Agree on limits

It may be that one partner does not want to go out because every outing seems to stretch on and on: "just one more errand." Set limits and stick to them, valuing your partner's trust and well-being more than the convenience of getting errands done efficiently.

Setting limits allows your partner to rest confident that you are not going to morph into a social monster and require him or her to go to parties every weekend or shop at four different stores every Saturday. Negotiate for what makes both of you happy.

Evaluate: If setting limits helps enough, great. If not and you are still disagreeing on the number of hours spent in public, see Test 3.

Test 3: Be independent

Perhaps the happiest medium for you as a couple is having more independent time. Try it. The person who needs more socializing can get more friends and the person who needs less can focus on hobbies that can be done in solitude.

Evaluate: If the problem has not been solved by this point, refer to Chapter 14, "Troubleshooting Reciprocity: Tips and Tricks to Create Support, Appreciation, and Respect in Your Relationship."

IDENTIFY: I DREAD INTRODUCING MY PARTNER TO MY FRIENDS. I WORRY HE OR SHE MIGHT SAY SOMETHING ODD OR EMBARRASS ME

Test 1: Evaluate your current approach

If you introduce your partner as if you are embarrassed of him or her, it will be impossible for your partner (or the people to whom you are introducing him or her) to form a good impression. Be admiring. Shine the light on your partner's best traits and people will see those best parts, often excusing the bad. Introduce your partner positively and see if it makes a difference.

If your partner makes odd hand movements, perhaps the introduction could be, "And this is my husband. He's an engineer by day and a musician by night." Such a description helps others dismiss your husband's hand movements as useful: "Perhaps he hears a rhythm and is composing," or "Wow, that's cool that he is so good at music."

It might be that your partner is borderline non-verbal. Find a way to help her appear as shy or quiet and as someone who finds it difficult to respond verbally. You could introduce her as, "And this is my partner. She is a writer" or "She is an artist." Find a stereotype that helps show the positive aspects of your partner's behavior.

Evaluate: If you change your introductions to be more positive and find this is the solution, fantastic. I have seen this positive introduction strategy in use many times and have been shocked at how pivotal it is to give a good first impression. After that first impression is formed, the person with autism can do all sorts of odd things and people will excuse the eccentricities. It is an amazingly easy solution, but if it is not sufficient, does not work, or if you are already doing this, then see Test 2.

Test 2: Be bulletproof

Imagine that you are wearing the coolest, sexiest set of armor ever made. When your partner does or says something embarrassing, you have a protective barrier. The comment is not a reflection on you (unless you respond in an unflattering way). Even if your partner insults you directly, let it bounce off the armor.

A personal example of this relates to a couple in our neighborhood who had been trying for eight years to have a baby. They were distraught over their inability to get pregnant. On one occasion my husband asked them, "So, why haven't you had a baby yet?" It was an inappropriate question.

It would have been easy to be furious with him. Instead, I was bulletproof. I was able to distance myself without emotional repercussion for me, my husband, or our neighbors. Of course I felt badly for both my husband (for his inability to see the harmful nature of what he had said) and of course I felt badly for the couple (for the pain caused by this too-intimate question); but since I was able to be bulletproof, there was no recrimination from me. I mentioned to him later that his comment was inappropriate, but only as an educational note. He made note of it and that was the end of it.

Evaluate: If you are fully independent—bulletproof—when your partner says or does something socially inappropriate, you will be able to continue to see the adorable, lovable side of him or her. If this does not work for you (it is exceptionally difficult!) then refer to Test 3.

Test 3: Prepare and set limits

Prepare ahead of time. Say to your partner, "We're going to talk to these people for three minutes. Don't check your watch, but remember that all you have to endure is three minutes."

Evaluate: If an embarrassing moment still happens even within a short timeframe, try Test 4.

Test 4: Set me free!

Give your partner a way out. Let your partner know that he or she is safe. If your partner needs to leave, he or she can tell you, and then go off to take a walk or wait in the car. There is nothing wrong with telling people: "Excuse me, but I'm not feeling well."

Evaluate: This one works if it helps your partner feel calm enough that he or she can dedicate more mental processing to the essential details of social interaction. Your partner will have more mental space for questions such as: "Will this comment be offensive?" If this is not enough, perhaps more control over the situation is needed.

Test 5: Be gone!

Agree ahead of time on a cue that means, "You need to leave now." Use a pre-scripted excuse. The cue can be physical (a particular type of tap on the arm), verbal (a particular word), or visual (a gesture or facial sign like a wink). Know that your partner will be on overload, so choose a cue that he or she can actually notice.

Evaluate: If the cue doesn't work or somehow backfires, do not be surprised. Once in a social situation it may be hard for your partner to hear or identify the pre-defined cue. Perhaps try Test 6.

Test 6: Just don't do it

Skip or go alone to any social events. Make everyone happy. If you are uncomfortable in a room of partnered couples, there are hundreds of potential reasonable excuses, ranging from, "He's sick," to, "He's deep in a project right now." Look for the benefits of being on your own. Make the best of it. Most important: do not, under any condition, say negative things about your partner who is not in attendance. It may feel good in the moment to vent your feelings, but has long-term effects that limit your future happiness; it makes any future social interaction with that group of people (or people who talk with that group of people) negative. Instead, if you need to let off steam about something, choose one or two friends who can help you to do so in confidence.

Evaluate: This last Test should work since it offers no scenario in which both of you are in public at the same time.

IDENTIFY: WE HAD A BAD EXPERIENCE IN PUBLIC, THE MEMORY OF WHICH IS MAKING IT HARD TO MOVE PAST IT

Test I: Heal

When an outing goes badly, the best you can do is try to heal. Healing is far more difficult when there are so many cues missed between the two of you.

The inability to heal the relationship, repair conversations, and mend miscommunication is part of the diagnosis. You have to be far more direct in your communication. Try one of these:

"I'm really sorry things went so badly today."

"I sure wish things had gone well."

"I don't really care why things went wrong, I'm just sad that they did."

"I want things to go back to the way they were before."

"All I want to do is pretend today never happened."

Evaluate: If a simple recognition that your partner had a hard time is enough, great. If not, see Test 2.

Test 2: Get rid of the pain

If your partner is still holding on to the angst and bad feelings, you can:

- Leave your partner alone for a while.
- Write your partner a note expressing your love and caring.
- Verbally express love: "No matter what happens, know that you have my unconditional love."
- Physically express love: Give a back rub, full body deep pressure, brushing, or any other type of physical input that would be calming for your partner.
- Verbally express appreciation: "I really appreciate the things that you do for me, even when they are difficult."
- Physically express appreciation: Do something nice for your partner such as take care of a task that needs to be done or make your partner's favorite meal.

Evaluate: If one or more of the above strategies works, great. If not, see Test 3.

Test 3: Let it go

If none of the above strategies have worked and you cannot think of anything else to try, then give it time. Supposedly time heals all wounds.

Evaluate: If time does not heal the bad experience, then perhaps it is simply just something in your past. Remember that the goal is to heal the relationship, not prove a point. Also, remember that some wounds leave a scar.

Summary/Maintenance

Respecting people means seeing them for who they really are, not who you wish they were. If your partner prefers less social time, you can show your partner respect by allowing that freedom.

This is crucial because there will be occasions when your partner is grumpy, unreasonable, and you may have problems getting along. You may look back at your day and wonder why your partner is being so irritable. You may reflect on the fact that you did the grocery shopping at the Farmer's Market and enjoyed each other's company, then ran some errands together, which made you feel great since it meant getting things crossed off your To Do list. You may relish the time you spent together, failing to notice that while you were being boosted, your partner was being drained.

One of the most crucial skills which you will develop as a couple is the ability to see the social pressures for what they are—difficult. With the world around you constantly telling you that social interaction should feel good, it is exceptionally hard for both of you to remember that this is not necessarily the case and be gentle with each other.

Give yourself a reminder, one you will see every day. For me, I have a graphic of a tiger on my phone. Every time I turn on my phone I remember that my partner is a loaner and will growl if I expect him to be a herd animal or a social one. I also have several pictures on the walls that have personal meaning, that remind me to be gentle and kind.

CHAPTER 19

Troubleshooting Obsessions and Priorities

CHOOSING WHAT YOU DO WITH YOUR TIME

The word "obsession" comes from the concept of besieging, surrounding, overpowering, overwhelming. Literally, a siege is when one army surrounds a building or city with soldiers until the people inside are forced to let the army inside the gates. It is an act of war, an imposed take-over, a forceful overpowering. It implies that the person who is obsessed has a lack of control over the outcome.

I am a firm believer that obsessions represent the best of the best while ironically, simultaneously representing the worst of the worst. Let's look at the worst part first (and get it over with).

The downside of obsession

Obsession can be synonymous with addiction, excessive attraction, compulsion, infatuation, and preoccupation. Some examples of obsessive situations include:

1. A man who is obsessed with (addicted to) video games.

2. A person who is obsessed with (excessively attracted to) one particular movie star.

3. An employee's obsession (preoccupation) with computer games which made it necessary for the employer to block his ability to access them online while at work.

4. A woman's obsession (compulsion) to gamble is overpowering.

5 A music fan's obsession (infatuation) caused a stampede in the crowd when the rock star appeared on stage.

The most essential element between a good obsession and a bad obsession is self-control. Look at the various negative consequences of the above listed varieties of obsession.

1 Is the video game player able to turn off the game at 11pm so that he can get a good night's sleep? Or does he lack the self-control to do so, then ends up sleeping in the next day, or worse, falling asleep at work?

2 Is the person obsessed with the movie star failing to devote her love to her significant other, instead channeling it towards someone who doesn't know her and never will?

3 Is the employee's obsession putting him at risk of being fired?

4 Is gambling consuming funds that should be used for food, home, the kids' college education?

5 Is the mob mentality putting fans at risk of stampede, something that has caused the deaths of an untold number of people at stadiums worldwide?

Obsessions that you cannot control can have devastating long-term effects. They can strip you of home, family, the love of others, and your own self-respect.

How to stop bad obsessions

Note that there are more solutions for this problem than I can fit into this book, so I will cover only one small subset of obsession-rerouting tactics.

First, however, note how different strategies are needed for people with autism. For example, a commonly recommended strategy for breaking a habit is to make a written note every time you feel the craving to indulge in your obsession. This is supposed to give you a moment of self-awareness, just enough time for the desire to simmer down.

For those on the spectrum, however, motor functioning is often interrupted. It would be ridiculous to ask someone who is resisting an obsession to sit down and write in complete sentences about what they are feeling. It would be akin to asking a Cirque du Soleil artist to do all the acts for all Cirque du Soleil artists all at once. It's asking too much of the human body and mind.

If typical habit-breaking techniques do not work, what will? This is a bit cheeky to mention, but perhaps use the same tactics that you would use with your cat? The book *All Cats Have Asperger Syndrome* by Kathy Hoopman (2006) gives insights into this frame of reference.

While we cannot cover all methods in this book, we can give a few ideas that are most appropriate: you can toxify the desired object/activity, make it illogical, use the element of surprise, and give consistent negative feedback for obsessive behaviors.

STEP 1: TOXIFY IT

Find a way to make the obsession dirty or otherwise unpleasant. If you are obsessed with computer games, move your computer to a physically uncomfortable location. (When I was a child, my parents put the television in the unheated garage. We did not watch much TV. It worked.) Work with your known physical anomalies to make the obsession unpleasant. If you are sensitive to noise, don't put your computer (if that's your obsession) in a quiet, remote room; put it in the family room, where there is noise and activity. It will train your brain to dislike the previously appealing activity.

STEP 2: MAKE IT ILLOGICAL

With the help of a friend, make a list of how illogical your obsession is. The list will only be part of the story. There will be many logical aspects of your obsession, because otherwise why would you have started doing it? Focus only on the illogical aspects, write them out in a list, and post this list where you can see it daily. The goal is for you to be able to scoff at the activity as being ridiculous (no longer appealing).

STEP 3: USE THE ELEMENT OF SURPRISE

If the obsession is something that you cannot eliminate fully, you may have to use more sophisticated methods. For example, if your obsession is based on your computer and you have to use your computer for your work, you can't put your computer in an uncomfortable location and you can't make it illogical without also hurting your work. If this is the case, use a timer with a loud beeper or some other reminder device to help you put limits on the behavior. In action, you would set the alarm for 30 minutes when you are checking in on your work at night, which is the habit you want to limit. Set an alarm for 30 minutes and the unpleasant alarm will train your body to not disappear too deeply into work.

STEP 4: CREATE CONSISTENT NEGATIVE FEEDBACK

Ask your partner to give you consistent negative feedback for any slips into bad obsessions. This is significantly harder than it sounds. It is common for couples to exhibit enabling behavior for self-destructive actions. When one partner is overweight (which is bad for one's health), the other partner is often also overweight or has a different equivalent self-destructive behavior. Use your skills to see the logic of it. If you want to stop tapping your foot, ask your partner to remind you when you start doing it.

Feel free to be creative. It does not have to be verbal feedback/words. When I wanted to stop tapping my foot, I asked my daughter to hiss at me like an angry cat every time she saw me tap my foot. She has such a fierce hiss that I was quickly trained out of foot tapping. Use any sound, touch, or physical sensation that best motivates you to change.

Pay close attention to whether or not these methods are effective for you. Changing behavior is one of the most difficult things we do. Evaluate logically, clinically whether or not the method is working for you.

The upside of obsession

If you browse the self-help aisles of a bookstore or library, you will find numerous books dedicated to helping adults find their "true calling in life," advocating that they find something about which they are passionate, something about which they could be obsessed.

One of the fringe benefits of having autism is that you probably know exactly what you love to do with your time. What engages your interest? What do you love to do, look at, study, work with, explore? It is common for someone with autism to have a strong preoccupation: a fascination with electronics, antiques, door locks (or picking those locks), fighter jets, tanks, computer chips, knitting, caring for cats, or any other interest. Obsessions cover the scope of human experience.

If you do have an obsession, there is a chance that it may be stronger than it would be if you did not have autism. Perhaps the lack of social awareness has allowed you a level of non-conformity. Perhaps it allowed you to maintain your obsession into adulthood where it can have the more socially acceptable title of, "a passionate pursuit."

There is a good chance that you saved yourself a lot of time and soul-searching by keeping your obsession alive throughout your formative years. There is a good chance that you are already intimately aware of what interests you.

Two common definitions for obsession are:

- a compulsive or irrational action

- an unhealthy fixation.

Both sound negative but are actually a matter of opinion. The first part of the definition assumes that "what is rational" is a non-negotiable rule, but what is rational to an NT (such as dressing nicely to gain the respect of others) may be irrational to someone with autism (dress is irrelevant to skill).

The second half of the definition is also tricky. Whether or not something is healthy is a matter of opinion. One classic example can be seen in the conflicting reports on various healthy/unhealthy foods. One day the news reports that eggs are the healthiest food you can eat; the next day eggs are causing high cholesterol. The same applies to wheat: the grocery stores are full of "healthy whole grains" yet, in the recent bestseller *Wheat Belly*, William Davis (2011) explains clearly how destructive wheat is in the average diet. (Personally, as I have celiac disease, like many on the autism spectrum, I happen to agree with *Wheat Belly*.)

Whether or not your obsession is healthy may be a matter of opinion. To determine whether your obsession is healthy or unhealthy, go through the following troubleshooting process.

Troubleshooting obsessions

IDENTIFY: IS THE OBSESSION HEALTHY OR NOT?

Test 1: Are you forgetting to take care of yourself?

If you are neglecting your body, not taking care of your family or you are otherwise shirking your adult responsibilities, then your obsession is unhealthy.

Test 2: Do you have the basics of life covered?

If you are able to support yourself and cover the basics of what you need to do as an adult, then the obsession is a healthy, perhaps quirky, aspect of your personality.

Test 3: Are you in control of the obsession or does it control you?

Are you able to stop doing it in order to go to bed at night? Is it consuming more of your personal funds than it should? Note that it is normal to have a hard time stopping the obsession in the evening in order to go to bed. It is hard to not overspend on it. That's what makes it an obsession rather than a passing interest. As long as you are in control of your obsession, then it qualifies as healthy.

Test 4: Does the activity make you feel alive?

Does it make you happy? A temporary, short burst of happiness is not sufficient. That short burst would be indicative of an addiction-type obsession similar to drug addiction. The initial pleasure response burns out and leaves devastation in its wake. To pass the "does it make you happy" test, it has to make you happy in the moment *and* long-term.

If your chosen obsession meets the above criteria, it is probably on the healthy side of the equation.

This is good for you to know personally, but when in an adult relationship there is one more factor to the obsession issue: your partner may disagree with you.

The comments below are indicative of a partner seeing your obsession as unhealthy (regardless of how you perceive your obsession):

"Why do you spend so much time/money on _____?"

"I need you to stop doing _____."

"I'm so sick of you _____."

"When are you going to grow up and stop _____?"

Young children tend to pursue their intense interests which often appear as obsessions. A toddler may be obsessed with blocks or trucks. A young child may be obsessed with a certain action figure. Typically, this type of immersive enjoyment of a toy or activity may be seen as a childish behavior.

In the mainstream, many children are "trained out" of their interests. They are taught to be well-rounded. You may come across stereotypes from your partner or from society that give you incorrect guidance, especially if your particular interest does not fall into the narrow definition of "What is a healthy adult interest?"

Troubleshooting disagreements over obsessions

IDENTIFY: ONE PARTNER BELIEVES THE OTHER IS ENGAGING IN AN UNHEALTHY OBSESSION

Test 1: Document the situation
Track:

- how many hours spent per week

- how much money spent per month

- level of happiness daily.

Since you probably cannot use the NT "Let's sit down and talk about it," then use your ASD-specific skills. Use your skill for detachment and look at the behavior as quantifiable and trackable.

Evaluate: I have listed only one test for this problem. There are many others, but this one is the most effective and the best place to start. It is effective if it helps you to get an accurate picture of the time you are spending on your obsession *and if that awareness helps change behavior.*

So that you can see this solution in action, read the following examples:

In Stephen King's book, *On Writing* (2002), Stephen talks about the many years he spent as an alcoholic. He was in denial of the problem until his neighborhood started a recycling program. Once he could see the bottles in his recycling bin, an accounting of how much he consumed, he realized that he had a problem. The bottles in the recycling bin were a clear-cut "tallying" of how much he was drinking. He quit drinking.

Another example, which is common in the community of people with autism, is video games. For my husband with autism, his obsession used to be MMOGs, massively multiplayer online games. He thought that he was "taking a little break," or "just checking in on the game," or "just checking on my character." There were numerous excuses that made it sound small, quick, and harmless.

I documented the game playing: two hours and ten minutes after dinner, five hours after tucking the kids in, one hour in the middle of the night.

He saw the evidence in black and white which gave him the opportunity to decide objectively for himself if that was what he wanted to do with his time. Admittedly, since I had tracked the time instead of him, he didn't fully believe that the times were accurate. Yet, he never did track it himself. The tracking helped him when pulling away from this addiction in that it did not pass the list of tests in the previous troubleshooting section, "Is the obsession healthy or not?"

The solution that worked for us was a clearly defined, black and white, binary, on-or-off ultimatum (see Chapter 6, "Using Binary Thinking to Your Benefit"). The ultimatum was: "Stop playing games cold turkey or I'll file for divorce and you'll lose your children." The fact that I had documented how little time he spent with his children helped him to realize how serious the consequences were of, "just playing for a minute."

He understood the situation in binary terms. He sold his characters, quit every game to which he had subscriptions. He had several months of mourning, then noticed that he enjoyed all the free time he had. Now, seven years later, he is programming games instead of buying them. He realized that MMOGs were a substitute for his real obsession: programming. He is a creator. He no longer feels trapped by the obsession. In his words, "It's harder, but I finally get to do what I want to do."

Putting obsession to work

There are many careers where an obsessive level of devotion to a particular task makes you more valuable than other employees. Research scientists performing tedious experiments again and again; teachers giving the same lessons year after year; engineers drawing an endless number of diagrams and following endless rules; all of these and many more are well suited for someone obsessed with the task at hand.

The ability to be obsessed can help you to get a job and even help you to keep that job. Imagine a situation where there are two programmers, one with autism and one NT. The NT programmer may be far more likely to take time off, answer personal calls during work, be easily distracted (lack of intense focus), and when the deadline comes will have no emotional investment in solving the problem, completing the puzzle. In contrast, the person with autism, if programming happens to be that person's obsession, will push harder, longer, and with greater devotion to completion. If it is Friday night and the programmer is three hours away from a major breakthrough, it is the person with the obsessive personality who is going to make the great discoveries.

Summary/Maintenance

Perhaps the high rate of people with autism in our history books is due specifically to obsession. Our history books record the work of artists who worked harder than their contemporaries; craftsmen who were so madly in love with their craft that they sculpted, carved, chiseled beauty beyond the norm; programmers who worked around the clock hammering out tough problems. I wrote about the massive potential benefits of people with autism in *Business for Aspies* (Stanford 2011). Both employers and employees would benefit greatly from recognizing the strengths unique to autism and supporting those unique traits whole-heartedly.

Personally, I love the concept of healthy obsession. Many of the great works of humanity come from the mental state of obsession, a besieging of your mental resources, to the point that all senses are focused to the benefit of the obsession.

As long as you are in charge of the obsessive experience rather than the obsession ruling you, your personal obsessions can lead to possibly the greatest creations of your life, your legacy.

CHAPTER 20

Troubleshooting with Children

WHEN A COUPLE BECOMES A FAMILY

This topic deserves its own book, or several books, but we will have to make do with a chapter for now.

Becoming a parent is an overwhelming experience for most people, but for a person with autism, since adding children to the family means adding social interaction to the day, it can increase the number of daily difficulties by an exponential amount. From birth to death, there are a mind-boggling number of potential difficulties all related to the autism diagnostic criteria: pregnancy, infancy, diapers, crying, toddler's random movements, young children, tweens, teens, young adults, adults, extended family, holidays with family, difficulties with special occasions, aging parents, even inappropriate behavior at funerals.

It can be so overwhelming that when re-reading the previous paragraph on a final edit of the book, I started shaking and felt tears well up in my eyes. Since I do have NT empathy, seeing all of the difficulties my husband faced was too overwhelming. He was able to do it one step at a time, but looking at it all in one broad, sweeping view showed the massive, and even crushing amount of work involved for him.

Being in a partnership, especially a sexually intimate one, brings up the possibility of pregnancy. Pregnancy leads to bodily changes that can wreak havoc on the sensory system.

Because this chapter is so jam-packed with content, I have used an abbreviated form of troubleshooting: the Simple List. It removes the Evaluate tool, and gives a quick 1, 2, 3 punch.

IDENTIFY: DURING PREGNANCY, A PERSON'S BODY CHANGES DRASTICALLY, CHANGING EITHER YOUR OWN BALANCE OR THE BALANCE AND SHAPE OF THE PERSON YOU HUG

A few fixes:

1. Take a touch sabbatical.

2. Study the physiological changes, understand them clinically.

3. Do OT/PT to rebalance your body as it grows.

IDENTIFY: CHILDREN MAKE NOISE. NOISE CAUSES OVERLOAD, WHICH LEADS TO MELTDOWNS

1. Use headphones or ear buds to dampen the noise.

2. Get support. Spend less time with the children.

3. Be the one who handles the quieter times such as eating time, homework time, or reading stories at night. Let your noise tolerant partner take the loud times such as bath-time, having friends over, or preparing for school in the morning.

IDENTIFY: CHILDREN MAKE RANDOM MOVEMENTS. IT STRESSES ME THAT THEY DO NOT MAKE SENSE IN THEIR MOVEMENTS, ALWAYS JIGGLING OR WIGGLING OR WANDERING

1. Look for pattern in chaos.

2. Do not try to limit their movements (unless they are in danger). Often, trying to get children to be quiet and calm only causes more problems. Instead, try to be calm yourself to role model calm for your children.

3. Minimize your time with the kid-crazies. We call the random movements of children playing "kid-crazies" because the way they move seems so crazy, and it seems to be a type of movement that only occurs in childhood.

IDENTIFY: THERE ARE TOO MANY THINGS TO DO NOW THAT I HAVE A CHILD/CHILDREN

1. Give yourself even more structure and routine than before. It is a well-known fact that children thrive with structure. Thankfully this can also benefit you by providing a framework for daily tasks, eliminating so many factors in the daily equation.

2. Do less. Kids are often overbooked anyway. Cut out as many activities as you can, especially those that your child never wanted to do in the first place.

3. Recognize that yes, there really is too much to do and seek the advice of someone who is good at minimizing the extras. Ask that person for advice.

IDENTIFY: MY KIDS ARE NOW TWEENS AND I DO NOT KNOW WHAT TO DO WITH THEM

1. Disconnect if necessary. Be present physically, but give them the space they need to make their own decisions. The best advice I ever received about raising teens came from a man who worked with teens at risk. His advice was to "Be there." That's all.

2. Tweens are beginning to realize that you are not perfect and that you have flaws. Be yourself and that is good enough.

3. Focus as hard as you can on their positive traits. A common saying for us has been, "Well, they may be _____ (playing video games too much, not showering, being so awkward that they embarrass you) but at least they aren't _____ (hanging out at dance clubs, going to parties, doing drugs, getting pregnant/ getting a girl pregnant). Be grateful for the best traits of your teen.

IDENTIFY: RAISING TEENS IS TOUGH! IT'S TOO HARD

1. Recognize that if your children are biologically yours, there is a good chance that they will be somewhere on the spectrum.

Recognize that if the teens were hard for you, it is certainly hard for them too.

2. Counter-point: If your teen is not on the spectrum and you are, your child may be embarrassed by you. The social rules of teens are often extremely strict. Remind yourself that these years are short and not indicative of your future relationship since issues you and your teen may have now can be healed as the teen becomes an adult.

3. Count your blessings. Focus hard in the teen years on what your child has become capable of doing. Expound on your teen's strengths. While it is important to not live vicariously through your child, do take credit for the good things you did teach your child.

4. If all else fails, count the days until your teen is legally an adult.

Note that this troubleshooting deals only with you and your own mental health, not the teen's mental health.

IDENTIFY: I DO NOT KNOW HOW TO RELATE TO MY YOUNG ADULTS/GROWN CHILDREN

1. Brainstorm for unique ways to stay connected. The standard family reunion surely will not work, but you can still spend time together by attending Comi-Con or the Game Developer's Conference or the Maker Faire, or any other number of events that may appeal to your particular interests.

2. Respect the other's choice of connection. If you want more time or less time with your adult children, let them know, then respect their response. Note that people change over time. Mark your calendar to check in with your adult children once a year to ask if they would like to spend more or less time together. This allows for growth and change.

3. Make a short list of the Top Five things you love most about your grown child. Keep this list in a memorable spot so that you can refer to it regularly. This will help you feel closer to your child by focusing on the best traits. Even better, send a copy of the list to your adult child.

IDENTIFY: I DO NOT KNOW HOW TO INTERACT PROPERLY WITH EXTENDED FAMILY

1. Try to determine what the extended family wants from you. It is to be hoped that this is a simple question with a simple answer. Some families do not mind if you don't visit for the holidays; some families would take life-long offense if you did not visit. Just ask.

2. Recognize the difficulties; isolate and simplify problems. Is the problem too much noise at large get-togethers? Find ways to do smaller groups, or skip the event and find another way to interact with family. Sometimes not seeing extended family is better for family relations than going to an event.

3. Make sure family is support for you; do not allow it to be draining. You may be under the false assumption that family is painful and hard. While it may be more difficult for you than for others to achieve and maintain family relationships, the end goal at least should be one of support.

IDENTIFY: AT FAMILY EVENTS, SUCH AS WEDDINGS/FUNERALS, I ALWAYS SEEM TO MAKE A MISTAKE OR ACT INAPPROPRIATELY

1. Remember that it is usually better to be quiet than talkative, which gives fewer chances for error.

2. Review appropriate behavior ahead of time with someone you trust.

3. Ask for forgiveness when someone informs you of a mistake. "I'm sorry. I wasn't aware that that was wrong. Can you overlook _____ (the mistake)?"

4. Always plan time to heal afterwards. It is probable that your sensory system and other systems will need time to recalibrate after any social event. A family-based event will be even more stressful. Be kind to yourself and plan relaxing time after the event.

Summary/Maintenance

People with autism can be fantastic parents. The diagnosis does not dictate an inability to parent.

Instead, how you problem-solve issues that crop up due to autistic traits determines whether or not you will thrive as a parent.

As I write this, my husband with autism is sitting at our dining-room table with two of our sons on a week-long programming marathon during the holidays. They are writing applications for cell phones, just for fun.

They have many modifications in place to make this work: no noise, and extremely comfortable clothes. Two of them are wearing black sweatshirts with the hood up, something not allowed in schools and shunned in public because of the gangster appearance. They all, however, love the soft, fuzzy feel of the fabric; the coverage of the hood helps to block light; and the weight of the hood gives just enough sensory feedback to calm them.

They will work from 9am to 11pm and will enjoy every minute of it. It is a unique type of family gathering. No big sit-down meals; no niceties to share; no social rules, just three guys with their laptops, a pan of lasagne and a desire to interact with others in the best way they know how.

Do what is best for you and for your children. The rewards of parenting make the effort worth it.

CHAPTER 21

Troubleshooting Meltdowns

If you are on the spectrum, you probably observe people's emotional reactions as bizarre, especially when the reaction is self-destructive.

Yet, humans have an illogical propensity to do self-destructive things. As I type this I am up too late, which is not good for my body, especially as I have an early morning plane flight to catch and I have not yet packed. I will suffer the consequences later. Is this self-destructive? Yes. Is it illogical? Yes. Is it typical of me? Yes.

Apparently I am not logical enough to let reason overrule my emotional desire to write about losing emotional control; which is ironical.

The universal meltdown

The term "meltdown" is not restricted to those on the spectrum. Meltdown describes what happens when a person's sensory system is overloaded, typically the result of too much input. A meltdown is a standard human reaction that can occur for many reasons.

The term "meltdown" was first used in 1965 in regards to nuclear reactors. Due to a defect in the cooling system, the reactor could overheat, causing the fuel rods to melt. This allowed radiation to escape. At the time this term was invented, the breakdown of a nuclear reactor was the most terrifying analogy people could make. It signified a traumatic event for a person who had internally freaked out.

Personally, the term "meltdown" has much meaning. I lived in northeast France in 1986 when a reactor blew at the Chernobyl nuclear power plant in Ukraine (near the Russian border). The winds carried radioactive fallout over much of Europe. I remember news reports telling people to throw out all fresh produce that had been harvested since the explosion. I also remember people not taking it seriously. France is so far from Russia. How could we get radioactive poisoning from so far away? Yet even now doctors are finding a rapid increase in thyroid cancers from people who lived in the area and ate the food that was poisoned.

The purpose of sharing this is to give you a visual image. It may seem like a meltdown is contained by space and time, but the repercussions are often felt far and wide. A meltdown you had with your partner when you were a young adult, may still be felt in your fifties, sixties, and well into retirement. Meltdowns need to be taken seriously and dealt with as best we can.

IDENTIFY: MY PARTNER IS HAVING A MELTDOWN AND I DO NOT KNOW WHAT TO DO

Test 1: Ride out the storm

During the meltdown your partner is in survival mode. Go into survival mode as well and do only what you need to do to survive for the next few minutes or hours or even days until your partner is feeling better.

Evaluate: If your partner can successfully come out of the meltdown in a reasonable amount of time without doing damage to him- or herself or others, then perhaps this is the best solution. If one or both of you want to minimize the meltdowns, see Test 2.

Test 2: Give your partner what he or she needs

During the meltdown the brain's survival mechanism is triggered. There is something your partner needs to see, hear or feel in order to turn off the blaring siren of the survival mechanism. One or more of the following may work:

- Give your partner a tight hug.

- Help your partner to climb under some covers (dark).

- Give your partner verbal reassurance that everything will be ok, that you love your partner unconditionally.

- Play loud music to override your partner's auditory sensitivity.

Evaluate: If you can find the right response to help your partner survive a meltdown, you have a chance that you will be able to minimize future meltdowns. If this is not sufficient, go to Test 3.

Test 3: Emergency protocol

Develop a list of emergency strategies: things your partner can do to survive once the meltdown has begun. A few examples which your partner experiencing the onset of a meltdown could try include:

- Stop, drop, and roll. Stop what you are doing. Drop, by going to a different room in the house. Roll with the physiological effects until it is past. Some people with autism may want to literally roll themselves up in a blanket to give sensory support.

- At the first sign of a meltdown, switch to a highly immersive activity such as a computer game or TV show. This will help you more easily avert meltdown.

- Cool the reactors in your nuclear plant. Find a way to literally cool the heat of the meltdown, preferably a physical solution such as cold water on your face or loud music in your ears. Force your body to cool down in whatever unique way you have found works for you.

Evaluate: If you can find emergency strategies that help avert and minimize meltdowns, fantastic. The goal is for meltdowns to be shorter and less frequent. If not, see Test 4.

Test 4: Fix whatever caused the meltdown

Prevent or minimize the meltdown pre-emptively. Look at the situation logically and identify the trigger. Was it too much loud noise? Was it lack of sleep? Was it a particular topic that you find particularly painful? Find what causes the meltdowns then figure out a way to eliminate those triggers.

Evaluate: If you can successfully eliminate the triggers to minimize future meltdowns, this worked. If not, see Test 5.

Test 5: Get professional help

Meltdowns can get serious. If the situation becomes dangerous for you, your partner, or others, seek professional help.

Evaluate: If the meltdowns decrease in frequency or duration, this has been successful. If not, perhaps try a different type of professional support.

IDENTIFY: MY PARTNER IS ACTING LIKE A COMPLETE IDIOT (AN INADVERTENT "SIDEWAYS MELTDOWN")

Test 1: Not just imagined

Understand that your observation is accurate. If your partner is under stress, he or she may be acting in a less-than-smart way due to the rational part of his or her brain being off-line. Also, it is more difficult to concentrate and nearly impossible to remember from one minute to the next what is being said. Following a train of thought is going to be next-to-impossible.

Evaluate: If a basic understanding of what is going on with your partner helps you be more compassionate with each other during a meltdown, great. If not, see Test 2.

Test 2: Imperfection is ok

Allow your partner to have imperfections. See Chapter 12, "Troubleshooting Perfection, Aiming for Imperfection, and Making Your Life Lighter."

Evaluate: If you can successfully give your partner the freedom to have flaws and it minimizes the frustration related to lowered cognitive abilities during a meltdown, great. If not, see Test 3.

Test 3: Give yourselves space

Spend time apart; allow yourself time to calm down. Recognize that with space and time his logical brain will come back online. Also, during this time your willpower and ability to be compassionate will be renewed.

Evaluate: If you are able to come back together feeling renewed and rejuvenated, this has worked. Don't be surprised if you both experience regression when you come back together. That's normal. Do your best to make consistent improvement over time and continue taking breaks as needed.

IDENTIFY: IT SEEMS THAT MY PARTNER IS USING A MELTDOWN TO MANIPULATE ME

Test 1: Define "manipulate"

There are two aspects to manipulation:

* skillfully influencing someone

* in an unfair manner.

Recognize that while the interaction may be unfair, it may not be skillful. Your partner may have learned how to get what he or she wants in a clumsy way that appears manipulative. Your partner may fail to see the unfair nature of his or her requests and actions.

Evaluate: If the realization that the manipulation is not intentional helps you get past the feeling that your partner is taking advantage of you, great. If not, see Test 2.

Test 2: Look for other motivation

Assess the situation to determine your partner's motivation. There is a good chance that your partner is motivated to do something that would benefit you both.

Evaluate: If your partner is "getting what he or she wants" which happens to be something that is good for both of you, or perhaps just good for your partner and not important to you, then just relax and enjoy the benefits of your relationship. If not, see Test 3.

Test 3: Treat it as non-manipulation

Do not let the manipulation get to you. Research manipulative behavior online and in books for what you can do to avoid getting wrapped up in it.

Evaluate: If you can stop the manipulation from ruining your relationship, you have succeeded. If not, refer to Test 4.

Test 4: Decide

Decide whether or not you want to live with the manipulating behavior. This is always the final test: if all else fails you are left with the final decision of staying or going. See Chapter 25, "Troubleshooting Whether to Stay or Go: The Decision Process."

Evaluate: The end goal is for you to experience happiness and fulfilment in your daily life. Whatever decision you make, in the case of a manipulative partner, the only factor to consider is what is best for you personally.

IDENTIFY: MY PARTNER IS TOTALLY OUT OF CONTROL

There may be times when your partner, on the spectrum or not, is out of control, "on the ledge," either violent or depressed on a dangerous level.

If your safety or your partner's safety is at risk, skip straight to the last test.

Test 1: Use all your resources to help de-escalate the situation

Refer to your favorite books, websites, and other resources for ideas that work for you. One idea might be to cancel all of your partner's responsibilities for the day and tell your partner to take a sick day, in his or her room with only his or her laptop. Do whatever usually helps your partner to de-escalate.

Evaluate: If you can help your partner to de-escalate, great. If not, start on Test 2.

Test 2: Be proactive

Improve your own personal health and encourage your partner to do the same. Even if you are mid-depression or mid-meltdown, regulating diet and exercise could be enough to solve or at least slow down the meltdown. Much research has shown that a healthy diet, particularly a gluten-free diet, can stabilize a person's hormonal levels and increase emotional resilience. Also, research has shown that various forms of yoga can help to regulate your ability to control emotion.

Evaluate: If you see a marked improvement in your ability to avert the difficulties of major meltdown, great. It is extremely important to keep up any exercise or dietary solutions that work for you. If this is not sufficient, then see Test 3.

Test 3: Latch on to any solutions, big or small

It is probable that you have experienced or will experience similar situations throughout the length of your relationship. When you find solutions, write them down and keep them in a handy place, perhaps a list on your phone or in a notepad in your bag. Your list may include:

- Evacuate!

- Eliminate all sound, or at least as much as possible.

- Dim lights.

- Say, "You're great just the way you are," as many times as your partner needs to hear it.

- Respond with logic, not emotion, or vice versa.

Evaluate: If you find that you can de-escalate emergency situations by using tactics that have worked in the past, great. If not, and all other solutions have been exhausted, refer to Test 4.

Test 4: Encourage self-awareness

As problems escalate, encourage your partner to be aware of what is happening on a physiological level. Common signs of stress are a rising and hunching of the shoulders, a furrowing of the brow, and a clenching of the jaw. When the person under stress brings awareness to his or her body, it reroutes the thought processes from emergency mode into self-awareness mode.

You can even test this on yourself next time you are under significant stress. By bringing awareness to the physical sensations that arise you are able to change them. Notice how the knot in your tummy or rigidity in your shoulders softens as you become aware of what is happening in your body.

Evaluate: If focusing on physiological self-awareness helps your partner (and you) relax instead of escalate, then you have succeeded. If this does not work, see Test 5.

Test 5: Give extra support

Recognize that someone with autism has spent most of his or her life focused on left brain logic instead of right brain emotion. This means that the right brain might be very weak, and perhaps many years behind in development.

The more heightened the argument or difficulty you are experiencing, the more the right brain hijacks all thought processes. Our "alarm center" resides in the right brain and alerts us to danger in the environment, be it emotional or survival-based. As a difficulty progresses, the cumulative effect is that the person with autism gets so amped up that even a stubbed toe will feel like a tragedy. Focus on calming the alarm center.

Evaluate: If you can give sufficient support to help calm your partner's alarm center, great. If not, see Test 6.

Test 6: If the situation has become dangerous, get help

Call a mental health professional for access to helpful resources in your area. If one is not available and the situation is urgent, call the police (in a situation of violence) or a suicide hotline (if depression has escalated to this point). Once you call for help, you will no longer be able to control the situation; police and mental health professionals will be in charge of what happens to you and your family from that point on. In some situations, however, it may be the right, or perhaps the only, choice.

Summary/Maintenance

Any work we do to eliminate problems in our relationships and in our lives helps free up more of the left and right brain to be ready in case of emergency.

If you are in an emergency situation, trying to talk your partner off the ledge, try your best to assist, and remember, that in the end, people make their own choices and are responsible for their own actions.

CHAPTER 22

Troubleshooting Complaints

TOXICITY IN RELATIONSHIPS

Complaints can make a good day bad and a bad day worse. In the long-term, complaints can ruin a relationship. Only a masochist would want to be around someone who whines and complains excessively. Yet, in many relationships, complaining is part of a regular day. Remove the complaining from your relationship and you will notice a distinct improvement overall.

First, what is a complaint?

A "complaint" is usually defined as:

* expressing dissatisfaction or resentment

* notifying others of physical pain or other discomfort

* verbalizing negative comments

* lamenting

* faultfinding.

Complaints are rarely ever useful. Nearly always they emphasize and magnify negative aspects or events. Negativity infects the relationship with a "dark cloud" that is hard to dissipate. Complaints are toxic.

A person with an NT brain may complain for a variety of reasons. One popular reason is that when you complain, you get social feedback from others. Complaining is often seen as a way of bonding. For example:

Person 1: *"I just hate the rain. It has been raining non-stop lately."*

Person 2: *"Me too. I haven't been able to stay dry all week."*

The "me too" type of social interaction is a common form of casual bonding. By agreeing with someone it makes people feel that they are part of a group. In some circles the "me too" complaints are a daily ritual, shared every time they meet during the course of the day.

The problem arises when the complaining goes beyond benign chit-chat. Complaining tends to become natural, a regular form of communication and the person who complained about the weather earlier in the day will not recognize the level of damage done when coming home and complaining about the messy house, the unmade dinner, the too-loud kids, and the nighttime headache. Complaints may sometimes be benign, but they can be used as a verbal sword, doing damage to anyone on the other end of the blade.

If you have autism, there is a twist to your way of interacting that will not apply to those who do not have an autistic brain. For a person with autism, a complaint is probably a statement of fact and only a statement of fact.

Fact and complaint are two entirely different things, yet, that statement of fact may easily be perceived as a complaint. Examples of this include:

"This house is dirty."

"Your clothes are wrinkled."

"This food tastes awful."

"This is the 27th day in a row of rain."

"My back aches."

It is important to differentiate between statement of fact and complaint. They are entirely different things, prompted by different motivation, different intention, and different desired outcome.

The difference between a statement of fact and a complaint is:

- Statement of fact = observation of a condition in the world.

- Complaint = an expression of discontent, regret, pain, etc.

Note the distinct difference between the two: one is a neutral statement; the other is an emotionally-charged expression.

The difference seems innocuous enough until you look at the repercussions of living with a partner who complains, especially a partner who complains a lot. The complaints can create an atmosphere of negativity, frustration, and a downward spiral of pain causing more pain.

Excessive complaints are a problem that needs to be solved.

IDENTIFY: MY PARTNER COMPLAINS OFTEN

Test 1: Differentiate

Differentiate between complaint and comment. Ask, "Are you just stating a fact or is there more that I should be aware of?"

Evaluate: It is probable that this simple, easy question will help your partner see that: 1) you do not like the complaints, and 2) perhaps you feel that your partner complains too much. If this is not achieved, see Test 2.

Test 2: Seeing the negativity

Explain that complaints are, "a negative comment." The concept of negativity is subjective and may be hard to grasp. Be patient in explaining this concept in a variety of scenarios. It may be hard to understand that, "It's raining again," is a complaint in certain circumstances, but in others, such as checking on the weather before going out, may be a helpful comment. These nuances may be difficult to master.

Evaluate: If you notice a distinct decrease in complaints, this method has worked. If not, see Test 3.

Test 3: Just the facts

Choose to interpret complaints as a matter of statement. Change your perspective. For example, if your partner says, "Dinner is burnt again," say, "Yes, it is and I think I can fix the problem by getting a better cooking pan." Un-charge the emotional aspect of the comment.

Evaluate: If you find it too hard to turn complaints into comments, go to Test 4 for further encouragement.

Test 4: Reaping benefits

Recognize the benefits of not being offended by complaints. Part of the difference between a complaint and a statement of fact is that a complaint is perceived as offensive by the listener.

Recognize that taking offense is a choice. No one can offend you without you choosing to be offended. There are big benefits in choosing not to be offended! When you are not offended, you can:

- keep your heart rate even and calm

- reduce physical and emotional stress

- be more easygoing with your partner's mistakes

- more easily admit any wrong-doing on your part

- see the situation more clearly

- respond in a helpful, supportive manner more easily.

Evaluate: If you are still annoyed by your partner's complaints, then none of the above methods have worked. If so, the final option is to simply accept that your partner is a complainer. Once you have accepted the complaints as part of your partner's character, you can ignore most of the complaints, allowing you more peace in your day.

What if the problem is reversed?

IDENTIFY: I COMPLAIN TOO MUCH

Test 1: Complaint versus comment

Notice the difference between complaint and comment. There is a good chance that you do not notice how often you complain simply because you are not differentiating between the two.

Evaluate: If noticing how often you complain helps reduce the number of complaints you make in day, great! If not, try the next test.

Test 2: Make it concrete

Make a mental (or written) tally of how often you complain.

Evaluate: Sometimes seeing how much you are doing something helps break you of the habit immediately. This is how Food Journals work—once you see what you actually ate in a day, you can control your food intake more easily. If noticing how often you complain does not work, try the next test.

Test 3: Bad choice

Give yourself physical Pavlovian feedback for every complaint. A commonly suggested method is to put a rubber band on your wrist and snap it every time you complain. It will hurt and should cause you to stop the complaints before they come out of your mouth. If a rubber band does not work, try biting your lip, flicking your arm, or (the most effective for me) do ten sit-ups or push-ups. Some people use financial consequences: you must put $1 in the Complaint Jar every time you complain, whether on purpose or by mistake.

Evaluate: Having a strong feedback loop should train you to stop the complaining. Yet, if you have sensory issues, the rubber band may not work. If you have financial issues, the Complaint Jar might not work. If none of the physical feedback methods work, try the next test.

Test 4: Ratios

Specifically increase the ratio of positive comments to negative comments (complaints). Focusing on positive comments improves your focus in many ways, helping you to see the good rather than just the bad.

John Gottman, a well-known marriage researcher, discovered that for a marriage to be successful, couples must average a ratio of five positive interactions to one negative interaction. He called this the magic ratio.

You will have to work so hard to give compliments that you won't have time to complain.

Evaluate: This method has been successful if increasing the number of positive comments helps transition your complaint-ridden relationship to one where complaints are rare.

Test 5: Flip the complaint/comment

Before voicing something that may be perceived as a complaint, flip it. For example, instead of saying, "It is rainy and cloudy today," say, "The rain and clouds certainly help me to appreciate the sunny days more."

Evaluate: If you can effectively flip the comments before voicing them and if this helps increase the positivity in your relationship, then this test has worked.

Prevention

There are several things which you can do to make complaints less likely. The ones listed below are specific to autism-linked relationships. The best prevention strategies are: appreciate, accept responsibility, self-soothe, and compartmentalize.

APPRECIATE

A person with autism may not hear comments of appreciation, instead responding with a "no-duh." For example, you may say to your partner, "I really appreciate how you take care of your body," after you have noticed how some adults let their bodies go but your partner has continued to exercise to keep his or her own body fit.

Your partner with autism may be bewildered, wondering why you would comment on something obvious, hearing it as something silly like, "You have two feet." Your efforts at appreciation may not have the impact you intended.

Do not give up offering appreciation simply because it is sometimes misconstrued. Instead, focus your efforts on the non-obvious. Comment on the things that your partner is working very hard to accomplish. For example, if it is hard for your partner to go to work every day, comment, "I really appreciate how hard you work," Or, if it is hard for your partner to eat dinner together with you, say, "I really appreciate being able to have dinner with you and talk together at the end of the day."

Comment on what is difficult for your partner with autism and it is more likely that your comments will be positively received.

ACCEPT RESPONSIBILITY

This one is the toughest, simply because the person with autism will not be able to see the responsibility as his or her responsibility. The lack of social awareness will make your partner with autism's view of personal responsibility very limited.

A few responsibilities that your partner may not see are the responsibility to:

- celebrate birthdays/buy presents on important occasions
- help you when you need help
- split housework fairly
- your children
- (the fuzziest) "be there for you."

The clincher: *Just because your partner does not see his or her responsibility clearly does not mean that he or she is purposefully trying to avoid it.* Work on identifying and outlining responsibilities clearly, linearly, and logically. This limits criticisms because when both partners are fulfilling their responsibilities to themselves and to each other, there is nothing to complain about.

SELF-SOOTHE

Soothing oneself is a huge benefit not only to the person with autism but also to the partner. On the flip side, allowing your partner to self-soothe is even more important since it shows respect to someone who needs time and space to achieve calm.

When people are uneasy, or uncomfortable—when they need soothing—they are far more likely to complain. Focus on soothing and minimize the complaints.

Allowing yourself time to self-soothe is more difficult than it sounds. Your way of calming yourself down may be odd, or may be seen as "unnecessary" by others.

Communicate to your partner how important it is. If you compare your type of self-soothing to a socially acceptable equivalent, your partner will be more likely to be supportive. For example, "I know that when I'm playing games on my laptop you see it as a frivolous waste of time, but I play games instead of golfing or going to sports games. It's how I unwind." Note that this may or may not make sense to your partner so you may need to remind your partner that your activities are important.

Allowing your partner time to self-soothe is probably even more difficult because you are not in your partner's body and do not understand what he or she needs. If you do not have autism, it may be exceptionally difficult to have empathy for what your partner needs.

In this case, try to find equivalents for yourself. If you need time to read or watch TV at the end of a long day, recognize that your partner needs time to do whatever he or she does to relax.

When both partners can calm themselves independently, life is much easier for both. Encourage your partner to take breaks.

COMPARTMENTALIZE

When my husband and I were first married, I questioned him on how he could ignore the problems so easily. He said, "I just put them in a jar and put the jar up on the shelf."

I misinterpreted this as denial. I saw only the negative aspects of compartmentalization. After many wasted years of trying to get him to "open up," I finally learned to respect and even appreciate this ability. I even learned to use it myself, to my own personal benefit.

Compartmentalizing the problems in your relationship puts a stop to complaints. Whenever you want to say a negative comment, put that comment in a "Hash List." A Hash List is a list of complaints that you can go over on a "Hash Night."

Once a week, at a time we have chosen that works for both of us, we sit down somewhere private and each of us lists the items on our Hash List. There are so many benefits to having a Hash List:

- It allows you both to have a complaint-free week.

- It gives you space between the complaint and the voicing of the complaint. When you give the complaint space, it usually seems much less important later.

- It allows you to evaluate if your complaints are one-offs or if the same problems are reoccurring each week.

- It gives you the comfort of knowing that your concerns will be fully addressed. During the week, your partner may not be able to give you adequate attention, but during a planned Hash Night, attention is given.

There are currently 17 items on my Hash List for my husband and 15 of them are all about the same topic. It would not do any good to mention them. He already knows, but I still have the desire to hash them since he is not doing anything about them. Putting these concerns in a Hash List allows me to get it off my chest and into a safe spot.

Make it dirty

A difficulty in a relationship is either solvable or not. If it is solvable, solve it and move on. If it is not solvable, however, then bouncing it back and forth between you two only harms you both.

Think of a relationship problem like a big ball of mud, mold, sticky phlegm, contagious bacteria or anything else you find disgusting. If you can wipe it off you (if it is solvable) then wipe it off! If you cannot, if it is too big, then do not toss it at your partner.

For unsolvable problems, discussing them (complaining) only increases misery. Just as tossing a mud ball back and forth increasingly covers you both in mud, arguing about an unsolvable problem gets you both dirty, irritated, uncomfortable, sad, and it takes time to clean up/heal after a mud ball tossing argument.

So, find a handy place to put the mud ball. For example, say your issue is that your partner is overweight. There is nothing he can do immediately to lose the weight. Your partner may be working on it with good diet and exercise, but mentioning it daily only makes him want to eat more and exercise less. Wrong direction!

The healthiest goal would be to not mention it, but that is hard to do. Having a safe spot where you can "park" these ugly issues allows you relief, and much relief for your partner also.

Here are some great places to store the filthy mud balls everyone has in their lives:

- on a piece of paper that can easily be thrown away later

- in a journal or diary, especially one dedicated only to this purpose

- in a Notes application on your phone

- in a document or spreadsheet on your computer.

I love the autistic brain. I love how so much of what could be considered a "deficit" can be used as an ability.

Use logic

I especially love the logic. Sure, a non-social-seeking, highly logical person is not a teddy bear style best friend, but he has skills that others could never have.

Logic can be especially helpful in conversations with people whom you see day after day. The ultimate logic, the logic that makes those around you happier and more satisfied, is this:

- If you state a complaint once, there is no logical reason to state it again.

- There is no emotional benefit, no background shaming, no guilt trip, no emotional tit-for-tat games.

Complaining more than once serves absolutely no purpose. Whining and moaning is ridiculous to the point of being funny. Have you ever seen a person with autism laugh at someone who appears to be in pain? Perhaps part of the laugh is due to the apparent silliness of stating the same thing over and over again, as if something would change if the person said it enough times.

If complaining is so illogical and without purpose, why do people do it?

For non-logical people

A complaint can often get attention from others. If they will not hear your positive comments, a complaint might be the second best way to get them to pay attention to you. Imagine a child in a grocery store: he tells his mom he is hungry (an unemotional fact). She ignores him. He says it again. Nothing. He whines and cries. Now she hears him, shoves a bag of cookies his way and goes back to shopping. This is a very common experience for young children and most of us are trained at a very early age that complaints get results and calm, logical, fact-based communication is to be ignored.

Complaints may feel familiar and comforting. If you grew up hearing others complaining about the weather, complaining about a long work week, you may consider it a normal way of interacting. Thankfully, people with less social attachment are less likely to copy others (outside of echoloialia or mimicking behavior).

Without the ability to see things logically, complaints can breed like fruit flies. Complaints lead to more complaints. Focus on the negative and you will get more negative. For example, in my own experience, once I see that my husband has not taken out the trash, I begin to see dozens of other things he has not done. The only way to stop the cascade of negativity is to switch to focusing on the positive. Positive and negative thoughts have a hard time residing in the same active thought process in the same mind at once.

The logical brain is better positioned to sustain a complaint free lifestyle than others. There are several reasons why, including:

- There is no purpose to a complaint. Facts are important, but complaints are irrelevant.

- Complaints are typically repetitive. The stereotype is of a partner nagging the other to "Pick up your dirty socks," or other naggy type of request, that may be said every day, or even several times a day for years. To the logical brain repeated requests are a ridiculous waste of time. There is no purpose to them.

WHY WOULD A LOGICAL PERSON COMPLAIN?

If you have autism, there are many reasons:

- You may have the misunderstanding that complaining is fun since people often smile and make other happy gestures when complaining. True, for some people they get emotional benefits from complaining. For some people, complaining is a way of life, a way of interacting. Look at the news, especially the political newscasters. Their professional lives are full of non-stop negativity and criticism, yet they seem happy. Odd, huh?

- You may have the misunderstanding that complaining is an expected form of communication. It does not need to be. Complaints are the cheap and easy way to communicate. Complaining about the weather or the traffic conditions is often an easy chit-chat level of communication. As a logical person, however, you are probably aware that when you focus on negative things, you see more negative things. It is a downward spiral. Complaint-ridden communication is only an exercise in encouraging depression.

- You may be copying others' ways of communicating because you have grown up on social scripting, direct teaching about how to "be in sync with" (copy) those around you.

WHY GO COMPLAINT FREE?

- As a logical person you have more to lose. When you focus on something, you focus on it with a laser blast of intensity. When others focus on negativity they get a little more negativity, but when you focus on negativity and you get a massive blast of negativity, frustration, depression, pain, obsession, and overall choking of the soul. It affects you more than it does others, both to hear the complaints and to say the complaints. It is hard to eradicate obsessive thoughts. Recognize that complaints are more potent for you and avoid them as much as you can.

- People generally like positive (non-complaining) people better. It is hard enough to make friends. Positive (non-complaining) people have an easier time making friends.

- It is easier for you to be complaint free. Yes, the consequences are more intense (first point in this list) but the actual transition to positivity is easier. Take the Switch quiz below. It will test your level of negativity while giving you the guidelines on how to switch.

Switch quiz

1. How often do you complain during the average day?

    a. rarely, maybe once or twice

    b. often, probably five to ten times

    c. frequently, ten or more times in one day

2. Are the repeated complaints useful? Do they get you what you want?

    a. rarely

    b. sometimes

    c. frequently

3. Does complaining feel good to you?

    a. no

    b. maybe

    c. yes

4. Would you lose anything you cared about if you were to stop complaining regularly?

    a. no

    b. maybe

    c. yes

5. Do you enjoy being around people who complain?

    a. no

    b. maybe

    c. yes

If you answered A on all questions, congratulations, you are a generally happy person. You may need to work with your partner on stopping complaints, but you, yourself are in a good position with a healthy level of looking on the bright side. If you answered mostly Bs, you are borderline between the two. If you answered mostly Cs, training yourself to not complain will bring a noticeable change for the better in your relationship.

This test can also determine the health of your relationship. For example, Question 2 asks: "Are the repeated complaints useful? Do they get you what you want?" In a dysfunctional relationship, complaints may be the main form of communication. Partners in a bad relationship will not hear each other unless requests are made at the level of loud complaint.

Complaints train behavior

Think of a child playing in her room before dinner. The parent calls out, "Dinner's ready!" The child ignores the parent until the third or fourth call, and usually by that time it is not a gentle, "Dinner's ready," but a, "Get down here now!" Why would anyone in their right mind live in a situation where only the most ugly format is the effective one?

Here is where your logical mind comes into play. You can take a step back and see the ludicrous, life-wasting pattern. People with autism, the geek gene, can often see patterns. There is a definite pattern in the yell-to-hear approach.

Before we vilify the child who is belligerently ignoring her parent's request, consider it from both angles. Perhaps the child has already tried coming down to dinner after the first call only to find that dinner was not actually ready and if she got there "early" she was given more chores: "Set the table," "Help me dish up the food," "Wash a few dishes," or worse, just be ignored and stand there bored while parents did not realize that they had been insincere in their "dinner's ready" request. This child would learn that tone of voice and what level of anger would truly mean "dinner's ready."

I happened to be blessed with wonderfully logical children. A false "Dinner's ready!" did not work at all and it took only one or two angry dinners to make us want to skip dinner altogether for a week or two. Thankfully this did not last long as I figured out what was happening. Until I did, however, the kids would end up eating their dinner in front of their computers. I would graze while cleaning up the kitchen and my husband would be "working late" and get cold leftovers later or just skip dinner entirely.

One day, out of sheer sadness, I sat down alone while eating my dinner. I thought, "My children are good, kind children. I am a good, kind mother. Why isn't this working?" I thought about it from their point of view—truth is appreciated. So, I went to my children's room and asked them to give me their attention for a minute. It has been many years since we had this talk, but it went generally like this:

> You are good people. I am a good person. We love each other and we do not like anger in our home. I like eating my dinner with you. You probably don't like eating with me yet, but that's probably because you haven't seen how it can be fun. Our biggest problem right now is that we all come to dinner angry and I think I figured out why.
>
> I have been saying, "Dinner's ready!" when it's not. From now on I will be honest. I will call, "Please come and set the table," or "Please come and do the dishes," instead. If dinner is truly ready and you do not need to do any other tasks before sitting down to eat, then and only then will I call, "Dinner's ready!" You can trust me and I will try to earn and protect that trust.
>
> My favorite time with my family growing up was when we played games. I loved laughing with my brothers and parents. They were witty and fun, a lot like you are. When I am old, I want to be able to remember many happy dinners with you. I want to start having happy dinners now. Please pick up your plates and come down to the table. We will clean off the table, get out a game and have our first Honest Dinner.

That was one of the best, most awkward dinners we ever had. The kids were incredulous, but their eyes and ears were open. I remember one of them looking at me out of the corner of his eye as we were cleaning off the table as if he was thinking, "Is this for real or is she going to ask us to do a dozen chores as soon as we let our guard down?" They gave it a try, however, and were open to the possibility that we might be able to have a logical, truth-based meal together.

That was the foundation on which we built our family dinners. We still go through phases when we do not have family dinners for a long stretch. Lately it has been because we are traveling extensively and are rarely ever all at home at the same time. At other times we have skipped the family dinner due to a new computer game being out. The most common reason for skipping the family dinner is because one or more of us is going through an intense experience (kids starting a new school year, one of us having a hard time at work) and not having a family dinner is a way to create more quiet, private, protective, and healing space for each other.

Back to Question 2 on the quiz. Repeated complaints can be part of a pattern of communication that is dysfunctional but effective. You may have patterns of communication that are hurtful, but are the only way that the other person can hear you. I will share a personal solution that is painful, but will hopefully be as useful to you as it has been to us.

At one point during our relationship, many years ago, I noticed that my husband only heard me when I yelled. I hated yelling. I hated yelling more than I hated anything. Yelling makes a person ugly, cold, and hard. Yet, when I spoke gently he did not hear me. When I yelled, things got done.

We went to see a counselor and in talking with the counselor, the situation became clear to both of us. When I yelled, I got results; when I was quiet, he did not hear me.

At that point we both had a choice: I could yell and stay in the relationship or I could not yell and have no relationship. I made the decision that yelling and anger would no longer be part of my life. I chose peace over my partner. If it had to be one or the other, I'd choose peace. I began grieving for the loss of my partner.

That left him with a similar set of choices: he could stay as is and lose his wife and children or he could figure out how to hear the non-yelling, regular voice communication.

He chose the latter. He wanted to figure out how to hear me. It was not the typical communication counseling and we were lucky to have a counselor who, while she was not a counselor specifically for autism, she did her homework and modified her approach to fit the particular dynamic of our relationship. As the counseling was infrequent the bulk of the work happened at home.

At home, we figured out the OT aspect: how to awaken his senses so that the ears were "turned on." We also figured out the environmental aspects: what needed to be in place for him to hear me and under what conditions it was useless for either me or him to try. Through trial and error we slowly transitioned.

During the time we were adjusting to the new dynamic, our relationship nearly fell apart. I would not speak loudly (yell) enough for him to hear me and he could not hear what he had previously relied on, my guidance on how to interact with the kids and participate at home. He was flying blind and I was on mute.

It was not just a distracted brain. It was not just the typical autistic inability to hear people call their name. It was not just the need for high affect. It was not just a low tendency to hear other people. It was all of them combined and more. I did (and still do) have great respect for what he went through to learn how to hear.

I am thrilled that now, after years of work, my husband can hear my voice whisper in crowded room full of dozens of people talking. I am so grateful that my partner, the love of my life, has attuned to me as I have attuned to him in a respectful, healthy way.

Super-abilities or scars?

This is one of the benefits of the logical, autism, geek brain. New tasks can be learned (not always, but it cannot hurt to try). If you do manage to master an ability through hard work, self-awareness and persistent effort, that new ability can become a super-ability.

> *Judge not*
> *JUDGE not; the workings of his brain*
> *And of his heart thou canst not see;*
> *What looks to thy dim eyes a stain,*
> *In God's pure light may only be*
> *A scar, brought from some well-won field,*
> *Where thou wouldst only faint and yield.*
>
> *...*
>
> *The fall thou darest to despise—*
> *May be the angel's slackened hand*
> *Has suffered it, that he may rise*
> *And take a firmer, surer stand;*
> *Or, trusting less to earthly things,*
> *May henceforth learn to use his wings.*
>
> (A. A. Proctor 1880)

These powerful verses run through my mind when I see the contrast between someone who has never had to consciously learn social skills with someone who had to learn the hard way.

Complaining can feel good, but it is still bad

Question 3 of the Switch quiz above asks, "Does complaining feel good to you?" The following is a mental image to illustrate this:

> Complaining is the junk food of communication. Fatty french fries may taste good from time to time, but eat them for breakfast, lunch and dinner and before you know it you will no longer feel comfortable in your own body.

There is nothing deep or mysterious about why complaints feel good—they probably give a good, temporary feel-good moment to most people, but then, like the fries, complaints leave a bad taste in the mouth, and a lingering sense of shame.

What would happen if you stopped complaining?

Question 4 of the Switch quiz asks, "Would you lose anything you cared about if you were to stop complaining regularly?" This is a revealing and thought-provoking question. It is common for people to do things without understanding them. Fortunately in a logical brain, it is easier to uncover (or resist in the first place) things that are illogical or wasteful.

If you or your partner has a habit of complaining, spend a few minutes trying to visualize what life would be like without complaints. If your relationship was based on complaints, with both of you complaining about work or other topics, then you may find you suddenly have very little to talk about.

Your happiness

The final question, Question 5, "Do you enjoy being around people who complain?" is pivotal. There is a chance that you simply have a sarcastic, biting sense of humor. For a person who has a sarcastic temperament, complaints can be a form of verbal jousting. For example, Person 1 may say, "It's *only* 7,408 miles from San Francisco to Sydney." Person 2 may respond with sarcasm by saying, "Now *that's* a useful fact!" Person 1 is sarcastic by saying 7,000+ miles is a short distance. Person 2 is sarcastic by commenting on the usefulness/ uselessness of the fact. Part of sarcasm is stating the opposite of what is true. Sarcasm is a particularly difficult form of communication for people with autism to grasp. If you are a partner or friend of someone with autism, then using biting sarcasm is cruel.

There are many benefits to purposefully stopping complaints, but it is important to note that there will be many times when a negative comment is necessary. If a car nearly hits you as you cross the street, it is ok to feel angry and negative.

Anger
Anger in its time and place
May assume a kind of grace.
It must have some reason in it,
And not last beyond a minute.

(Lamb and Lamb 2007, p.55)

When our family was trying to reduce negativity in the home, I printed out the verse above and taped it to the wall. Within weeks, all of us were expressing ourselves better and complaints had dropped to nearly none.

Stopping the complaints

It is hard to change patterns of behavior and many of us are not even aware of the complaints we say. To test how often you complain, wear a "complaint bracelet," any type of bracelet that you can switch easily from hand to hand. Even a piece of string works well as long as you can slip it on and off. If sensory issues get in the way of you doing a complaint bracelet you can also move an object from one pocket to another. The only qualification is that it has to be a physical act that you do every time you complain.

For me, it is a chain-mail bracelet, Renaissance style that my son made for me out of chain-mail rings. I began the process of "de-complaining" my life many years ago when I was at a low point. I checked out the audiobook *A Complaint Free World* by Will Bowen (2007). While I did not agree with the religious context of the book, I did whole-heartedly agree with how important it is to stop the complaints and the author had a proven, effective method for getting it done.

I listened to the audiobook on my way home from the library. The author explained the bracelet concept and I thought, "Ok, here it goes. As soon as I think a complaint I will switch my bracelet."

My very next thought was a complaint, "Sheesh, I hate it when I'm late." I switched my bracelet but before I could get it on to the other hand, another complaint came flooding, "I can't hear the CD if I'm paying attention to my thoughts." I turned the CD off but it did not help.

The drive home was slow. I pulled over many times to switch, switch, switch. It was ridiculous, a stream of complaints to which I had become accustomed, but it became extremely clear what was happening in my head. The first non-negative thought was the "ah-ha" moment when I realized that I had found the solution which I had been looking for. I had been sad and depressed in part because I had a constant stream of negativity going through my head. No wonder things had been difficult!

I kept the bracelet on for the next year and still wear it occasionally. It took approximately three months before I could wear the bracelet all day without having to switch it. Everyone around me noticed the change. One friend said, "It's like a light came on in your face." Since I am accustomed to living with people who interpret things literally, this phrase was particularly funny to me.

For someone who may be prone to OCD, the bracelet switching may not work for you. You may feel a compulsive need to switch the bracelet. You may end up complaining simply for an excuse to move the bracelet.

Several non-bracelet options are to:

- pinch yourself every time you complain

- keep a notepad with tallies: every day try to beat the score of the day before

- put a coin in a jar for every complaint: this one gives a powerful visual image of what the complaints are costing you in lost relationships, lost time, and lost value.

Summary/Maintenance

Many marriages have ended because the toxic complaints were allowed to flow freely like dirty oil on a white couch. Stopping the complaints may make the difference between keeping your marriage together or dissolving your ties to each other.

PART 5

WHEN TROUBLESHOOTING DOES (OR DOES NOT) WORK

CHAPTER 23

Rebooting

When you reboot a computer, either intentionally or unintentionally, it clears any pending errors or events. Rebooting brings a system back to normal condition usually in a controlled manner. Typically it is usually done in response to an error in processing. A reboot also occurs when it is impossible or undesirable for a process to proceed and all error recovery mechanisms fail.

Rebooting works for a relationship by similarly clearing out errors: physically, mentally, and behaviorally.

Rebooting is a problem-solving technique rather than a specific area of difficulty so we will be discussing rebooting in a what, when, where, why, and how format.

What?

Rebooting is a process whereby you turn off the computer either completely (a hard reboot) or partially (a soft reboot). Rebooting stops ongoing processes, allowing the computer to begin again, restarting processes in a "clean" order.

Couples in nearly every modern culture are already rebooting, just using different words to describe it. You may hear people describe this process as:

- "renewing vows"
- "celebrating an anniversary"
- "having a weekend get-away"
- "taking time to rekindle the fire."

If, however, you have a frame of reference that aligns with the spectrum, these processes may not work because:

- a "vow" is a reciprocal promise and reciprocal interactions are difficult

- "celebrating" often means socially-overloading parties

- a "get-away" means being away from beloved routines, causing the opposite of the desired result

- "rekindling the fire" is a metaphor. Fire? What fire?

Sometimes all we need is new language to help us see how a mainstream concept is simply a misunderstanding of the much-needed equivalent for people with autism. In the highly logical brain the term "rebooting" may make more sense than any of the other common terms.

In some ways rebooting is more effective than the common mainstream ways:

- People with autism typically are loyal on a level more exacting and precise than the word "vow" indicates.

- "Celebrating" is time-consuming and often unproductive; skipping it may actually improve your quality of life.

- "Get-aways" often do not achieve the happiness of the couple long-term. In fact, get-aways can often be negative points in a couple's history, "Remember that time we went to Tahoe and fought the entire time?"

- "Rekindling" is a returning to a previous way of interacting, usually an attempt to return to "the way things used to be," but trying to hold on to old patterns of behavior in new environments (perhaps the birth of kids or a change in housing) does not work. The only way to return to the past is in one's memory.

In contrast, rebooting is a process that allows the partner to incorporate "updates" in his or her core self and in the relationship. When you install a new program (or under several other circumstances) the computer will prompt you to restart before you start using the new program. It may also prompt you to restart after bug fixes and/or security fixes.

We need to do the same in relationships. When new software is installed (one of you takes a new job, a new child is born), reboot, making sure that you do not carry old, now dysfunctional processes into the new relationship.

When?

There are several big clues that a reboot is needed whenever:

- you see problems that seem to have no other answer
- a major life event happens
- you notice things around you are "wrong"
- you get too many "bug reports" (complaints) from your partner
- someone you trust says, "You need a break/vacation/nap."

Where?

There are various articles and books discussing how NTs can reboot their lives to be more authentic, but an NT's way of rebooting will probably look very different from the rebooting of a person with autism.

The go-to location for rebooting with your partner is out to dinner, or perhaps dinner and the movies. For relationships that take autism into account, the reboot may be different, based on certain sensory needs:

- Stay at home for three days straight. Stock up ahead of time to make sure that you have everything you need.
- Go to a secluded hotel.
- Disappear into a project/computer game/something that jolts you mentally out of your everyday life.
- Take an hour or a full day to mentally step back from your life and reset the rules.
- Go to a museum and walk silently through the entire museum.

Rebooting can occur anywhere, anytime, so do not use the excuse that, "We don't have the money/time to take a vacation so we can't reboot." Even just closing your eyes can be a short rebooting. In fact you do it every night by sleeping. It is how our bodies physically reboot every night. If we do not reboot at night with sleep, our body will force itself to sleep through micro-sleeps which last from fractions of a second to 30 seconds.

For the "where" of a relationship reboot, the possibilities are endless. Find what works for you, specifically for *you*. If you reboot best by removing yourself from your normal environment:

- have date nights (short)

- take small weekend trips (medium)

- do significant vacations on your own (long).

Since a love of routine comes with the territory, a change in daily schedule or a change in routine may actually be unwelcome.

If this is the case, do not change the physical environment, change the behavioral environment. Change what you do for:

- an hour (short)

- a day (medium)

- a week or more (long).

Take your vacation days from work at the same time as your partner. Stay home together, but do, "what I wish I could do with my time."

If both a physical and behavioral reboot do not work, then do a "To Each His Own" break. Do what you want to do, but do it separately.

If you do individualized reboots, one of you can do a physical reboot (travel) and one can do a behavioral reboot (home), or any variation of what each of you needs specifically. While our kids were young, this was the solution that worked for us. I would travel, even if it was just camping, and he would stay home. It worked.

Why?

The standard answer goes something like this: to keep your computer in good working order, you need to do system software updates occasionally. These updates make changes to core operating system files, and that cannot be done while the operating system itself is in use without having an impact on the stability of the programs that are already running. Rebooting lets the changes be made in a safe way. It also lets system security monitor changes to system files to ensure that unauthorized changes are not made.

In relationships we reboot to wipe out old rules that are no longer useful and that could easily cause glitches. For example, when a new baby is born, your previous rule of "sleep in on Saturday" will not work. You need to update to the next version, the next phase of your life. If you do not reboot your behavior, you may be frustrated, wondering why your partner used to enjoy sleeping in with you, but now sleeping in is not appreciated anymore. You may have crashes (arguments) with your partner simply because you have not reset the rules in your mind.

To live happily as a couple, reset the rule from:

"Sleep in on Saturday so that my partner feels closer to me," to

"Wake up when baby does so that my partner feels close to me."

If you do not reboot, you end up using old rules that no longer apply in a new environment. You end up with glitches (misunderstandings) and crashes (arguments).

For a deeper understanding, let's dissect the first paragraph of "Why?":

- "To keep your computer in good working order, you need to do system software updates occasionally."

  To keep your relationship smooth, you need to make adjustments occasionally.

- "These updates make changes to core operating system files…"

  Updates adjust the "rules" of the relationship.

- "…and that cannot be done while the operating system itself is in use without having an impact on the stability of the programs that are already running."

  These updates cannot be done during a typical day. If you try to do these core changes while all the regular activities are going on, you risk upsetting the stability of your relationship.

- "Rebooting lets the changes be made in a safe way."

  Rebooting, stepping away from the regular activities of everyday, is the safest, easiest, and most reliable way to adjust as your relationship adjusts naturally with time.

- "It also lets system security monitor changes to system files to ensure that unauthorized changes aren't made."

  It protects you and your partner against outside impact such as affairs or other invasions into your relationship.

The last portion of the concept—protecting your relationship against "unauthorized changes"—is possibly the most important. If you are the loyal partner, this information is good to know. If you are a partner who is missing the loyalty gene (perhaps due to insufficient vasopressin secreted from the hypothalamus) Chapter 16, "Troubleshooting Monogamy and Faithfulness" is a crucial chapter to read since it highlights the logic of being faithful to one partner.

How?

There are so many ways to reboot that this section alone could be an entire book. Here are only a few quick ideas, grouped by length of time needed.

SHORT

- A verbal cue such as simply saying, "Reboot!" and your partner will recognize that you both need to adjust your behavior.

- A visual cue such as making the "time out" sign with your hands.

- A physical cue such as the hug my husband gives me when both of us need to reset on the concept of "He loves me; I love him."

MEDIUM

- Set aside time when both of you can think clearly and schedule either a get-away or a get-in (a staying-at-home vacation).

- When rebooting at home, prepare for it ahead of time by defining what is acceptable during that time and what is not. If you take vacation time from work to reboot at home but end up checking in at work and then working half the day, that is not a reboot. Define parameters ahead of time.

When rebooting away from home, make sure that you do not bring too much of home with you. Bring only those things with you that you think will improve the relationship: a Kama Sutra book, a special fuzzy blanket, or an extra soft pillow which you love.

LONG

- A Sabbatical, anywhere from three months to one year, either on your own or as a couple.

- A work assignment. If there is a possibility of working at a different site for a week or longer, and you both need a reboot, then use it as a free way to get a good, solid reboot for your relationship.

- Perhaps the holidays can provide a successful reboot. For many of our holidays, one of us would take the kids to visit their grandparents while the other was "on a deadline at work." That "deadline" was actually one of us rebooting, staying home, doing the things we needed to do to reboot fully. We saved ourselves endless difficulty by being flexible about how we handled the holidays.

There are three types of reboot: a hard reboot, soft reboot, and random reboot.

Hard reboot

To do a hard reboot, the power to the system is physically turned off then turned back on. In a relationship, a hard reboot would be one partner ceasing communication or physically walking out of the door; all system functioning is shut down. Since the operating system does not have the opportunity to perform any shutdown procedures, data loss or corruption may occur.

When a computer starts again after a hard boot the filesystem may be in a corrupted state, requiring an integrity check: "Checking file 1 of 72." In a relationship, there is significant time spent during this process. It is the period when you re-establish the rules of the relationship.

In a worst case scenario, corruption may affect files that are required for the operating system to start, thereby preventing it from booting again (the result for the relationship would be divorce or permanent separation).

A hard reboot may be caused by power failure, by accident, or deliberately as a last resort to reset an unresponsive system. In a relationship where one or both partners has autism, a hard reboot can occur for any number of reasons, including when:

- social cues are misread

- sensory issues interfere with physical closeness

- reciprocity is needed by one partner, but not given by the other

- mindblindness causes misunderstandings.

For people with autism, a hard reboot can erase some of the inequality by taking both partners back to the starting point of the relationship. The drawback is that a hard reboot may be too severe a change in routine for someone with autism. For a person without autism, the "emotional baggage" may make a hard reboot difficult.

A hard reboot happens when the system crashes (a big fight) or when power interrupted (an external event such as a death in the family). A hard reboot is not planned and is harder to recover from than a soft reboot.

Soft reboot

A soft reboot involves restarting a computer "normally" under software control: pressing the power button or selecting Shut Down without suddenly removing power or otherwise triggering a hardware-based reset as in a hard reboot. A soft reboot means that you have restarted the machine by doing an orderly Shut Down or Restart. In a soft reboot, you are safely flushing any cached write operations to persistent storage. This means that the information in "short-term memory" is flushed, erased, removed, or cleansed.

A soft reboot in a relationship might be:

- Seeing a counselor or therapist who is familiar with autism.

- Reading a book on autism, such as this one, then using those ideas to change how you interact in your relationship.

- A simple realization that a certain process needs to be stopped and another process implemented. For example, you may discover that your partner needs something different sexually. Change the behavior and reset how you interact during your intimate moments together.

- A short 10–15 minute time to yourself to think, meditate, or, as Temple Grandin did with the "hug box," find a type of sensory feedback that calms your body and mind.

- A planned trip, whether for time away from each other or for time together.

A soft reboot preserves the integrity of the system and prevents data loss or corruption (general problems). In a relationship, the soft reboot protects against having troubles post-start up.

In order to protect the relationship, prepare for the reboot the same way you press the Power button and allow the computer to prepare itself for the process. An example of a relationship soft reboot:

> One partner to the other: "I really need some time on my own for a bit. I will be back in two hours. I love you."

We developed a 1, 2, 3 process when we were having too many hard reboots, causing problems on top of problems. We agreed that every reboot would include the following three components:

1. State what you are doing. Saying, "I need time," is very different from stomping out (hard reboot). Without stating what you are doing, your partner may make inaccurate assumptions such as, "He is leaving me!" or "He misinterpreted what I said and I need to get him back for a long conversation so that I can clarify." If you were very angry or shut down, perhaps your partner will assume that you may not be safe being out on your own. Be clear. State what you are doing.

2. State the parameters of your leaving; give clearly defined limits to what you will be doing. Maybe your partner needs to know where you will be: "I will be the library," or "I will be walking along the marina." Maybe your partner needs to know what you will be doing: "I will be thinking," or "I will be exercising." For us, I need to know how long he will be gone: "I will be gone two hours." If you have children, this will probably be your desired information so that you can answer the kids when they ask, "When will Dad be back?"

3. State that your relationship is not at risk. The act of powering down, rebooting, may leaving your partner feeling abandoned or rejected. Give a simple statement of, "I love you," or "We're ok," or "Nothing is changing; I just need a little time."

A soft reboot is the most effective way to preserve the strength and integrity of your relationship.

Random reboot

Random reboot is a non-technical term referring to an unintended (and often undesired) reboot following a system crash. The cause of the crash may not be evident (or even discoverable) to the user.

If you are having an argument with your partner and you are completely baffled by what he or she is saying, there is a good chance that you are in the process of a system crash. In common lingo, you have blue-screened, referring to the blue error screen that is shown when a non-Mac or non-Linux computer crashes. This error screen is also known as "the blue screen of death."

If you are baffled by what is happening in an interaction, tell your partner that you have blue-screened and ask for a reboot. For example:

Him: "I have no idea what you are talking about. Reboot?"

In response I usually continue to ramble for a few seconds before the reboot request sinks in, then I pause, dumbfounded, and then I reboot:

Me: "Well, I love you and was just asking if you loved me back." Whatever problem we were discussing—mowing the lawn, caring for the kids, picking up his clothes—was a sign of love which I needed to see.

Him: "Ah! Ok."

The previous example is a very simple random reboot. A more serious random reboot could be due to life-long difficulties, larger misunderstandings, physiological reactions to external input. In all random reboots, you may not be able to determine what caused the problem in the first place.

The micro-restart for conversations

A restart is shutting down a single program in order to restart the program, the hope being that by resetting the program any problems will be eliminated. A restart in a relationship is a way of starting a conversation from the beginning, checking the initial "settings" or assumptions behind the conversation. A restart is a simple set of actions.

Partner A thinks, "It sounds like she sees me as a big, mean monster, but that can't be right. Restart."

Partner A asks, "Do you really think I'm that bad?"

Partner B says, "No! I think _____."

The misunderstanding of a person's character, motivation, and intent are reset to default. The default should be: you are a good person who wants the best for both of us.

A micro-restart is an even shorter resetting of assumptions. If you do not understand what your partner is saying, a micro-restart may be similar to this:

Partner A thinks, "She's upset about how I care for the kids and nothing I've said or done is helping. Restart."

Partner A asks, "Are you upset about how I care for the kids?"

Partner B says, "Yes!" and clarifies or, "No!" and clarifies. For us, it is usually "No!" followed by a clarification that resets the interaction to default settings.

A micro-restart deals with a specific instance or situation. A restart deals with an overall belief. A restart differs from a reboot in that a reboot is a full shut down of the relationship whereas a restart is a simple resetting to default during a conversation or interaction.

Summary/Maintenance

A computer's reboot function is an important aspect of the system's design. The ability to reboot your relationship is equally crucial.

Many everyday electronics are able to reboot/reset/restart: television, audio equipment or the electronics of a car, portable media players, and many others. Some, particularly cell phones and computers, are prone to freezing or locking up. The lack of a proper reboot ability could otherwise possibly render the device useless after a power loss or malfunction. This is called "bricking" the device since the phone (or other device) becomes as useless as a brick when all functionality stops.

System administrators, techies, or probably you, will reboot computers as a technique to work around bugs in software, such as memory leaks or to stop processes that hog resources to the detriment of the overall system, or to terminate malware. While this approach does not address the root cause of the issue, resetting a system back to a good, known default state may allow it to be used again for some period until the issue next occurs. The other sections of this book deal with "addressing the issues" while this section will have shown you how to return to baseline when things go wrong.

CHAPTER 24

When Troubleshooting Does Not Work

OTHER PROBLEM-SOLVING METHODOLOGIES

This chapter contains a full range of methods above and beyond the standard ITE troubleshooting method primarily used in this book so far. Perhaps some of these methods may be a better fit for you and your partner or perhaps a better fit for certain circumstances.

Methods for solving problems

1. Abstraction
2. Analogy
3. Backward chaining
4. Brainstorming
5. Cause and effect
6. Diagrammatic reasoning
7. Divide and conquer
8. Eliminate possibilities
9. Generalizations
10. Guess and check
11. Hypothesis testing
12. Lateral thinking

13 Means-end analysis

14 Morphological analysis

15 Proof

16 Reduction

17 Research

18 Role play

19 Root cause analysis

20 Seek the source

21 Subdivide

22 Trial and error

23 Use symmetry

METHOD 1: ABSTRACTION

Abstraction is solving the problem in a model of the system before applying the solution.

Abstraction is the opposite of role play. In role play you act as if you are someone else in order to understand the other person's point of view. In abstraction you act as yourself while someone else acts as your partner.

For abstraction, you act out the problem in order to script solutions. For example, if you are having a hard time communicating to your partner that tickling is not allowed and never will be allowed, find a friend who can stand in for your partner, preferably someone who knows how your partner thinks and feels.

A sample script might read as follows:

You: *"Jon, I need you to know that tickling is not allowed and never will be allowed with me."*

Jon: *"But you're so cute when you're mad."*

You: *"I don't know what to say to that."*

Jon: *"Try saying, 'Thank you for the compliment, but this is a rule and there are consequences,' then outline consequences."*

You: *"Ok, let's start over."*

Note that during the discussion with your partner, these helpful tips will probably not be part of the conversation. This valuable information comes *in the abstraction interaction only*, where the person acting as your partner can give insights that your partner may not realize.

As you work through the problem in a "model of the system" you will work through issues before talking to your partner. This gives you the chance to deal with the problems methodically, increasing your chances of success when you have the conversation with your partner.

METHOD 2: ANALOGY

Analogy entails using a similar previous situation to solve the current problem.

This technique is very useful if your partner is feeling defensive, hurt, or has a tender ego. Think of a time:

- when things were particularly good in your relationship
- when your partner did something particularly brilliant
- when your partner showed exceptionally good problem-solving skills.

Use that information to help solve your current problem. Imagine that your partner is gaining weight. Perhaps he or she has little control over how much he or she eats, but has exceptionally good control over how much money he or she spends. Therefore, you might say, "You are so good at keeping our finances in great shape. You have excellent self-control. That is a really rare and wonderful thing. I am worried that maybe your body could use similar attention. Can you try using the same self-control with your food intake and exercise that you do with our finances?"

A strong, sincere compliment, especially when it refers back to a specific concrete event, can often cushion difficult issues. For the previous example, you could also add, "Remember that time you wanted _____ but you resisted getting it until we had the money in the bank to pay for it? That was amazing self-control."

METHOD 3: BACKWARD CHAINING

Backward chaining is when you start with the end goal in mind, and work backwards towards the nexus of the problem.

Backward chaining is a go-to method for any situation where you have a clear vision of what you want. Imagine that you are frustrated with your finances.

Starting point: Recognize that you are not happy with your financial situation. Identify that you want to be financially secure.

Chain back 1: Define what financial security is for you. Perhaps it is, "No debt, $x in the bank for emergencies, and $x invested in my retirement account."

Chain back 2: Research how people work towards this type of financial situation. Research: "How do I get rid of debt, save emergency funds, and invest in retirement?"

Chain back 3: Implement these strategies in your own life.

The backward chaining technique is also valuable for arguments that happen repeatedly and many other types of situations.

METHOD 4: BRAINSTORMING

Brainstorming involves visualizing many different ideas that could be potential solutions, then reviewing the ideas until an optimal solution is found.

Imagine that you are having a hard time with getting meals prepared each night and the dishes cleaned up. Say to your partner: "I would be so much more relaxed if we had better solutions for preparing our evening meals and cleaning up afterwards. Can we brainstorm together for ways to make that part of our evenings more enjoyable?"

If the issue is sensitive, such a sexual performance issue, you may wish to brainstorm with a trusted friend or medical professional first. A mental health professional is particularly good at brainstorming.

Brainstorming is a powerful activity especially if you approach the problem both logically and imaginatively. If possible, create an environment of safety where your partner feels free to suggest any option no matter how oddball. This sense of freedom and safety keeps the flow of great ideas coming. For example, if one of you wants to have sex more often, ideas such as, "Put it on the calendar," and "Do it whether you want to or not," might be the ultimate solutions you are seeking. Mentioning these ideas within a brainstorming environment is ok; mentioning them without the clarification that you are brainstorming may easily make the suggestion appear inappropriate and perhaps offensive. So, remember that brainstorming is just that—brainstorming—and the ideas that are suggested do not need to be implemented, they are only ideas.

The biggest benefit of brainstorming is that it brings unusual suggestions to the surface. Sometimes it is the odd, creative, wouldn't-have-thought-of-it-otherwise suggestions that end up solving the toughest problems.

METHOD 5: CAUSE AND EFFECT

Identifying the problem as an effect allows you to trace back to the cause and thus eliminate the problem.

A few common examples of cause and effect in a partnership include:

You spend more time than usual with your partner → Your partner pulls away

You haven't been home much lately → Your partner overspends

You have been preoccupied with a new project → Your partner is not sexually interested for long periods of time

The problems will present themselves as the "effect" and will give you little clue to any potential solutions. It is only the cause that leads to solutions. In the second example above, if all you know is that your partner is overspending, you may try to fix the problem in ineffective ways. Ironically, if your partner is overspending, you may react by working harder, taking a second job or staying later at the office for a bigger bonus. If you have not looked for the cause of the overspending, you could just make the problem worse.

Cause and effect problem-solving is a simple, stripped-down way of looking at problems. It many situations, especially the simple situations, cause and effect helps keep things simple.

METHOD 6: DIAGRAMMATIC REASONING

Diagrammatic reasoning means drawing a picture of the problem to see if it leads to a creative solution.

Many people with autism have strong visual abilities. If you or your partner happens to be visually oriented, this technique may solve many problems.

Before we tried this method of problem-solving, I noticed that we often had the same problem over and over again—I would ask Carl to help with something, but he would ignore me until I had asked many times and was quite upset.

His view: "She gets so angry over such little things."

My view: "I give him so many chances to hear me, but he never does pay attention until I am loud and angry."

One day I tried diagrammatic reasoning by drawing a cartoon of the problem on a scrap of paper. The cartoon is included in Chapter 8, "Troubleshooting Mindblindness: The Universe is Us."

When I showed the cartoon to Carl he laughed. The humorous nature of a cartoon helped him let down his guard long enough to recognize a familiar pattern. Once he was aware of the pattern, he was able to recognize, "Maybe my wife is giving me a chance to hear her and I'm just missing it?" Once he was open to the possibility, he was able to change his behavior.

METHOD 7: DIVIDE AND CONQUER

Divide and conquer entails splitting large, complex problems into smaller, solvable problems.

This technique is crucial to anyone with executive function weaknesses. Need to clean your desk? Impossible! Can you, however, throw away three things off the desk every day? Probably. Divide and conquer seems, at first, as if you are getting nowhere, but once you have a few successful divide-and-conquer experiences, you should be convinced of the power of tackling big problems in small steps.

Divide and conquer is particularly useful for couples with children. If taking the kids out to dinner is overwhelming, have just one parent go. If attending your child's springtime concert is sensory hell, have just one parent go. Eliminate the guilt by recognizing that everyone has limits and it is most important to take care of yourself so that you can function.

Divide and conquer works for everything from home chores, to communication, to sex. If your partner is good at compartmentalizing, maximize that skill by using it to break down larger problems into smaller, solvable bits.

METHOD 8: ELIMINATE POSSIBILITIES

Eliminating possibilities is the opposite of brainstorming: you can eliminate possible solutions to reveal the most likely solution(s).

Sometimes eliminating possibilities will give you clarity. If you are overwhelmed by a problem, go into elimination mode and identify the solutions that are least likely to work.

Imagine that you need a new car, but that there are too many choices. Make a list of cars you are considering then go down the list, eliminating those that will not work for one or both partners.

It is important to notify your partner when you are in eliminating possibilities mode. If your partner is not aware that this is what you are doing, you will appear argumentative.

To notify your partner that your goal is to eliminate the least likely options, you can say, "There are so many possibilities that I can't see straight. Let's eliminate the ones that won't work for either you or me and see what we have left."

METHOD 9: GENERALIZATIONS

Using generalizations allows you to take a solution that is successful in one area and use it across the breadth of your relationship.

Generalization is a large-scale way of making mass improvements to a relationship. Imagine that your partner has auditory issues. S/he is very sensitive to noises of all types. It became a huge problem when you were playing music on weekends, but you both addressed it and now you listen to your music on your headphones. Your weekends are now much more enjoyable.

After this one problem is solved, you notice your partner still seems agitated and annoyed most of the time you are together. You ask your partner if other noises are bothering him or her, but he or she may not be consciously aware of what is causing the irritation. So, try eliminating other noises. Only run the dishwasher, washing machine or other large, noisy appliances when your partner is not at home or in another room with headphones on. Switch all phone calls to your cell phone and put it on vibrate in your pocket. If it rings (vibrates) step outside to take the call. In a few days, take note of whether or not there has been an improvement.

Finding solutions that work in relationships is tricky, especially when unique sensory issues are brought to play. Once you find a solution for one problem, it is in your best interest to use that solution to benefit the rest of your relationship.

METHOD 10: GUESS AND CHECK

In this technique you make a random guess at how to solve the problem, then check to see if the problem is solved.

Since people with autism miss so many cues, they have far less information to use in any situation. When you do not have enough information, the guess and check method is probably your go-to way of interacting.

Here is a good example: your partner is angry with you and is not talking, not telling you what is wrong or how you can fix it. Without enough information, you have to take your best guess. You keep guessing until the problem is solved or one of you gives up.

If you offend your partner with one of your guesses, let him or her know that you are using the guess and check method because you do not have enough information to try a more sophisticated technique.

METHOD 11: HYPOTHESIS TESTING

Hypothesis testing means forming a theory for a possible explanation to the problem, and then trying to prove or disprove the theory.

You would start this type of problem-solving by asking your partner, "Hypothetically…" Imagine that you do not know how to approach your partner physically for an intimate encounter. Instead of trying a type of touch or move you have read about that supposedly will work, you can ask, "Hypothetically, if I reached down to kiss you on the neck, would that feel good to you?"

Your hypothesis is that kissing her neck would feel good to both of you. You float the idea (suggest it as a possibility) before doing something that might be a mistake.

Hypothesis testing works in many situations. Perhaps your partner is angry at you and you do not know why. Forming a hypothesis and simply asking if it is true helps to show your partner that you care. Note that you have to be careful not to offend. For example, if your girlfriend seems grumpy, do not ask, "Is it your period?" Alternately if your boyfriend is grumpy, do not ask, "Is it because you haven't had sex in a while?"

It may be a mystery to you why certain questions are offensive, so it helps to make a Never Ask list in your own personal journal. Your list will vary based on your culture. Some comments are offensive in some cultures, but not in others.

Offensive comments will be rare with hypothesis testing, but they are important to note that if your question is on the Never Ask list, the results of your hypothesis testing will be invalid.

If you are in a situation and are not sure if you are making the correct choice, try hypothesis testing. Floating a theory is a great way of gently improving your relationship.

METHOD 12: LATERAL THINKING

Lateral thinking entails approaching solutions indirectly and creatively.

For touchy situations, it is often helpful to approach the problem indirectly to see if your partner is able to handle talking about a certain subject.

Imagine that you have both arrived home from work and you do not want to interact in any way that evening. Perhaps you have had a tough day and need silence and time to yourself. As you cannot read facial expressions or body language, however, you have no way of knowing if this request will offend or has offended your partner.

Instead of saying, "I need time alone. Don't disturb me," say, "How was your day? How are you feeling?" If your partner sounds irritable, then spend a few minutes asking your partner about his or her day and telling your partner about yours. Once your partner hears that you are overloaded from a too-busy day, hopefully he or she will suggest that you take some time to relax on your own. If not, then you can ask more directly.

By asking indirectly you were able to avoid offending with a too-abrupt request/solution to a problem.

This also works with sexual issues, which are almost always delicate issues. Instead of, "That didn't feel good. Don't do that again." You can say, "That was an interesting move. I don't think I've felt that before. I didn't like it."

If you cannot think of what to say, consider that many issues are multi-faceted. If approaching from one direction does not work, you simply need to approach from a different direction until you find one that gets to the problem (and thus the solution).

METHOD 13: MEANS-END ANALYSIS

This technique means undertaking one small action at a time, evaluating whether or not the incremental steps get you closer to a solution.

If one or both of you does not enjoy problem-solving, you probably feel low motivation to fix the problem. When you engage in problem-solving you may encounter internal resistance on top of a naturally weak executive function, a double-whammy. Means-end analysis is a way of compensating for mental blocks that would otherwise inhibit a solution.

Means-end analysis is most appropriate for the big issues such as merging households, whether or not to have children, or how to handle a job-related move. Any massive task that needs to be broken down should use, at least in part, means-end analysis.

Means-end analysis is particularly powerful for people with autism who have a strong ability to compartmentalize. First, you break down the problem into smaller bits, then solve one bit at a time, compartmentalizing all other bits into the mental storage area of "Will Solve Soon."

Choose only one action per day. In the example of a house move: "Today we will agree on where each person puts his or her stuff in the bathroom. Tomorrow we will decide whether we will put our clothes in the same closet or find different closets/storage spaces for our clothes."

A few suggestions to make it more successful:

- You do not need to outline every step up-front. In fact, it may be too overwhelming to do so.

- If you do not have a comprehensive list of all steps, just attack the issues that are most obvious first.

- If you are having a hard time staying motivated, work on the parts that would give you the most pleasure first. If you are organizing the kitchen, organize the part where you make your breakfast every morning first, if that is the part that would make you happiest. It will help motivate you for the next task.

Colloquially this tactic is called, "eating an elephant one bite at a time," but some people may find that visual image unpleasant and potentially confusing. Instead, consider means-end analysis as:

- programming one line at a time

- painting one brush stroke at a time

- showering, washing one body part at a time

- reading one sentence at a time.

I like means-end analysis because it allows for progress to be made without overwhelming either person.

METHOD 14: MORPHOLOGICAL ANALYSIS
Morphological analysis means evaluating end results and interactions of an entire system over time.

Morphological analysis is the appropriate method for dealing with big problems such as, "Do we stay together as a couple or not?"

Evaluate results over a period of time. Are you generally happy or generally miserable together? Do you both help each other? Are your needs being met in some way by the person you are with? Do you enjoy meeting the needs of your partner/can you reciprocate in mutually acceptable ways?

Once you look at your relationship as a whole, you can put the current problem into perspective: is the current problem a small aspect of the overall relationship or is it a recurring difficulty overwhelming the bulk of the relationship? If you are on the spectrum, you can probably complete a morphological analysis easier than most people. The ability to review something logically is crucial to morphological analysis.

Morphological analysis also works for problems that are small but pervasive, such as, "Are we communicating effectively?" and "Do I get my way significantly more or significantly less often than my partner does?"

METHOD 15: PROOF

Start by trying to prove that the problem cannot be solved and the point where the proof fails will be the starting point for solving it.

I confess that I try the proof method too often. It is the pessimist's approach and perhaps the least fun method for your partner. That said, if one or both of you is a pessimist by nature or by habit, this method may prove particularly beneficial.

Imagine that you have been fighting recently. Proof problem-solving may sound like this: "We have been fighting far too much. It hurts and drains me. There is nothing we can do about it." The solution is in the sentence right before the, "nothing we can do about it," or similar phrase indicating that there is no solution.

The proof is: We fight + hurt x drain = no solution. The starting point for the solution is, "It hurts and drains me." At this point we can say, "As soon as I feel the hurt, I can stop and take a look around for exactly what is happening in that moment." Perhaps your realization will be something as simple as, "We are arguing about something ridiculous. We have both just got home from work. We are both tired."

At that point you can see the solution. If the problem is that you are tired, the solution is to rest. You can tell your partner, "We both need time to rest before joining up as a couple after work." Change your routine to involve a solitary 30 minutes of quiet alone time after work every day and you may find that your relationship improves. Find the concept that comes right before the "no solution" comment and you may find the core of the problem.

METHOD 16: REDUCTION

This means transforming the problem into another problem for which solutions exist.

Reduction is the quick fix for times when you have a must-solve problem, but do not have a lot of time to analyze it. You simply look at the current problem, relate it to a similar problem that you have already solved as a partnership and presto, you have a solution.

Imagine that your partner plays computer games on Friday nights when you really wish that you were going out, maybe to a restaurant or to the movies. By analyzing why your partner does not like going to the movies or does not like eating out may be too time-consuming. The reduction method may work for you both.

In this example, transform the Friday night problem into the Sunday morning solution. You found the Sunday morning solution when you mentioned to your partner that you really like to spend Sunday mornings going for walks in the countryside. Your partner said, "Sure," and you have been enjoying the mutual experience ever since.

Ask your partner if you can apply the same technique to Friday nights. Reassure your partner that you will not be asking to overtake his or her gaming schedule, just asking for a few scheduled times when you two can be together. It is probable that your partner will gladly agree to it, when framed within the context of, "We have already succeeded with _____, let's also succeed with _____."

Reduction technique is powerful because it defuses the problem, taking a new, unknown difficulty and transforming it into something solvable, similar to something you have already solved.

METHOD 17: RESEARCH

Explore ideas used by others and/or developed by professionals and adapt those ideas to your own situation.

The research technique is the one I use most. When there is a problem, search for answers online, read books on the topic, or otherwise research the topic. It is one of the hardest, most laborious methods of problem-solving so I suggest it hesitantly.

Unless material has been written specifically for people who have autism or work with those who have autism, the problem-solving suggestions could prove problematic or even have detrimental outcomes.

On a number of occasions my husband and I have tried suggestions from relationship books only to find ourselves in a worst shape a week later. I could fill another book, which wouldn't help anyone, with mainstream methods that *do not work*.

To use the research method, you need the ability to sift through a large amount of inappropriate material. Not much research has been done on adult relationships where one or both partners are autistic. If you are able to read the mainstream research, incorporate it into your particular relationship and revise the suggestions to fit your particular situation, great.

Imagine that you are both less-than-satisfied sexually. If you refer to mainstream relationship books, they may suggest talking it over, discussing what you like, exploring and experimenting, all of which could be disastrous and even scary for someone who is already venturing into the unknown by just being in the relationship in the first place.

In this case, a different problem-solving technique might lead you to a solution. Perhaps the reduction technique works better (see Method 16). You know that your partner is able to do certain things better when only one sensory system is activated: if he or she is speaking, then he or she is only speaking, not eating, folding laundry, or even giving eye contact. You use this same method in the bedroom, recognizing that during sexual contact your partner will be communicating only physically. You can switch from expecting words to instead "hearing" your partner's body language. If you allow him or her to channel all his or her senses into the one singular expression and allow all the others to switch off, perhaps you will see a more attentive partner.

METHOD 18: ROLE PLAY

Act as if you are another person in order to see a different point of view.

In role play, you assume the attitudes, actions, and communication patterns of someone else. You do this in a make-believe situation in an effort to understand a differing point of view or social interaction.

Role play can be effective for situations such as:

- one partner under-appreciating the other

- one partner doing the majority of housework, but wanting a more equitable division of labor.

For role play, typically you will role play as your partner and vice versa. It can be illuminating to see how your partner really feels about certain things.

Imagine that you are role playing a physical interaction:

Partner A: *"Now at this point I put my arm around you and pull you in close to me."*

Partner B: *(does what husband describes then explains)* *"At this point I start to feel claustrophobic because you are holding me too tight."*

It is likely that the revelations that occur during role play will help you both interact more thoughtfully and appropriately with each other, all of which leads to deeper love and greater intimacy.

If you find your partner cannot role play, do not be surprised and do not force it. Some people with autism are mindblind and are not wired to be able to do this.

METHOD 19: ROOT CAUSE ANALYSIS

Root cause analysis is done through the process of discovering, identifying, and then eliminating the cause of the problem.

This is my all-time favorite technique, annoyingly so. I love, with a passion, looking at root causes. Once I can see the root cause to a problem, the problem is pulled out of your relationship, hopefully to never re-appear.

I find it similar to gardening. If you see a weed, you pull up its entire root and it will be unlikely to ever re-infest your garden.

To pursue root cause analysis, look at your partner's actions and find what caused them originally: "My partner is misunderstanding me when I say _____." Instead of having the same miscommunication over and over again for the next 50 years of your life, find the cause of the miscommunication. Find it. Expose it. Remove it from your relationship.

Sometimes it is difficult to find the root cause. Your partner may be working off erroneous information received at the age of five from siblings, parents, or someone else. Your partner may be using information read in a magazine or seen on TV.

Find the core belief and identify it. For example, if your partner grew up with the ever-painful "look me in the eye" comment from adults in his life, he may have retained that message regardless of how many times you have said you do not care if he gives you eye contact. "Are you angry with me because you think I want you to look me in the eye but you don't want to?"

It is quite common for people to be unaware of the root cause of their problems day-to-day, but it is also common for people to be miserable in their adult lives. The purpose of this book, and others like it, is to eliminate pain. The goal is to increase the peace and happiness in your home.

Sometimes finding the root cause is easy to the point of being funny. My favorite example occurred one day when I was particularly grumpy. My husband thankfully took the root cause analysis approach and said, "I know you say that you are angry about a lot of things I'm doing wrong lately, but is there anything else that might be causing this anger in the first place?" After a minute I realized that I had been wearing a terribly uncomfortable pair of shoes. I had been expressing anger at everything else around me when all I really needed to do was slip off my shoes, relieving the grumpiness which allowed peace and happiness to flow back into our home.

METHOD 20: SEEK THE SOURCE

Identify the problem, then look at your own behavior for a potential solution, or possibly for an understanding of where the problem originated.

The only person you can control is yourself. If you see a problem in the relationship, flip it back on yourself to check to see if you were inadvertently the cause of the problem.

The problems we see in others are most likely problems in ourselves. In fact, those traits in others that most annoy us are often traits that we are most eager to repress or otherwise control in ourselves.

Since taking care of your own problems is much easier than trying to get someone else to fix his or her problems, it makes sense to work on your own problems first.

Two anecdotal examples of seeing the problem in your partner, then finding the solution in your own behavior are:

- Your partner is spending too much money. You recently purchased a new computer which your partner interpreted as a free license to make other non-necessary purchases.

- Your partner is no longer interested in you sexually and has been rebuffing your advances. Look at your own personal hygiene and how well you are taking care of your body. If you have stopped exercising, stopped brushing your teeth, or stopped getting your hair cut regularly, perhaps that is causing your partner to lose interest in you.

There will be times when you find that you were not the cause of the problem. If your partner had a bad day at work, or is experiencing health problems, there is little you can do from your end to solve the problem independently without your partner's cooperation.

There will also be plenty of times, however, when you find that you were the cause and you have the power to quickly and easily fix the problem. The only person you can fix is you.

METHOD 21: SUBDIVIDE

Divide the problem into smaller sub-problems and solve only one at a time.

This technique works well for problems that are mind-bogglingly large. Say your problem is: "We are too busy. It is causing sensory overload day after day." This problem is common in nearly all households with children.

To subdivide successfully, write the problem on a piece of paper without worrying about it being solvable or not. Then, brainstorm for all other problems related to that main problem.

Main problem: we are too busy.

- I have to drive the kids to karate after school nearly every day.

- I have to get up for work too early in the morning.

- I have a headache when I come home from work at night and there is nothing I can do about it. I have to just keep going.

- I never have a day to myself.

- I do not have a private place where no one will disturb me.

After you have a long list of the many sub-problems, attack only one. In the list above, you could attack the last one: "I don't have a private place where no one will disturb me." Choose a spot, even if it is just your bedroom and claim it as a sanctuary. If it is a spot that others need access to, then limit your time. Put a sign on the door indicating that you need the space uninterrupted for an amount of time.

I have a "Secret Writing Room" sign that I have taken with me from house to house. I have put it on closet doors, bedroom doors, all sorts of doors when I needed to have quiet, uninterrupted time with my laptop. It works.

Needing this visual, written indication of my own personal space was a sub-problem of a monstrously large overarching problem. If we had not subdivided the problem and attacked the bits one at a time, I doubt we would have solved the problem.

METHOD 22: TRIAL AND ERROR

By using trial and error test possible solutions until the right one is found.

Trial and error is the foundation of troubleshooting outlined throughout this book. It is the go-to solution for any problem that is plaguing you. If something is not working, try something different.

It is insane to do the same thing over and over again, not realizing that it does not work. The trial and error method is a simpler way of viewing the ITE method described throughout the book. I mention it here in case the concept of troubleshooting does not work for you, but the concept of trial and error does.

METHOD 23: USE SYMMETRY

To use symmetry entails recognizing that partners tend to balance each other.

When you see a problem in the relationship, check to see if you are counter-balancing the behavior. This is also called "enabling" in mainstream literature on relationships. In terms of highly logical people, Newton's Third Law of Motion makes much more sense: for every action there is an equal and opposite reaction.

A common scenario is where one partner (most likely the one with autism) is cold, distant, avoidant, passive, not engaged. The other partner (most likely the one without autism) becomes co-dependent, overly connected, needy, clingy. The co-dependence counter-balances the disconnected partner.

Summary/Maintenance

Even though this chapter contains more than 20 problem-solving strategies beyond the standard ITE troubleshooting methodology, there are many other problem-solving methods beyond the ones listed here. If you have tried all the problem-solving methods listed to no avail, please know that this book is not definitive. There may be other methods that will help you and your partner with whatever issues you face.

CHAPTER 25

Troubleshooting Whether to Stay or Go

THE DECISION PROCESS

The decision-making process for maintaining or severing a relationship may be quite different from the perspective of someone with autism as compared to the mainstream perspective. Some reasons for this may be:

- Loyalty is worth more to a person with autism.

- Emotional connection may be worth nothing.

- Physical and emotional safety may be worth more since it is harder for someone with autism to get and maintain safety with other adults. That relationship may be a rare and highly valuable part of the person's life.

- Severing a relationship may contain little to no emotional charge for a person with autism.

- A person with autism who also has sensory processing issues, may perceive a physical separation as an intense physical loss.

While we can make generalizations about how a person with autism will perceive the dissolution of a relationship, they are only generalizations. The perception is specific to each person and yours may not align with this list. For example, someone with sensory processing disorder may have next-to-no physical connection with his partner and may find the loss of physical intimacy a relief.

Weighing the decision accurately

In order to specify the details for yourself, as the person with autism, it helps to use one of the aspects of whom you are—your autism—to its best advantage. If you do not have autism, but your partner does, also use this method since it will put you in the same frame of reference which a person with autism will probably use naturally.

Make a Pro/Con chart to see the problem more clearly. Unlike most Pro/Con charts, however, for this one, give each line item "weight." For example:

Pro

My partner always remembers dates (birthdays) +10

My partner has nice eyes +3

My partner has a job +25

Con

My partner never knows what to do to celebrate a birthday -7

My partner always gives the same present -5

My partner does not take good care of his body -20

My partner does not support me in my job -5

In this example, if you were measuring the chart by how many line items were on each side, you might give too much importance to an item that is only a small issue while the larger issues are only a single line. By weighting each item, you can get a better view of what is truly important to you.

In this example, there are four cons and only three pros, so if counting only line items, you might deem the relationship as not working well. Yet, if you count up by weight, identifying how important each item is, you would find that the cons are -37 and the pros are +38 showing more clearly that the bad stuff is not as bad as you thought it was and perhaps the good stuff is quite important to you.

For example, your partner not supporting you in your job is only -5 since you are able to get support and encouragement from friends and you do not rely on your partner exclusively for emotional support. In contrast, it is extremely important to you that your partner has a good job since you saw one of your parents (or other role model) unemployed and equate unemployment with hardship, which is why you give your partner's employment a +25.

Weighting line items allows you to deal with large issues that might be inconceivably large otherwise. For example:

Pro

Rubs my back and gives me the physical input I need +10

Leaves me alone when I need my own space +17

Does my favorite activities with me +5

Is a good person whom I like to be near +10

Has many other attributes

Con

Had an affair -300 (or perhaps -300,000)

There are some people who rate an affair as unforgivable, an infinite weight that no other pro could out-weigh. There are others who see it as a human mistake and would weight it in the same range as other human "foibles." It is up to you to make that determination based on your own personal beliefs.

By weighting each line item, you get a clearer, more accurate picture of what you want in a relationship. It also allows you to put big issues into perspective.

Indecision

Once you have a clear picture of how well your relationship stacks up, you may be faced with a decision: should I stay or should I go? Indecision may be extremely painful, particularly for a person with autism who needs stability and routine. Just the thought of instability may cause the person with autism to not be able to think clearly.

Keep in mind that people without autism may actually enjoy indecision, seeing decisions as final and finality as lifeless. The illogical NT way of interacting with the world may be extremely difficult for a person with autism, ripping you in and out of indecision, leaving you with whiplash and permanent confusion. Make note of what each of you prefers: stability/finality or flexibility and adaptability.

Sharpening the saw

The next step in determining whether to stay or go rests in determining what you want for your own life. Remember that you are not trapped (and if you do feel too threatened to leave, that is a matter for the police).

In order to get this long-term view, you can do a "sharpen," a term generated from Abraham Lincoln's famous quote: "Give me six hours to chop down a tree and I will spend the first four *sharpening* the axe."

Since the issue you will be thinking about will probably be extremely difficult, prepare for the sharpen a week in advance. Do any of the following activities that are good for you:

- Prepare yourself physically. Take a hot shower and brush your whole body with a loofah pad if that is what helps your sensory system to "align."

- Dress in clothes that comfort you most.

- Exercise regularly for a week to improve blood flow and improve mental functioning.

- Cancel social engagements to reduce social stress and drain.

- Get to bed earlier at night, shutting off bright light sources such as your TV or laptop at least one hour before attempting sleep.

- Appeal to whatever sensory needs you may have—go and swing at a local playground, twirl in the air; jump on a trampoline; listen to heavy metal music; do activities that clear your mind.

- Organize your home; clean and sort so as to also tidy up your mental processes.

- Eat healthy foods that give you the most energy and clarity. If you react badly to gluten, dyes, or other additives in foods, avoid them with increased rigor for a week before your sharpen.

Schedule the sharpen for several hours on a day when you will not be disturbed. Take the day off work or otherwise give yourself space and time. A few sharpens we have done include:

- a weekend at a hotel with nothing but the items from a backpack

- a day home alone from morning till afternoon, making sure the house was cleaned and food pre-made before the sharpen

- a week-long cruise, an extreme sharpen for both of us, but it worked as long as we did not get distracted by the cruise itself

- taking a drive—give yourself time to think either in a moving vehicle or while parked by the side of the road, inspired, it is to be hoped, by the scenery.

During this sharpen you have only one goal—to identify and define what you want to do with the rest of your life.

A few questions that may prompt your thinking:

- What type of person do you want to be? How would you describe your preferred personality?

- What do you want to be doing day-to-day? 10 years from now? 20 years? 30, 40, or 50 years?

- Describe what your life will look like, in visual detail, many years from now.

If you have weak executive function, this process will be extremely difficult. Be kind to yourself as you work towards discovering what you want out of life. Any insights you can gain will be golden, precious. Write them down in a journal that you keep private. This will encourage you to be fully honest with yourself and will help you to remember what you discovered during your sharpen.

Once you have taken the time to look at the wider view of the rest of your time on Earth, it will be much clearer whether you are wasting your life and should move on, or whether you should work to stay with your partner.

During this sharpen it should become clear whether or not your vision includes your partner. If it is not clear, perhaps talk to your partner or a trusted friend until it does become clear. Then do what you need to do.

> *To decide and not to act*
> *Is not to decide at all.*

> *(Japanese proverb)*

It is probable that you, like many others, will find it very difficult to act on your decision. You may have become so comfortable with the daily misery of your life that you do not want to change. If you have autism, this desire to not change will be particularly strong.

If you are still having trouble making this decision, the following questions may help you:

- Who are you trying to please?

- Are you caught or stuck?

- Who is telling you what to do?

If you know you want to leave, but have not, complete or answer the following:

- I want to leave because…

- I want to stay because…

- I am indecisive because…

- What am I waiting for?

- Is this a bad investment?

- Am I avoiding responsibility for the years already wasted?

- Am I hoping someone will make the decision for me? Script the behavior.

- How does it feel now, standing still?

- What is my catastrophic fantasy?

Barriers to clear decisions

There are three big barriers to seeing what you want clearly:

- authenticity

- anxiety

- avoidance.

AUTHENTICITY

It may be extremely difficult for the person with autism to be in tune with feelings because so much of social behavior has been taught. Books about "being authentic" make no sense. The authentic self was, at least originally, a little kid who was likely to bang his or her head against the wall, scream at nearly anything, and have meltdowns due to smell, sight, touch, and especially food (a description of one of our sons at three years old). The "authentic" self may be something you do not want to be.

ANXIETY

Accept anxiety as a positive fundamental human experience. Autism may heighten anxiety, but the anxiety should not control your decisions. It is hard for me to write this "advice" since I know first-hand how intense anxiety can be. Regardless, you need to control your life, not allow anxiety to control your decisions for you. The main reason is that a life ruled by anxiety is a miserable life.

AVOIDANCE

Conflict in itself is not the problem. It is how we handle it. Conflict in itself is neither negative nor positive. It is neutral. What makes it either constructive or destructive is the way we manage it. If you have weak social skills and an inability to deal with conflict well, avoidance may be your method of operation, your modus operandi, or normal way of interacting. Unfortunately, a life ruled by avoidance is also a miserable life. Accept conflict as part of life and allow it to happen, then deal with it as best you can.

THREE QUICK WAYS TO OVERCOME THE BARRIERS

- Authenticity: You are what you want to be, not who you were.
- Anxiety: Do not let anxiety rule you. Think "problem" not "threat."
- Avoidance: The problems are neutral, not good, not bad, just problems to be solved.

If you decide to stay, but are unsure, one way to solidifying your decision is to make a contract with your partner, each of you completing the following.

1 This is what I expect of you: _____

2 This is what you can expect of me: _____

If you decide to leave, you can also make a similar contract, which may prove helpful, but the details are more likely to be delineated by lawyers instead of you or your partner.

Still unsure?

If you have arrived at the end of this chapter and are still unsure or perhaps unable to follow through on your decision, perhaps the following visual will help: stop behaving like a cat tangled in yarn.

If, in your mind's eye, you can see the cat tangled in yarn and can learn from the cat's experience when tangled, it may help you disentangle yourself from the current problems more effectively.

If you are not a visual person, but instead are a linear thinker, perhaps the following questions and advice will give you one last assist in helping you build a happier, better life either with or without your partner, whichever suits your future vision best.

- What do I want to accomplish by the time I am "old"?

- Is there anything I want to experience but have not yet?

- What would I want to do with my life if I could do whatever I wanted?

- What makes me happy day-to-day?

A few guidelines for how to put yourself in the right mindset to solve these tough questions include:

- Take responsibility for your situation—stop blaming others.

- Strengthen your willpower through healthy eating, exercise, and routine.

- Be conscious of unconscious conflict—then eliminate it.

- Build confidence by giving yourself credit for what you do well.

- Fully live your own life in your own unique way.

Summary/Maintenance

Severing a long-term relationship, especially an intimate one, is worthy of a lot of thought and attention. Don't make the decision when you are angry or otherwise not thinking clearly. There are many factors to consider, but the ultimate factor is your own personal health and well-being.

CHAPTER 26

When It Works

IDENTIFYING AND CELEBRATING IMPROVEMENTS

Celebrating our accomplishments is a natural and important way to encourage future accomplishment. The purpose of this chapter is to explore the purpose of celebration and how a person with autism may experience it differently. While the celebration experience may be markedly different, the same need for recognizing accomplishments exists in us all.

It is human nature to be remarkably short-sighted. The troubles of the day loom large; yet the successes we experienced last year or even yesterday, have been forgotten. This blocks us from recognizing bad patterns and from enjoying the chances for improvement.

What we are rewarded for, we tend to repeat. Sometimes we reward each other for things that make us both unhappy. Reward is sometimes tied to bad behavior, which is akin to eating a slice of chocolate cake when you are not hungry

If you want a happy, healthy relationship, work hard to reward the happy, healthy achievements you have.

IDENTIFY: ONE OR BOTH OF US DO NOT LIKE CELEBRATIONS

Test 1: Check your understanding of what it means to "celebrate." Ask, "What do you think I mean by 'celebrating'?"

The word "celebration" may invoke memories of loud children's parties with massive sensory overload, or large adult parties where people are chatting and social skills are needed. There is a good chance that the word, "celebration" carries a negative connotation for a person with a social disorder.

Evaluate: If discussing your perception is enough to help you both reach a common understanding and fix the problem, great! If simply understanding your different perceptions is not enough, however, try Test 2.

Test 2: Define "My celebration/our celebration"

Describe what would feel like a celebration to both of you. A celebration is a reward, therefore it should feel good. It should motivate you to do it again. Write a list of a dozen things or activities that feel good to you. Compare lists to see what overlaps.

A few ideas for how to celebrate in a way that may appeal to autistic sensibilities include:

- visiting your favorite museum

- spending time at the library

- visiting a location that focuses on your particular interests (if you are interested in astronomy, you might visit a planetarium)

- doing something that you normally would not do but that you really enjoy

- asking yourself, "What do I never have enough time to do?" (whatever comes to mind may be a much-desired activity)

- sneaking in on a college lecture if you live close enough to a university

- playing a favorite video game together

- making your favorite meal three times in a row

- invoking a "Silent Celebration" where all sounds are silenced for several hours

- taking a "Social Sabbatical" where you stay home for two days straight with zero social interaction outside of each other

- purchasing a new, heavy, extra fuzzy blanket

- working on your laptops side-by-side for an entire day.

Whatever you do, make sure your reward is specific to you.

Evaluate: If there is enough overlap in your lists and you are both ok with the activities you have in common, then you now have new, unique tradition(s) between the two of you. The goal is to create your own way of celebrating together. It must feel good. If, for whatever reason, this does not work, try Test 3.

Test 3: Celebration = capitalizing on positive events

Remind yourselves that there may differences in motivation behind a celebration. A person without autism may instinctively turn to others to share his or her good news (termed "capitalization"). This sharing is supposed to increase positive emotions and lead to greater intimacy, commitment, trust and stability.

For a person with a social disorder, there is no instinctive turning to others and there is no capitalization of experience. Without that social feedback, the celebration needs to be more personal, more appealing on a non-social level.

Evaluate: Sometimes it is a recognition of differences that solves the problem. If this realization helps you both achieve a positive way of reinforcing the good parts of your relationship, then it has worked. If not, see Test 4.

Test 4: Semantics

If one of you associates "celebration" or "party" too negatively, then choose another word:

- commemorate
- exalt feats/extol virtues
- fete/feast
- honor
- make merry
- memorialize
- revelry.

You can also give your celebration a code name, the significance known only to you two. If you celebrate by going to an observatory or a museum, then you could say, "I have noticed that there has been a sharp decrease in negativity over the last month. I think we should museumize this improvement." It is the personalized equivalent of your own type of celebration.

Evaluate: This works if you can both let go of past memories enough to fully enjoy your current experience. If rescripting the celebration experience as something enjoyable is not enough then, try Test 5.

Test 5: The PTSD of bad celebrations: the anti-celebration

There is a chance that any type of celebration, no matter what it is called, will not feel good because of a deeply ingrained post-traumatic stress that happens when bad memories are invoked. Perhaps your partner experienced too many overwhelming birthday parties as a kid or is in mental lockdown in regards to any type of celebration.

If so, have an anti-celebration. Do not do anything. On your anniversary or other celebration day, what naturally flows into that blank space and time will probably be what your partner likes doing most.

The only drawback to this is that one partner may feel left out and want to celebrate, especially when it is something widely recognized such as an anniversary. Celebrate it! Just do not call it an anniversary. Recognize that simple semantics are allowing your partner to heal. You can still celebrate, but be clear that your partner is doing it as a favor to you, not as a required celebration.

Evaluate: The anti-celebration works if afterwards you have experienced some type of physical or mental reward. It has not worked if one of you has a negative experience or feels resentful at the fact that, "My partner can't even call it a celebration." If so, see Test 6.

Test 6: The party is on!

If you find that even an anti-celebration does not work, have your own celebration independently or with other friends. Do something you truly enjoy. For me, it is going to a hotel for a writing weekend. I bring a bag with my favorite treats and check-in as early as possible and check-out as late as possible, using the hotel's pool and hot tub in the evening.

Evaluate: The desired end result is for both you and your partner to be rewarded. If you find a type of celebration that works for you both, congratulations.

IDENTIFY: I DO NOT SEE ANYTHING IN OUR MARRIAGE/ RELATIONSHIP WORTH CELEBRATING

Test 1: Learn to see progress

Due to the malleable nature of memory, people cannot accurately track progress mentally. So, record your progress scientifically. Keep a journal, blog, consistent emails that tell about your life events, any type of tracking system that allows you to compare current experience with previous experience.

Warning: When you are doing this memory-recording, it will seem a relatively random, useless task. You may get little or no satisfaction out of the task or may actively dislike recording your memories. Do it anyway.

Evaluate: If looking back on these recorded memories is enough to help you see progress, great! If not, or if you find you simply cannot get the memories recorded, see Test 2.

Test 2: Try a different type of journal entry

There are many different ways to record your memories. Perhaps you just have not found the one that works for you. Try the following variations:

One word entry

Monday: Orchestra

Schedule entry

Monday: Woke at 7am. Got to work by 7:45, early just like I like it. 11:30 company lunch, horrific. 5pm commute while listening to newscast about autism. 6pm went on walk with partner. 7pm dinner, reading. 9pm collapsed on bed, no talk, snuggled.

Snapshot-of-one-moment memory entry

Monday: After work, we went on a walk together and it was actually quite nice. We were both silent but noticed the plants that are blossoming. It is spring and we can see buds on so many trees in our neighborhood. He held my hand. It was only for a few blocks, but so nice.

Adjective entry
Thursday: Good, tiring, loving.

Dialogue entry
Monday:

> **Me:** "Do you want to go out on a walk?"

> **Him:** "If I don't have to talk, I'll go on a walk."

We both laughed at the rhyme.

If you are an auditory person, capturing dialogue might be the most powerful and enticing method of recording your experience. Remembering the sound of rain on the roof as you fell asleep at night, the sound of a cat purring, or other sounds can bring back memories vividly.

If you are a visual person, describing scenes, giving a glimpse into what your life looks like will be most effective. Use whatever method of recording works for you.

Evaluate: If you able to consistently record your memories over time, that is proof that this method works for you. If it does not work, try Test 3.

Test 3: See patterns over time: the scientist
You may not be able to keep a journal because you honestly believe that it is a ridiculous waste of time. If so, track a different aspect of your life to prove to yourself that tracking works. The saying, "You make what you measure," is similarly used in relationships, "You can see progress in what you record."

The easiest way to prove this is to spend a week tracking the food you eat. Make a chart that lists the following:

Time	Food	Mood
7am		
8am		
9am		

Keep this journal for a full week from the time you wake up to the time you go to sleep. When you look back at it, you will find patterns and it is highly likely that you will find improvement in what you eat and how you feel throughout the week. It seems like ridiculous waste of time, but the results will be in front of your eyes, the best type of proof.

You may feel weird tracking every bit of food you put in your mouth and your mood/energy levels, but here is the truly weird part—many people live their entire lives not knowing that certain foods cause fatigue (sugar, fats) and certain actions (stretching, going on a walk) help boost energy.

People tend to not connect action and consequence. A person may not notice that he is fatigued and has a headache every Saturday morning. He may not notice that he feels lethargic 45 minutes after eating white bread. Most people's analytical abilities are not strong enough to look at the patterns and in a logical and detached way.

Evaluate: If doing a test on a different part of your life works to convince you to try it for your relationship, great. If not, Try Test 4.

Test 4: Test bugs—the engineer

The act of journal writing may still be too heavy a task. Then try documenting bugs. When you have an argument write out actual bug reports:

Problem:

Steps to reproduce it:

Expected result (what it should do):

Actual result:

How they differ:

Example bug report

Problem: I asked for time alone but she kept talking to me when I needed quiet time.

Steps to reproduce it: 1. Ask partner for time alone. 2. Observe response.

Expected result: I get alone time.

Actual result: A fight.

How they differ: I got the opposite of what I wanted.

Once you file this bug report in your journal, you can refer to it quickly by a code name. Bugs are often categorized by:

* severity

* priority

* category.

The problem above (one which we had as a couple) could be categorized as "Needed quiet not given—Priority 3," or any type of name that works for you so that you can reference the bug easily the next time that it happens.

The goal is to identify the problems, work on solving them, and notice when they increase (so that you can find new solutions) or decrease (so you that can notice the improvements).

For programmers, engineers, and others in similar fields, a lack of bug reports is cause for celebration.

Evaluate: If the bug reports work to help you see where the problems are occurring and stop the negative patterns in your relationship, great. If not, see Test 5.

Test 5: Make sure it is fair and balanced—the anthropologist

The bug reports might not work if one or both of you needs to hear plenty of positive along with the negative. (The bug reports work for me, but not for my husband who needs a higher ratio of positive to negative.)

You or your partner may perceive the bug reports as a line-by-line, blow-by-blow recounting of your difficulties. It may cause you both to look back ten years later and think, "Wow, all we did was fight," when in reality, the argument lasted only a few minutes and was forgotten the next day. The method that may work for you is to make your written record as accurate to your current experience as possible.

For the anthropologist test, record both the good and the bad in accurate proportions. To make sure the memories are accurate, do not censor the unpleasant parts, just make them short and factual.

Evaluate: If you are able to use the scientific reports to show progress, this works. If not, see Test 6.

Test 6: When the bad memories are too bad

Some memories may be too bad to include and are best forgotten. For the bad memories:

1. Edit. Rip out the pages either figuratively or literally. Press "delete." Heal. Rewrite history (different from denial). Denial is saying, "It never happened." Rewriting history is saying, "It may have happened, but it doesn't need to be preserved."

2. Reminisce about the good to the point that the bad fades into oblivion. Hang up a new picture of you two in a happy place on a happy day. Create lots of visual reminders of your togetherness.

3. If you find that reviewing the journal is making your partner feel bad, especially if your partner becomes defensive, put the journal back in storage. The journal is to be used as a tool to build a happier relationship, not to be used as a weapon.

Evaluate: If the bad memories are fading, allowing more room for positive celebrations of improvement, then you are succeeding. If not, try Test 7.

Test 7: Count the little things

If none of the above strategies work, there are still things you can do to celebrate your accomplishments as a couple. Count the little things! Write a daily list of what has gone right for both of you in a small notebook. Mine includes romantic, funny, odd memories and often little realizations of gratitude:

- I am grateful that Carl kissed me awake. (Romantic)

- I am grateful that my husband and I have a linguistically odd child who says erudite things that make us appreciate life and the world around us. (Funny)

- I am grateful that I did not run over the dead wolf in the road while going 75 mph/125 km per hr. (This actually happened.) I am grateful that Carl appreciated my driving skills. (Oddball)

- I am grateful for a gluten-free toaster. (Little things)

Evaluate: These are little daily celebrations. It may take the pressure off having the bigger celebrations such as anniversaries (a good thing). If counting the little things does not work for you, try Test 8.

Test 8: Celebrate time markers—the linear thinker

If none of the above strategies work, just celebrate time markers like most people do. Celebrate birthdays, anniversaries, Valentine's Day, and holidays and call that good enough.

Evaluate: If these traditional markers are sufficient for you both to feel like a successful couple, great! It probably works best with people who prefer consistency over improvement. If you or your partner need more celebratory feedback, see Test 9.

Test 9: Celebrate not going backwards

If all else fails, celebrate not going backwards, not divorcing, not falling apart, not becoming a mean, nasty old couple. It sounds like an awful, almost morbid thing to celebrate, but I know for us, it can be quite valuable to give ourselves credit for simply holding the relationship together.

Evaluate: If this realization is enough of a celebration to give you both positive feedback, great, it works. If not and you actually are going backwards in your relationship, perhaps other chapters in this book can shine light on the problems. Perhaps devote your energies to problem-solving first so that there is more to celebrate later.

Why celebrating is so important

The following are reasons why celebrating is crucial to your long-term happiness:

- It gives a start and a finish to specific improvements. Once you have stopped criticizing, you do not need to continue to work on it. When you celebrate an improvement, you finalize it.

- It creates a sense of joy around fixing a problem. It gives positive feedback for dealing with something that was initially negative.

- It creates a tradition. Couples who have regular rituals and traditions form stronger, healthier relationships.

- It creates an overall goal for your relationship: improve so that we can do fun things together.

- Most important: it gives you something to look forward to! I have tried this myself. When I had the goal of, "Stop nagging," it was much easier to stop when I knew that I had a reward coming up. Now, years after setting the goal to stop nagging, I still have an immediate, easy "Stop!" reaction when I feel a nagging thought that I want to say.

Summary/Maintenance

Celebrating successes is the adult form of ABA, Applied Behavioral Analysis, where progress is tracked, "We've been married for one full year," and a reward is given, "We celebrate."

You may not call it celebrating; you may do things that do not look like celebrations at all, but in the end, if you are both giving yourselves and each other positive rewards for successes, the level of happiness and peace in your relationship will increase.

The ultimate reward

In the pale light of the evening I see his face, happy, fading into sleep. I put my hand on his cheek and feel rough warmth. In the dim light filtering through the white curtains I can see his eyes are a light Tahiti ocean blue.

His cheek is still warm from too much sun earlier that day. His hair, once a Viking red has faded to amber with hints of white. It is the sexiest color I have ever seen. He has grown his hair long like a rock star and its softness is enviable.

He closes his eyes slowly once, twice. Silence. I whisper words I cannot remember, breathing in his scent. I feel my heart rate slow to a calm, steady beat. I feel a smile tickle around my lips. There is a poignant peace. I feel deep, abiding love and loyalty in that moment. This type of soul-deep satisfaction is worth everything.

"This is what I always wanted in a relationship with another human being."

I push the bliss of these moments to the front of my thought-stream, the central position of remembering.

I push back, push out the moments of negativity, the memories of missed opportunities, failed dinners, bombed birthday parties, and awkward moments. So many awkward moments. I turn to my journal lying beside me and edit out the ugly parts in my daily journal entry.

"Holding on to ugliness makes one ugly." Plus, those earlier parts were worthless. They add nothing: only pain.

By conventional standards our relationship is irrevocably flawed. We have fought. We have cried. Individually we have ached unbearably: surgery without anesthesia.

But the pain becomes the past: faded, distant, soon forgotten.

The delight becomes the present and the future. We choose our present; we choose our future; we even choose our past by reminiscing on the good parts and letting the bad parts fade.

So many happy moments accumulated in a treasure chest—in my chest—of memory. Moments when things worked. Moments when the body felt good and the mind was safe and active. The moments were not those that others reminisce about: the wedding day, the birth of a child, a birthday party. The memories of love are abundant, but different, modified by sensory needs and perceptual differences: playing a computer game, reading books side-by-side, talking about physics, laughing about the world, building devices, solving a tough puzzle. These colorful, happy moments fill volumes and I amplify them.

Now I set my journal aside and turn back towards my husband. I watch his sleeping face, hear his even, deep breath, smell his warm, masculine scent, and kiss his rough cheeks. I feel a physical oneness with him. I am an adult; he is an adult, and together, autism intermingles with us as our legs and arms intertwine.

That relationship, the intermingling, is beautiful.

REFERENCES

Allen, D. (2002) *Getting Things Done: The Art of Stress-Free Productivity*. New York: Penguin Books.

Berman, L. (2011) *Loving Sex: The Book of Joy and Passion*. New York: Dorling Kindersley Publishing.

Bowen, W. (2007) *A Complaint Free World: How to Stop Complaining and Start Enjoying the Life You Always Wanted*. New York: Harmony.

Chandler, S. (2006) *The Story of You: And How to Create a New One*. Pompton Plains, NJ: Career Press.

Chapman, G.D. (2009) *The 5 Love Languages: The Secret to Love That Lasts*. Chicago, IL: Northfield Publishing.

Clifford, D. (2008) *Quick and Legal Will Book*. Berkeley, CA: Nolo Press.

Davis, W. (2011) *Wheat Belly: Lose the Wheat, Lose the Weight, and Find Your Path Back to Health*. Emmaus: Rodale Books.

Hockschild, A. and Machung, A. (1997) *The Second Shift*. New York: Avon Books.

Hoopman, K. (2006) *All Cats Have Asperger Syndrome*. London: Jessica Kingsley Publishers.

King, S. (2002) *On Writing: A Memoir of the Craft*. New York: Simon & Schuster Adult Publishing Group.

Lamb, C. and Lamb, M. (2007) *Poetry for Children*. Whitefish, MT: Kessinger Publishing.

Levine, A. and Heller, R. (2010) *Attached: The New Science of Adult Attachment and How It Can Help You Find—and Keep—Love*. New York: Tarcher.

Love, P. and Stosny, S. (2008) *How to Improve Your Marriage without Talking About It*. New York: Three Rivers Press.

Lucas, M. (2012) *Rewire Your Brain for Love: Creating Vibrant Relationships Using the Science of Mindfulness*. New York: Hay House.

Proctor, A. (1880) *Songs of the Soul: Gathered out of Many Lands and Ages*. New York: Robert Carter and Brothers.

Stanford, A. (2002) *Asperger Syndrome and Long-Term Relationships*. London: Jessica Kingsley Publishers.

Stanford, A. (2011) *Business for Aspies: 42 Best Practices for Using Asperger Syndrome Traits at Work Successfully*. London: Jessica Kingsley Publishers.

Tatkin, S. and Hendrix, H. (2012) *Wired for Love: How Understanding Your Partner's Brain and Attachment Style Can Help You Defuse Conflict and Build a Secure Relationship*. Oakland, CA: New Harbinger.

Thomas, K. and Thomas, T. (2005) *The Modern Kama Sutra: The Ultimate Guide to the Secrets of Erotic Pleasure*. Boston, MA: Da Capo Press.

Volkmar, F.R. and Wiesner, L.A. (2009) *A Practical Guide to Autism: What Every Parent, Family Member and Teacher Needs to Know*. Hoboken, NJ: Wiley.

HOW TO LOVE

Everyone has their own personal perception of love, but if you don't know where to start, here are a few ideas. As you get to know your partner, make your own personalized How to Love list.

- Do something enjoyable with your partner.

- Give your partner what he or she needs, even if that is leaving him or her alone or giving him or her silence and/or space.

- Give your partner something meaningful to him or her. (Don't give chocolates to a partner who doesn't like sweets. Give your partner a book if he or she likes reading.)

- Do something for your partner, especially if it is something that makes your partner's life easier such as cleaning up or doing the dishes.

- Pay attention to the particular words and phrases your partner likes most and say them often.

- Encourage your partner towards good eating, exercise, and sleep habits to help him or her live a happier, healthier life.

- If your partner chooses a career path or schooling option he or she loves, encourage and support him or her as much as you can.

- Be clear in what you need: loving someone means giving your partner what he or she needs *and* making it easy for your partner to do the same in return.

- Establish visual remembrances of your love by putting photos of the two of you in an easy-to-see location in the home.

- When in public, act like you are together by holding hands or standing near to each other.

- Remember details about your partner.

- Take care of yourself so that you can be a healthy, loving partner.

- Get your body in the best shape possible so that you can enjoy physical intimacy together.

- Be patient with your partner's mistakes: sometimes love is the lack of negative emotions.

- Ask your partner what he or she likes. Make your own How to Love _____ (partner's name) list.

APPENDIX B

SIGNALS OF LOVE

For the purpose of simplicity, this list is split into:

1 physical love/lust, and

2 long-term love that comes after years together.

Physiologically the two types of love are very different, with different hormones circulating in your body as you feel these different types of love. They both, however, come under the same umbrella of "love" so they share the same appendix.

Some common signals of early love (lust) are:

- blushing—the rush of blood to the cheeks
- pupils widening
- fidgeting with hair/twirling hair around finger
- brushing a finger over lips—a non-verbal pre-kiss gesture
- tilting head slightly to the side
- flipping hair back (for long hair)
- walking with back straight, chest out
- for women, walking with the hips swaying; for men, walking "cowboy style."

Some common signals of long-term love are:

- an instinctive reaction to turn to your partner (rather than away)
- standing close to your partner, holding hands in public
- when your partner walks in the room, you smile
- many habits of helping and supporting your partner.

Signs that an NT will give that are not received/not given by someone on the spectrum include:

- prolonged eye contact, visual foreplay
- body language cues such as feet turned towards the partner and other body positioning cues
- gentle touching while talking
- seductive handshake or an intimate advance in the form of a "hello hug" when meeting.

Signals for NT long-term love include:

- spending more time together
- naturally giving comfort when subtle cues are given to indicate an increased need for support
- talking about suggestive topics, "dropping hints."

Note that this list is not complete. It is merely a sampling of signals of love you may see.

If your own signals are not standard signals, make sure that your partner is aware of them. For example, tell your partner, "When I am happy to be near you, I am bouncy," or "When I am feeling loving, I nuzzle." Share these details as you become aware of them so that your partner can respond well to them.

APPENDIX C

TEST FOR CO-DEPENDENCY IN ASD-LINKED RELATIONSHIPS

This is a generalized set of statements often found on self-tests for co-dependent behavior, where the respondents have to say "yes" or "no," depending upon whether the statement is true or not for them. All questions have been adjusted to fit within the context of ASD-linked relationships.

1. I often give advice, even when it isn't requested. Yes ☐   No ☐

2. I tend to befriend people who need help with their problems. Yes ☐   No ☐

3. I do other people's work for them, assuming their responsibilities. Yes ☐   No ☐

4. I often lose sleep worrying about others. Yes ☐   No ☐

5. I often feel the weight of responsibility for others' happiness and well-being. Yes ☐   No ☐

6. I can't say "no" without feeling guilty. Yes ☐   No ☐

7. When I am able to fix others' problems, I feel strong and valuable. Yes ☐   No ☐

8. I feel that I have to protect people, especially those who have problems. Yes ☐   No ☐

9. I live in such a way that no one can ever say I'm selfish. Yes ☐   No ☐

10. I often relive situations and conversations to see if I can think of some way I could have done more or spoken better. Yes ☐   No ☐

⑪ I feel very frightened of angry people. Yes ☐　No ☐

⑫ I am quite offended by personal criticism. Yes ☐　No ☐

⑬ I often forget to take care of my own needs. Yes ☐　No ☐

⑭ I often try to get people I love to change their attitudes and behavior. Yes ☐　No ☐

⑮ I believe I can't be happy unless others are happy. Yes ☐　No ☐

⑯ My thoughts are often consumed with the troubles and needs of other people. Yes ☐　No ☐

⑰ I sometimes feel responsible for another person's actions or mistakes. Yes ☐　No ☐

⑱ I feel that I need to fulfill the needs of another person before my own needs. Yes ☐　No ☐

⑲ I suppress thoughts or feelings about helping another, only to "explode" in anger later. Yes ☐　No ☐

⑳ I feel rejected or angry when another person does not want my help. Yes ☐　No ☐

㉑ Arguments with my partner make me want to change my partner. Yes ☐　No ☐

㉒ I sometimes think that if my partner could see things my way life would be much better. Yes ☐　No ☐

Answering "yes" on up to five statements indicates that you are at low risk for co-dependent behaviors.

Answering "yes" on six to ten statements indicates that you have several co-dependent behaviors that interfere with your daily happiness. Your ability to live a happy, healthy life will increase the more you can eliminate the issues you answered "yes" to above, so work to improve in one area at a time. For example, say you answered "yes" to Statement 20, "I feel rejected or angry when another person does not want my help?" Perhaps you could:

① Identify what is happening when you experience this unpleasant feeling. Ask yourself, "Am I upset because ___ does not want my help? Is this making me feel rejected?" Sometimes identifying the instance is enough to turn the situation around.

2 Create a mantra that you can say to yourself silently whenever you feel this emotion. For example: "There may be many reasons why ___ does not want my help and it may have nothing to do with me," or "It's great when ___ doesn't need my help because it gives me more time to do what I want."

3 Develop a self-calming strategy specifically for this situation. It can be a simple act such as taking a few deep breaths or snuggling under a warm, tightly wrapped blanket for a few minutes. Or, it could be a more sophisticated technique such as downward dog, a yoga position known to defuse even the most intense anger. (To do downward dog, start on your hands and knees like a dog. Next, straighten your legs so that your body makes two sides of an equilateral triangle with your buttocks being the apex of the triangle. As you ease into the position, straighten your arms, neck, and back to make one flat side of the triangle.)

Answering "yes" on 11 to 16 statements indicates that you may be co-dependent (or other factors are at play). Since significant issues need to be addressed, it may be easiest to begin researching co-dependency and implementing fixes to heal from the negative consequences of being too deeply affected by the acts of others.

Answering "yes" to 17 or more statements means that you may need professional help. Please do not be offended or intimidated when seeking professional help. Personally, I know co-dependency well since I fell into co-dependent behaviors and I needed help fixing the dysfunctional behaviors. Thankfully a counselor who was willing to consider ASD as part of the equation in my marriage was able to help me revise and eliminate the co-dependent behaviors. It is fixable.

Know that the more co-dependent behaviors you can eliminate, the more secure, calm, happy, and satisfied you will be with yourself and your partner.

INDEX